A SHADOW OF WAR

Sidestone Press

A SHADOW OF WAR

Archaeological approaches to uncovering the darker sides of conflict from the 20th century

Claudia Theune

I would like to thank Niall Brady, for ensuring the translation retained my voice while also reaching an English readership.

Published by Sidestone Press, Leiden
    www.sidestone.com

Lay-out & cover design: Sidestone Press
Design concept by Marta Klement, Buro Millennial
Photograph cover: Berlin Wall, Bernauerstraße, by nikhg | stock.adobe.com

ISBN 978-90-8890-454-7 (softcover)
ISBN 978-90-8890-455-4 (PDF e-book)

CONTENTS

PREFACE

Contemporary Archaeology, that is the archaeology of the 20th and the 21st century, has been experiencing tremendous growth over the last 10 to 15 years. There is now an almost unmanageable abundance of small and large excavations, projects and publications. However, initial approaches and important precedent-setting projects are older. In the Anglo-American world, the first investigations began about 50 years ago, while in continental Europe, initial projects started in the late 1980s at sites of the last 100 years and their material remains. It is obvious that objects of all kinds are an essential part of our actions and therefore provide deep insights into small and large events, human structures and behaviour. The analysis and interpretation of the recent past through the lens of very dense and broadly-based written, oral and visual sources remains incomplete without taking into account the colossal number of things with which we surround ourselves. The material culture at these sites is now seen as an important witness to contemporary history, not least since the so-called 'material turn'.

Different scientific traditions around the world have led to different approaches and nuances. In the Anglo-American world, the focus was initially on projects related to everyday life, and to economic and social history. In Europe, the first work was achieved by German and Polish research, whose focus was on places of National Socialist terror, especially concentration and extermination camps. Shortly afterwards similar investigations were carried out in many other European countries, but also far beyond them. The field expanded more and more, and this was in part fuelled by the frequency of years of commemoration. Many investigations began at sites associated with the world wars or with liberation movements and revolutions. Excavations also took place at other types of sites of conflict, including where local wars were fought and at sites of international terrorist attacks. Places where people were oppressed, imprisoned or murdered, and where people expressed their protest against arbitrariness or governmental authority have also been considered. In many cases, the remains show the direct or indirect affects of war on people. The shadow of war embraces objects and features from all such sites. The material remains testify to death, armed violence, armament, repression, imprisonment and much more. However, they also reveal rebellion and the efforts of the people against this oppression and the fight for survival.

The research trigger was often the examination of our own history, also our unpleasant history. The need to remember and to commemorate drove the first studies. It led to the discovery and reappearance of details associated with former camps, battlefields and other remains of war. It helped to understand historical sites and rediscover forgotten sites. The work expanded to include other types of narrative, including industrial monuments and other places important to cultural history and no longer visible above ground. Although we have countless other sources reflecting the history and catastrophes of the 20th century, with the archaeological features and objects we have a further, very lively medium, which makes the former structures easier to grasp.

A pervasive motif of contemporary archaeology lies in the revival of memories, which can now be recalled by visible material structures. A culture of remembrance once initiated needs to be consolidated. The focus may be on official (state) history. It is also possible to give a voice to people who would otherwise be heard less, to marginal groups. The uncovering of former prisons and camps, battlefields or mass graves is therefore carried out in particular to commemorate the atrocities committed there, giving identity to the victims and a voice so that their suffering will not be forgotten. Material remains seem to be particularly suitable for making past events visible through finds and other remains, making them tangible and thus keeping memory alive. This central motif will appear again and again in this book. It is linked to the fact that archaeological remains also reflect our common cultural heritage, whether it is a heritage of which we are proud or a heritage that recalls dark times.

The enormous variety and quantity of archaeological research into our recent past has led to a multitude of publications dealing with surveys, excavations or material analyses. Young researchers increasingly take up these topics and write their theses in this field. General summary works have been published that focus on particular areas, such as the world wars, the Cold War, internment camps and archaeology and remembrance. It was very inspiring to read these publications and my own research has benefited greatly from them.

In 2014, I contributed my own overview study, published in German. Even then, the idea of publishing an English version was present. The first edition of the German book sold out after less than a year, and a second, slightly expanded edition was printed in 2016. When planning for the English version, it quickly became clear that the former structure did not cover all aspects of contemporary archaeology, in particular the comparative perspective. The structure of the book was completely redesigned. Numerous case studies from global contexts have now been taken into account, particularly as a result of the increasingly global character that is clearly reflected in the archaeological assemblages. Weapons and soldiers from all parts of the world have been and are used in conflicts all over the world; people are interned worldwide and react to imprisonment with similar survival strategies.

Another motive was to present the numerous published studies in German to a wider international audience who has no ready access to German-language publications. Many projects carried out in Central Europe or the German-speaking countries are less well known in English-language publications. Of course, my work speaks from a Central European, even German perspective, as a German living in Austria.

The present volume also expands the spectrum away somewhat from places of conflict, to include subjects such as infrastructure, private and public life, living and working, leisure, religion and worship. Some of these topics have their own developed history of research.

Based on these considerations, I start with some basic and essential thoughts on the history of the contemporary archaeology of the 20th century (and now also the 21st century), on ethical aspects and on the potential of the multi-faceted and manifold sources for contemporary archaeology. This is followed by remarks on places and remains of the two world wars, local wars, totalitarianism and resistance to state power. The internment camps that exist(ed) in many parts of the world play an important role in this book. Investigations on protest movements offer a new field of research in contemporary archaeology. The topic of borders has been dealt with in archaeology for a long time and it is discussed here, too. A crucial theme of the book deals with the dead and the tribute we pay to them. One of the core aspects of archaeology concerns objects of all kinds that shed light on human behaviour and actions. This leads on to comments on global perspectives that can be made based on the findings. In addition to the topics on war and its effects, I also like to focus on archaeological topics beyond wars, which can demonstrate the broad potential of contemporary archaeology for research into recent history. The final chapter is addressed to a very essential motivation of contemporary archaeology, which runs through the entire book like a common thread: remembrance and commemoration. Special finds or sites are briefly presented as the starting point of each chapter.

I am aware that many of the examples in the chapters could crop up in other chapters, and this reflects the fact that much of this information can be considered from different perspectives. References to the respective chapters and figures provide the reader with the corresponding information. The book concludes with a detailed bibliography and an appendix that lists numerous memorials.

The present book is written by me, but it would not have come into being without the invaluable help of many colleagues and friends from around the world.

I would especially like to thank those who translated my German text into English; these are Tanya Armbrüster (Berlin, Germany), Joris Coolen (Vienna, Austria), Desiree Ebner-Baur (Graz, Austria), Barbara Hausmair (Esslingen, Germany) and Paul Mitchell (Vienna, Austria). Niall Brady (Bray, Ireland) brought these parts together, edited them and took great care to ensure that my voice is present in English. I would like to express my very special thanks to him. He also had the idea for the title of the book. Furthermore I like to thank Daniel McNaughton (Chicago, U.S.) for proofreading the final manuscript.

My sincere thanks go to the many colleagues with whom I have been able to collaborate and with whom I have spent the past years discussing issues of contemporary archaeology intensively. I would like to mention Anders Andren (Stockholm, Sweden), Reinhard Bernbeck, (Berlin, Germany), Gillian Carr (Cambridge, England), Elizabeth Crooke (Belfast, United Kindom), Attila Dézsi (Hamburg, Germany), Marek Jasinski (Trondheim, Norway), Thomas Kersting (Wünsdorf, Germany), Rob van der Laarse (Amsterdam, The Netherlands), Thomas Lutz (Berlin, Germany), Laura McAtackney (Aarhus, Denmark), Anne Kathrin Müller (Berlin, Germany), Susan Pollock (Berlin, Germany) and my colleagues at the University of Vienna: Christiana Köhler, Bertrand Perz, Sybille Steinbacher, Tim Taylor, Lioba Theis and Stefan Zahlmann. In addition, Barbara Hausmair, Natascha Mehler (Bremerhaven, Germany), Paul Mitchell, Ulrich Müller (Kiel, Germany) and Niall Brady added many constructive criticisms to the manuscript and raised numerous discussions. Your suggestions prompted me further.

My special thanks also go to the heads and staff of numerous memorial sites and to many colleagues in Germany and abroad for their extremely good cooperation and the generous provision of archival material: Barbara Glück and her team from the Mauthausen Memorial (Austria), Günter Morsch and his team from the Sachsenhausen Memorial and Museum Sachsenhausen (Germany) and Jörg Skriebleit and his team from the concentration camp memorial Flossenbürg (Germany) are just a few examples. I would also like to express my sincere thanks to the monument conservation authorities in Germany and Austria, in particular to the Brandenburg State Office for Monument Conservation and Archaeological Museum (Franz Schopper and Thomas Kersting) as well as to the Federal Monuments Authority of Austria, Department of Archaeology (Bernhard Hebert, Heinz Gruber, Jörg Fürnholzer, Eva Steigberger) for the excellent cooperation in the projects of the past years. I am happy to add the University of West Indies (Campus St. Augustine, Trinidad and Tobago: Christian Cwik, Sherry-Ann Singh) and the National Trust of Trinidad and Tobago (Valerie Taylor, Ashleigh Morris).

My thanks go as well to countless colleagues all over the world who kindly and uncomplicatedly granted me the rights to sources and images. Beside those I have mentioned already are: Iain Banks, Ute Bauer, Joanna Brück, Jeff Burton, Lisa M. Daly, Torsten Dressler, Elisabeth Crooke, John Daniel Gilbin, Alfredo González Ruibal, Francesc Xavier Hernàndez, Detlef Hopp, Ryszard Kazmierczak, Wolfgang Klimesch, Zdzisław Lorek, Gavin Lucas; Randall McGuire, Anne Kathrin Müller, Adrian Myers, A. Fanjul Peraza, Peter Petchey, Gilles Prilaux, Ivar Schute, Oula Seitsonen, Caroline Sturdy-Colls, Pavel Vařeka and Johannes Weishaupt. In particular my scholars in Vienna, Judith Benedix, Isabella Greußing, Peter Hinterndorfer and Iris Winkelbauer have supported me in many ways.

The University of Vienna, the Faculty of Historical and Cultural Studies, the Institute for Prehistory and Historical Archaeology and the faculty key research area 'Dictatorships – Violence – Genocides' is my scientific home and has also contributed significantly to the research. The university library invests a lot to facilitate easy accessibility to worldwide scattered but online literature, which has allowed me to study the numerous interesting projects of my colleagues. It is an honour for me to thank the Faculty of Historical and Cultural Studies for their financial support to aid in printing the book.

Numerous students in Berlin and Vienna have shared in my research. They work with me with great commitment to investigate the crime scenes of the 20th century and contribute to the advancement of my research in talks on contemporary archaeology or with their own theses.

My children and their partners take part in my research, sometimes accompanying me on my travels to memorials and places of past terror and discussing the way of remembrance. It is through them that I understand the perspective of the younger generation on the history of the last 100 years, the shadow of the war and the commemoration of all victims.

Finally my heartfelt thanks go to Sidestone Press and especially to Karsten Wentink. He has supported my book in English from the very beginning and has always supported me – even if there have been delays. I would like to thank him and his team for their careful publishing work.

Dealing with the shadows of the wars of the 20th century is also an examination of one's personal past. It is a past that we, our parents and grandparents have experienced and shaped and which is passed on to us through first-hand stories. That we are often personally affected is obvious. Scientific research in contemporary archaeology is often characterised by personal motives, in my case as well. Many closely related members of the next older generation of my family fought as soldiers in World War II on the Eastern or the Western Front, some were killed or taken prisoner. They were anti-aircraft auxiliaries, members of the confessing church ('Bekennende Kirche') and also on occasion members of the National Socialist women's organisation. Among my parents' belongings are documents and objects that serve as memories for my siblings and me, and their grandchildren and great-grandchildren. Some of the 'finds' I include in this book. The members of my generation are children of the Cold War and we have actively participated in various protest movements. Here too, personal memory is still alive.

Although many of our generation in the Western World have the enormous good fortune to live in areas not directly affected by war, there are, however, far too many people in many regions of the world who are confronted by the terror of war on a daily basis and who are therefore often traumatised throughout their lives.

I have carried out my research primarily at former concentration camps and war sites. Using archaeological methods, my focus is on the expressive possibilities and interpretation of objects with regard to living conditions, survival strategies and the death of the victims. I want to keep the memory of the victims of these wars alive, to give them a voice, to help them achieve justice, to highlight their suffering and misery, to help them recover their identity and their own history. I want their memory to stand out from the shadow.

Chapter 1

THE BEGINNINGS OF CONTEMPORARY ARCHAEOLOGY DURING THE SHORT AND THE LONG 20TH CENTURY

INTRODUCTION

Periodisation means categorising the past into stages that are as strongly defined by local conventions as they are built on perceptions of past events and developments. The periodisation of the history of humankind is based on approximations of dates that mark significant change and, possibly, disruption. Normally these points in time are determined retrospectively, be it by the occurrence of new economic strategies such as, for instance, the Neolithic transition, or by turning points brought about through the invention of new materials such as ceramics, copper, bronze and iron for the prehistoric periods or porcelain, aluminium and synthetics during the modern era. The rise and fall of dynasties and other elites who altered the history of Europe or other principal regions around the globe have equally shaped our concept of the past. Normally, the transition between eras is barely recognised and is only perceived by a few contemporaries. An impressive example of greater perception is that by the 16th-century Italian artist, Giorgio Vasari, who described his time and the first stirrings of the Renaissance as the rebirth of the ancient world and dawn of a 'new age', in contrast to the Gothic medieval period. The fall of the Berlin Wall on November 9th, 1989, however, coincided with the beginnings of technological change that brought about the invention and spread of the World Wide Web and the so-called third industrial (digital) revolution. That event was recognised instantly and widely as a significant point of change in a way that signalled the end of one era and the initial moments of a new one; those events caused dramatic political change and triggered a huge economic turning point.

The very terms 'medieval' or 'the modern period' must be understood within their geographical and cultural contexts. To avoid difficulties with their communication, they should be related principally to absolute data. A more general standardisation of era classification from a global perspective did not exist before the beginning of the modern age. It was the invention of wireless telegraphy that acted as a catalyst and became one of the major game changers at the end of the 19th century, since it connected all continents in near real time. Another important factor that brought the world ever closer together was the emergence of new and swifter means of intercontinental transportation.

Where are the borders of contemporary archaeology and of the history of the 20th century? These two categories alone do not necessarily mean the same thing. Strictly speaking, both are categories that have no sharp borders since the term 'border' would emphasise the discontinuities rather than the commonalities between

Uncovering Gestapo prison cells in Berlin

In May 1985, a first and largely symbolic excavation took place on the grounds of the former headquarters of the GESTAPO, SS and the 'Reichssicherheitshauptamt' (Reich Security Main Office in Berlin), initiated by 'Berliner Geschichtswerkstatt' (Berlin History Workshop) and in cooperation with the joint venture 'Aktives Museum Faschismus und Widerstand in Berlin' (Active Museum of Fascism and Resistance in Berlin).

According to the motto 'Dig where you stand; and if you face the injustice of the past, ask what happened', a clear sign was to be set against the official policy of silence and forgetfulness. From the start, the idea that remembrance of the past could be guaranteed by uncovering foundations was set firmly.

It was the first excavation at a site of National Socialist terror. Although it cannot be seen as a scientific excavation in the truest sense of the word, the dig attracted a great deal of attention. Campaigners and survivors of the National Socialist terror carried out the site work as a clear statement against the deliberate forgetfulness. They were certain they would find the foundations and other remains of the former Gestapo headquarters.

The activities continued in 1986 and uncovered the remains of cellars in the north-east wing and also the apparently well-preserved prison cells. Such discoveries made it very clear that the scenes of crime and terror had not simply ceased to exist but were still present and only barely concealed under the present-day surface.

The results were quickly realised as being for the common good and are now permanently visible within the memorial grounds of the 'Topography of Terror' in Berlin.

A first uncovering of a National Socialist terror site took place on the grounds of the command centre of the GESTAPO (Secret State Police) (today the memorial Topography of Terror) in Berlin in 1985 (© Jürgen Henschel, © Stiftung Topography of Terror, Berlin).

the two. When referring to epochs, overlaps are defined as incipient occurrences heralding new developments that continue to have a longer after-effect. Many historians, however, have come to agree on defining the term 'contemporary history' exclusively as a history of those who lived to bear witness to the epoch. This makes contemporary history a term with an inherent dynamic that sees continuous changes in relation to its temporal brackets. At the time when the term was originally created and introduced during the 1950s, it encompassed the first half of the 20th century. Subsequently the focus shifted to the period between 1945 and 1989, while currently it has become the era of the turn of the millennium.

THE SEGMENTATION OF THE 20TH CENTURY

Even a sensible distinction of the 20th century cannot be based on the dates of the years 1900 and 2000 alone. Historians distinguish the so-called short and the so-called long 20th century. In the first case, Eric Hobsbawm uses the beginning of the First World War in 1914 or the Russian October Revolution of 1917 and the collapse of the Soviet Union in 1991 as the most defining turns. The Age of Extremes, according to Hobsbawm, is comprised of three individual stages: first, the Age of Catastrophes (1914–1945) saw the world shaken by two world wars. As one consequence among many others, from 1918 onwards, old world orders started to show progressive instability and empires collapsed. While a first wave of political democratisation reached some nations, fascist and totalitarian systems were installed in other countries. Another significant event was marked by the victory of the (allied) capitalist West and the communist East over a fascist-National Socialist Germany in 1945. Both world wars (1914–1918 and 1939–1945) had global dimensions and, for the first time, they targeted civilians to a hitherto unprecedented degree; those wars left deep traces that can be felt today. That Age of Catastrophes also saw the Armenian Genocide in 1915 and the Holocaust, where National Socialists were responsible for the mass murder of almost six million people.

The second stage of the 20th century is referred to as the Golden Age (1945–1970s); it begins with a second wave of democracies, the foundation of the United Nations (1945) and its different entities; but at the same time new totalitarian regimes appeared across the globe. The era coincides with a period of extraordinary demographic and economic growth, to an extent that it inspired an unbridled faith in progress as well as a firm belief that all its latent risks could be controlled, and that humanity could exert unprecedented power over Nature. It is the era of the Cold War (1946/47–1991); the so-called East-West Conflict that was accompanied by the proxy wars, but it was also the period when colonialism ended in several parts of the world. Many nations in Africa received their independence.

The third stage is considered a time of crises (1970s–1991). It began with the oil crisis of 1973–74, but those decades were equally defined by the Deténte, where politicians from all involved nations focused their best efforts in 'un-freezing' the Cold War. It also saw the emergence of the North-South Divide, as a sign of growing conflicts between a so-called First and Second World, and the poorer Third World. A further worldwide wave of new totalitarian regimes arose. Mass murder and genocide were perpetrated again, for instance in Cambodia (1975–1978), Rwanda (1994) and Srebenica (1995). It was an era when the dangers and risks of unchecked military build-up, environmental pollution and ecological calamities became increasingly evident and were met by political countermovements and global protests, the demand for equal rights or the upholding of human rights, which went against militarisation and environmental pollution. The fall of the Berlin Wall and the Iron Curtain (1989) concluded that era, along with the collapse of the Soviet Union (1991) and the end of the Cold War. It led to a third and further wave of political democratisation. It is not restricted to key events across Europe, and it is global.

Ulrich Herbert, in contrast, suggests a different perspective. He characterises the century either as the long 20th century or the high modern era, and his approach is based primarily on economic and socio-cultural aspects; the years 1870/90, 1990 and 2008, serve as the temporal brackets for him. He points to the so-called Second (Technological) Industrialisation or, in his words, the High Industrialisation, which began in England around 1850/70 and is evident in other places across continental Europe, America, Australia and Asia from around 1870/90, where it triggered an explosive economic growth. It resulted in profound economic and socio-cultural changes and permitted a more comprehensive sense of globalisation, which brought the world closer together. The rapid progress in transportation, communication, armaments industries, electronics, chemical industries and other fields at the end of the 19th century was so thorough and all-encompassing that the development was no longer limited to certain parts of the world, as had been the case during the First Industrialisation of the late 18th and early 19th centuries. Furthermore, colonies made it possible to tap into new markets while the commercial relations – old and new – intensified and thrived, and resulted in even more economic growth. A large-scale industrial development of this type had an equally strong and predictable impact on the First World War: the use of machine guns, tanks, aeroplanes, submarines and poison gas was essentially a product of industrial development and progress. It also advanced urbanism and is a causative factor behind an explosive increase in population. Big cities began to grow incredibly fast with the bourgeoisie on the one side and the working classes on the other side. New York, London and Berlin exemplify such modern big cities, or metropoles. The rural landscapes were similarly affected by technological change, where advanced equipment and machinery made farming much more profitable and helped to feed the growing population. The industrial era saw the formation of a number of new socio-political movements, such as the Labour Movement or the Women's Liberation Movement, but also alliances of international or global organisations like the League of Nations (1920). It also saw the onset of a new orientation towards people and race that mutated rapidly into anti-Semitism, fascism and national awakening. Religious principles – a pretextual argument in the later medieval period – were no longer the basis of anti-Semitism; now the hatred was more clearly influenced by political goals with a clear emphasis on racial distinctions and the foreignness of Jewish people.

Several plausible choices are discussed concerning the question of when the long 20th century ended. The year 1989/1990 (fall of the Iron Curtain) aside, as suggested by Herbert, one obvious choice is the rapid coming together of the European nations between 1992 and 2002. The process was consolidated by the Maastricht Treaty and the Schengen Agreement, and these two were followed by EU expansion that culminated in the introduction of the Euro currency. The September 11th 2001 attack

and destruction of the World Trade Centre (New York City, USA) is another turning point and signalled the growing threat of global Islamic terrorism. During that event 3,000 people died. It represents the culmination of various conflicts, including the crises and interventions in Afghanistan, Iraq and Syria with all their long-term challenges and consequences. The most recent date of significance would be the global economic crisis of 2008. But then again, viewed from the present day's perspective, we could add the current migrations of refugees, another effect of the globalization.

Wars, both civil and global, totalitarianism and oppression, violent or non-violent protests against state authority as well as civil disobedience have been permeating both the short and the long 20th century, even defining these eras, and they have left their shadows behind. There is a broad variety of focal points of the 20th century for archaeologists to access – an archaeology that focuses on the key parameters and so becomes a tool and a lens with which to reflect on the history of the 20th century and to illuminate it.

THE EMERGENCE OF CONTEMPORARY ARCHAEOLOGY

Archaeological studies of the short and long 20th century began in Europe some 30 years ago, a decade after such studies had started further afield. The discipline is a part of Historical Archaeology and came into being only in the final stages of a 70-year-long process that saw archaeology become a modern scientific discipline. Modern archaeology has benefited particularly from the intensified collaboration of the past decades between the Natural Sciences and the Humanities, which has contributed significant methodological advances to the discipline. At the same time, theoretical approaches informed by Post-Processual and related shifts in thinking were infused into these changes, creating a very dynamic intellectual environment. Multi- and interdisciplinary approaches have become increasingly the standard by which new questions are considered and engaged, resulting in exciting new results that are also informed by an extended spatio-temporal dimension to archaeological research.

The time frame was extended from prehistoric and protohistoric eras to the Middle Ages, the Post-Medieval period and the Modern period, including contemporary archaeology. Archaeologists are now broad-minded and are far more inclusive of visual and written sources, appreciating their strengths and their limitations as further sources in their own right. The complex array of data and how their examination is orchestrated is what makes archaeology interesting today, and it is where contemporary archaeology in particular has a real contribution to make.

As appreciation of the 19th and 20th centuries grew, contemporary archaeology came into being and demanded very tight cooperation with many ancillary fields in the cultural and social sciences, and included a broad theoretical and methodological base to provide new insight to the most recent past.

Contemporary archaeology or the archaeology of the recent past has several backgrounds. Looking at our own (material) culture led to the 'archaeology of us', focusing on garbage and modern technology, industrialisation and industrial remains, and also to the archaeology of everyday life, studied in abandoned places like houses, malls, industrial estates or urban or rural settlements. Such topics are closely related to cultural anthropology and ethno-archaeology; they can be set up as long-term studies. There has been a focus on decolonisation or post-colonial studies, conflict, terror, dictatorship and war.

Investigations in war-damaged cities after World War II became a catalyst for this process in Germany. In the same way that the archaeology of the medieval and early modern periods was initially focused on urban archaeology, so too it is with contemporary archaeology that villages and rural landscapes only became of interest subsequently. New categories of sites and contexts were highlighted and include industrial monuments, battlefields, execution places or concentration camps of the National Socialists.

The traditional study of archaeology tended to draw a line at the end of the early medieval period. Its ending does not mark a last point; humanity and the landscapes as well as the cultural environments occupied and developed through human agency continued to be dynamic. The realisation soon triggered efforts to expand the finite archaeological boundary, to glance ahead at what lay beyond. At first the focus shifted to the high medieval period, but soon it extended further through the Reformation, early modern and modern

periods and into the period of industrialisation. This process has led ultimately to what is now contemporary archaeology. Similar developments have taken place in other parts of Europe.

There are differences in how individual historical events are categorised as points of change. In the 'New World', for instance, in the Americas and Australia, the start of colonialism generally marks an important caesura. In African Archaeology, in contrast, the start of contemporary archaeology is based on written sources and the reports of witnesses that survive from a slightly younger moment.

When the chronological scope of archaeology was extended to include the medieval, post-medieval and contemporary periods, its spatial scope also expanded to encompass structures above the ground. Building archaeology plays an important role alongside archival research into historical written documents and images. In many cases, there are contemporary witness reports. These materials pose challenges across the globe, whether the cultural resource is based on a strong written-source tradition, or is grounded in long-standing oral tradition.

In contemporary archaeology, as with any archaeological study, the small and large artefacts or objects that people used on a daily basis and that are embedded in a specific context and landscape become the most important research field. Whether they were used during peacetime or wartime, for recreational or economic purposes, for eating and drinking, as clothing, or for religious or ideological reasons, these assemblages are vitally important to scientific enquiry.

Extensive material remains provide profound insights into daily life and human behaviour that other sources and disciplines often fail to observe. Photographs may capture commonplace items, and contemporary texts and contemporary witness reports may also mention them, yet it often requires archaeological finds to illustrate aspects of everyday life that are ignored by pictures, paintings, films and written sources alike. Archaeological investigations at sites from the recent past invariably produce sources that yield new insights.

The European Convention for the Protection of the Archaeological Heritage, also known as the Valetta Treaty or Malta Convention, was agreed in 1992. It brought together agreement on a European level and lifted the earlier chronological limitation on the periods of archaeological enquiry. In doing so, it ratified the existence of contemporary archaeology. The convention was built on important points of the Charter for the Protection and Management of the Archaeological Heritage that was ratified by the International Council on Monuments and Sites (ICOMOS) in Lausanne (Switzerland) 1989. Within the meaning of this convention, all remains and items, including structures and buildings among movable objects and other traces of human existence, became archaeological heritage. These assemblages must be preserved and investigated to help piece together the human past. The convention further declares archaeological heritage as a source for the European collective memory. After the ratification of the Valetta Treaty, federal or national heritage protection laws became modified in a way that renders redundant any strict limitations to certain periods of history. While different European states may take slightly different approaches to signaling when the medieval and modern epochs began, the important point is that archaeological materials and observations are now accepted as a testimony and resource for the history of humankind and, as such, are a legitimate source of knowledge. Non-European countries have developed similar principles. Acknowledgment of the importance of a preservation of cultural assets in Europe and across the world also led to a convention that covers underwater sites (UNESCO Convention for the Protection of the Underwater Cultural Heritage, 2.11.2001); this includes a codex of procedural rules that helps to govern the resolution of archaeology within the context of urban development and planning (Strasbourg, France March 10, 2000), and the UNESCO resolution for the protection and preservation of the global cultural and natural heritage (World Heritage Convention).

COMMEMORATION AS MOTIVE FOR EXCAVATIONS

The notion of a shared European past and memory had become a crucial motivating factor for various activities since the turn of the millennium. Historical sites that once staged significant events of the recent European or national past, and that have long since fallen into oblivion or are badly degraded, are frequently chosen for excavation. The excavations of such sites are normally informed by an objective to reveal previously unidentifiable remains

and to expose forgotten history. It is particularly true for remains of the two world wars (see Chapter 4) and other wars (see Chapter 5) and international conflicts, and especially those of the National Socialist era and the often torn-down and apparently no longer visible concentration camps (see Chapter 6) and to commemorate the dead (see Chapter 9). It is also the case for special national events because they can be made visible once again and in this way become a piece of the present-day population's shared memory. It suggests that the primary goal of such archaeological work is to reveal and document the find that has become hidden under the turf or pavement or even beneath walls and grout. Many visitors tend to understand and appreciate these newly visible sites of their close past more easily and more readily than the explanatory notes, maps, images or videos that are compiled to tell the narrative. A key objective of many archaeological activities is to capitalize on vision because that makes the most impact on a visitor's experience and re-lived memory.

Accordingly, many recently excavated sites of contemporary testimony relate to the idea of commemoration, memorial sites and museums in one way or another (see Chapter 13), which lends an important role to archaeology in terms of civic education. Young people from all over the world attended the excavations; while they help to uncover structures of the contemporary past they become familiarised with what remains of tyranny, civil protest and resistance and this strengthens democratic values and promotes tolerance.

Since the mid-1980s Germany has experienced increasingly vigorous demands for the intensified investigation of National Socialist rule and the murder of the European Jews and other groups. Historians were appointed to conduct research. The first excavations uncovered foundations at sites of National Socialist terror. The conscious exposure was aimed at preventing the fading of memory. We cannot be allowed to forget or to let these atrocities fall into obscurity once again. The uncovered structures will be reminiscent of the injustice and pain suffered by millions of people since the National Socialists seized power in 1933.

The Second World War (1939–1945), or more specifically National Socialist Germany (1933–1945) through its reign of violence, terror and destruction, brought incredible suffering over larger parts of Europe and beyond; that experience has had a great impact on the second half of the 20th century, a time that is also known as the Cold War period (1946/47–1991). Countless remains around the world are left behind from these twelve years of Nazi dictatorship; it is a particular period that is frequently highlighted in retrospectives of the 20th century, and this book will revisit those years repeatedly. The Pacific War, however, may be less firmly embedded in the European common memory, but the way it affected the populations of East Asia and America is equally encompassing. When the Japanese attacked China in July 1937, an event that was followed by the Massacre of Nanking in December of the same year, they started the Pacific War. But it was the Japanese attack on Pearl Harbour on 7th December 1941 that made the Pacific War part of the Second World War, with the American entry into the war the following day and the declaration of war against Germany and its ally Japan on 11th December 1941. While the German capitulation on 8th May 1945 marked the end of the war in Europe, the Japanese capitulated on 2nd September 1945 – only two weeks after the nuclear bombing of Hiroshima and Nagasaki (Japan).

THE FIRST EXCAVATIONS AT DETENTION CAMPS AND SITES OF CONFLICT

Archaeologists began excavations at former extermination and concentration camps around 1990 (see Chapter 6). A small investigation was conducted in the German extermination camp at Chełmno, (present-day Poland) in 1986/87. Another early project was at Witten-Annen (North Rhine-Westphalia, Germany; see Fig. 1.1) a sub-camp of Buchenwald (Thuringia, Germany), where the initial field campaign revealed the layouts of the barracks. In Bełżec, another German extermination camp in present-day east Poland, geophysical prospection was employed to locate the exact position of buildings and the gas chambers (see Fig. 1.2). More activity at other sites

Fig. 1.1. A small memorial was erected after the first excavation in the former sub-camp of Witten-Annen (North Rhine-Westphalia, Germany) (© Claudia Theune).

Fig. 1.2. Buildings were uncovered during the excavations in the former extermination camp in Bełżec (present-day Poland), which probably belonged to the killing facilities (© Ryszard Kazmierczak).

of National Socialist terror followed closely afterwards. It was often inspired by plans to create a new memorial where all traces had vanished long ago, or to redesign an existing memorial. In other instances, archaeological work was carried out to address questions concerning the relics of local history. It turned out that many of the surviving documents such as building plans and written records are incomplete and lacking, so archaeological measures were required to determine the correct layout of the facilities. Descriptions and images of structures and places, for example, sometimes fall surprisingly short in terms of perspective and dimensions, and demonstrate how different perceptions can lead to different interpretations.

Archaeological enquiry has continued and has progressively moved out from the main camps to include the sub-camps, the forced labour, prisoner-of-war or internment camps, and such work has extended beyond Germany and Poland. Since the early 2000s, the work has reached sites in Austria, The Netherlands, Norway, Great Britain, Finland, France, and even in Greece and other parts of Europe. It is especially the injustice that countless forced labourers suffered at the hands of National Socialists that has drawn the attention to forced labour camps in recent years. At the same time, investigations are extending further to include the factories where the captives were deployed.

After archaeologists became aware of National Socialist internment camps, the questions widened to include the Allied prisoner-of-war camps. The first

approaches were usually aimed at locating any extant remains through general survey. Once the layouts of barracks were uncovered and highlighted for future visitors, more detailed research helped to reveal the individual stages in the development of these facilities from their early beginnings, through the periods in which they were used for internment, to what became of them afterwards. The objects recovered have tended to occur in large quantities, and their context of discovery informs aspects of the captives and their guards, sometimes hinting at their origins, or illustrating the means that were available to them on a daily basis.

The erection of prisoner-of-war camps as well as detention camps, where German and also Japanese or other enemy aliens were imprisoned, spread through many parts of the world; the warring parties ran such camps in their motherlands and also in their colonies. After the end of the war, the Allies held countless German Wehrmacht soldiers in the so-called Rheinwiesen camps in summer of 1945. The soldiers had to sleep under the open sky, it was dirty and wet and the nutrition and hygienic standards were bad at least during the first few months.

Excavations have been carried out mainly at contemporary sites in the USA, Canada, Finland and Germany so far, but even more remote locations like Trinidad provide evidence. German war prisoners of the Africa Corps, for instance, were kept in a camp near Whitewater in the Province of Manitoba (Canada, see Fig. 1.3) or in Fort Hood (Texas, USA), where the layout

Fig. 1.3. Prisoner-of-war camp in Whitewater (Prov. Manitoba, Canada) where investigations took place between 2009 and 2011 (© Adrian Myers).

of the barracks was revealed and many finds have been uncovered. All such discoveries underline the strong global dimension inherent in their era. Captives of war from all involved parties were shipped to and held in many parts of the world, and the evidence left behind gives an impressive example of the global perspective of a contemporary archaeology. The same applies in reverse at concentration camps, where people from all around the globe were imprisoned by the National Socialists and deprived of their rights. The world wars signalled the 20th century as the century of globalisation, and contemporary archaeology by association deals with the multitude of these aspects all the time.

War zones all over Europe, from Greece to Norway and beyond, are marked by battlefields and defensive systems, with many airplanes crashed, and many submarines and war ships sunk. Particularly in less densely populated areas, such as the High Alps or in Northern parts of Europe and the American continent, wreckage from both world wars can still be detected. The conservation authorities are equally responsible for protecting such objects in all their diverse forms, including bunkers and batteries / gun emplacements of the Atlantic Wall, many of which still exist along the shores from Norway all the way down to France, or remains of the Western Wall with its various bunkers and anti-tank barriers that have now become

accepted sites of archaeological and historical interest (see Chapter 4). Such sites pose a challenge of huge proportions because of their invisible structures, which lie underground.

2014 marked the centenary of the outbreak of the First World War, an anniversary that saw various activities get under way to provide an opportunity to catalogue the remains of this first significant catastrophe of the 20th century. In France and Belgium the first excavations of the large Western Front battlefields played an important role. Archaeological investigations at the site of a prisoner-of-war-camp from the First World War near Quedlinburg (Saxony-Anhalt, Germany) also received much attention. The stretch of land that lies between Nieuwpoort and Ypres in Flanders (Belgium) or the regions around Lille, Arras, Reims and Verdun (France) are riddled with discoveries of the gruesome tactical warfare that defines the social memory of trench warfare. Several of the trenches and former positions of artillery batteries have been uncovered, repeatedly exposing adjacent solitary or mass graves, yet every so often victims turn up who were left without a burial. In some cases it is possible to identify the killed soldiers by their identity tags, and this creates an opportunity to give them a proper burial or even to return them and any personal items to their families. Apart from mortal remains, large quantities of

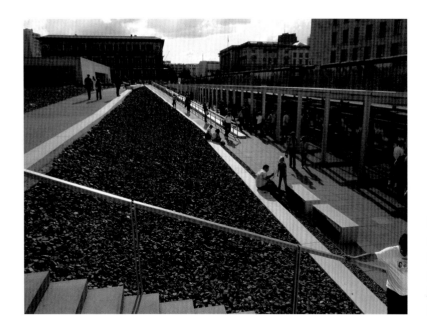

ammunition are a frequent find. Among them, the so-called trench art constitutes a very distinct category of object from those contemporary battlefields, where the soldiers would craft objects typically from the shell and bullet casings (see Chapter 10).

At the end of the war, long-standing state entities and several monarchies collapsed and were replaced by new – now democratic – states in the Western World within modified territories. The 20th century started out under the impression of a number of dramatic global-scale events that have recently come into focus again to be publicly revisited and commemorated. Related material remains in places that played a role in the events are included and now archaeologically investigated.

The Berlin Wall, for its part, has also been a focus of early research. After the Wall 'fell' in November 1989 and was rapidly dismantled in the course of the German Unification, parts of the Wall have been excavated and turned into memorials (see Fig. 1.4). It is the quintessential icon of the Iron Curtain, which once divided Europe from Finland all the way down to former Yugoslavia, and other sections of this divisive boundary have been targeted by several excavation projects in recent years (see Chapter 8). Other categories of sites have also attracted attention as, for example, the continued use of some former concentration camps as Soviet Special Camps after the end of the Second World War (until 1950).

Contemporary archaeology of the 20th century in Europe has focused on the principal finds and features associated with these sites. Smaller-scale and local initiatives of remembrance and reconciliation will also employ archaeological methods to promote awareness. Many archaeological projects were recently created around the world to investigate monumental or material remains that shed light on totalitarian, fascist or dictatorial regimes. Excavations conducted in Argentina during the past decades are as important as those in Spain, where the archaeological focus is on sites of the Spanish Civil War (1936–1939; see Chapter 5).

Mass graves and with it the victims of the atrocities of the 20th century have been repeatedly targeted by excavations. This began even during the Second World War when, for example, the Katyn (Smolensk, Russia) mass graves were discovered that held the Polish victims shot by Stalinist death squads in spring 1940. It is seen in other parts of the world where people have been murdered because of their political opinions, in places such as Cambodia (1975–1978), Rwanda (1994), Argentina (1976–1983), Spain (1936–1939), Bosnia and Herzegovina and other sites of the Balkan Wars (1991–1995). The meticulous forensic methods of archaeological fieldwork and its detailed documentation are allowing the determination of the causes of death and the recovery of personal items that can help to identify the deceased. After that, sites of commemoration can be set up or the victims buried in the proper way with dignity. In some cases the evidence gathered has even been provided to help with investigations of the International Criminal Tribunal in The Hague (The Netherlands). Those activities are all signs of the ongoing debate regarding the national histories of the recent past, with the rule of dictators, with the first and perhaps most important step being the recovery of the victims from the anonymity of mass graves (see Chapter 9).

One of the youngest fields of the 20th- and 21st-century archaeology focuses on places of resistance, protest and civil disobedience. Various places of social and political uproar have been investigated lately, among them sites that played a key role during the conflicts in, for instance, Northern Ireland (1969–1998) or remains of the first nuclear tests (1951–1992) in the Nevada (USA) desert. We can also include Greenham Common Women's Peace Camp (1981–2000) in England, which was established as a protest against the deployment of cruise missiles. Further examples include the Gorleben Anti-Nuclear Protest Camp (Lower Saxony, Germany, 1980), which developed from protests against plans to build a national deep geological repository for radioactive waste. In Prague (Czech Republic) a former travellers' camp became an archaeological excavation site. The last example in this short list is that of Ludlow (Colorado, USA), where in 1914 striking miners and family members were shot, an event known as the Ludlow Massacre; the former tent site of the families was investigated some years ago (see Chapter 7).

The most recent topics considered in archaeology are very prescient, and concern migration and exodus. Traces of illegal migrants, for instance, are being uncovered along the Mexican-American borders or even in Europe (see Chapter 8).

Archaeology can also help to broaden the perspective beyond the historical dimension and lend a voice or give a past to those whose low status rarely afforded them the opportunity of doing it themselves. It offers a new narrative that can stand apart from the well-known official reports.

CONTEMPORARY ARCHAEOLOGY BEYOND WAR AND CONFLICT

Topics such as world wars, fascism, civil disobedience and protest are a frequent occurrence, but not all research is inevitably related to those fields. Another subject with a relevance for human society is garbage, or waste (see Chapter 12). Archaeologists will often find it an unavoidable fact that they are excavating human detritus and they have paid little attention to this material as disposed waste for too long. Now their perception of the ambiguity of waste is currently changing and it is becoming the case that objects and traces of refuse are equally well recorded. A glance into the waste bin of the individual household or at a huge urban dump site can reveal a fascinating array of details about the daily routine and our ways of life. It offers many more dimensions for exploration. Excavation and investigations at U.S. communal dump sites of the 1970s, for instance, have shown for the first time that the waste was comprised of surprisingly huge quantities of paper. This led to pilot projects aimed at collecting old paper separately from households. It also led to the idea of paper recycling. It is only one among many examples that demonstrate how archaeology can contribute effectively to a country's socio-political development.

Contemporary archaeology has a relevance in 19th-century studies too. Industrial Archaeology, for example, falls into this category (see Chapter 12). The subject was first established in England, where people took a special interest in the national industrial heritage. British archaeologists were among the first to create inventories of monuments of the industrial past, to invent measures for their preservation and to make the sites publicly available. These developments included even the biggest monuments, such as the oldest iron bridge spanning the Severn River at Coalbrookdale (Shropshire, England) or the extended canal system that preceded the British railway. First endeavours at sites in Germany focused on the famous early pottery factories, and were followed by investigations of coal or ore mines and steel plants of the Ruhr district (North Rhine-Westphalia).

Open-cast mining has for centuries devastated enormous parts of the German coal districts in the Rhine area, south Brandenburg and Saxony. Several small towns, villages and farmsteads have been sacrificed to mining over the course of time, including very recent cases, and these have created a unique opportunity for archaeological research (see Chapter 12). It seems only logical not to linger on the medieval and early modern evidence alone, but instead to extend the investigations to include the first and the final stages. The unique combination of different sources such as landscape features, objects, images, recorded texts and contemporary witness reports allow for an exceptionally detailed and complete reconstruction of their history over time. In the western parts of the Czech Republic modern deserted villages are targets of archaeological research. The villages were abandoned by a largely German population during the displacement out of Czechoslovakia in 1945/46. A study of the settlement remains as well as the former cemeteries hint at the processes of abandonment and transition. Similar investigations were conducted in settlements that were totally destroyed during the Second World War, for example at Küstrin/Kostrzyn nad Odrą (Poland).

The variety of archaeological investigations at sites of the 20th century has now become very great. However, it has to be stated that many surveys and excavations are only known through short reports; only a few are published comprehensively.

The pattern within contemporary archaeology has been to consider places that once staged important historical events or sites that played a major role for the history of regions, states and even entire continents. However, archaeological methods and research should always strive to do more. It is its underlying task to cast a glance beyond well-known records and to consider a wider base of aspects of 20th-century history. Places, assemblages and objects of past infrastructure, of life and death, of a more domestic character or one associated with work and labour, of actions, leisure-time activities, of public institutions, religion, cult and deposits; all of these facets are within the scope of archaeological research, and the aspects of war, violence and protest are inherently present. It is the case that erosion of these cultural remains is constant; not only the huge and now mostly abandoned industrial facilities, but also a multitude of small craftsmens' shops, older service enterprises and even routeways and earlier infrastructure are forever being lost before they are studied and understood fully.

Archaeological research of the modern periods must normally include the 19th century to enhance its potential and provide deeper insight to the course of the past 100 years. The standing and the buried remains provide a multi-facetted testimony of past events. The majority of 20th-century sites are reminders of traumatic events resulting in negative connotations rather than the opposite, while sites reminiscent of joyful and positive events scarcely exist, or at least we do not highlight them. Since the painful distressing moments are an inevitable part of our local, national or global history, this situation cannot be avoided and has to be part of our conversation with the past. The documentation through archaeological means makes history a physical, even tactile experience, literally, and hence inspires higher acceptance while paving the way towards a more conscious perception.

The fact that concentration camps and battlefields were the first categories of sites to be investigated has inspired labels like 'Concentration Camp Archaeology' (German: 'KZ Archäologie'), 'Holocaust Archaeology', 'Combat Archaeology', 'Internment Archaeology' or 'Aviation Archaeology'. Excavations at places that have played a special role in specific wars resulted in the creation of even further labels such as 'Archaeology of the First World War / Great War' ('Grande Guerre'), 'Archaeology of the Second World War', 'Archaeology of the Cold War' or 'Post-War Archaeology' and, with regard to investigations at sites tied to events of civil disobedience, the label 'Archaeology of Civil Protest' has been applied. From my point of view, all these labels are too narrowly considered and fail to encompass the breadth of the multi-layered and complex dimensions of the places and the people and their roles in the history of the 20th century. The term 'Holocaust', in the strictest sense of meaning, is solely applicable to the mass murder and destruction of the Jewish peoples; without attempting to downplay this awfulness in the slightest, it needs to be observed that the bulk of those camps were never intentionally designed for mass murder, although it cannot be denied that many people were detained and murdered there. Another fact is that not all of the Second World War camps were closed immediately at the end of the war, since we know of at least a few that apparently changed hands and were then used over longer periods of time into the ensuing Cold War era. Often, we are not able to distinguish the layers exactly and assign the objects to one or the other phase of use. These few examples may suffice to demonstrate the limits of the labels mentioned above. The term 'Contemporary Archaeology' is therefore used consistently in what follows.

Chapter 2

CONTEMPORARY ARCHAEOLOGY AND ETHICS

INTRODUCTION

Archaeology has a long-standing and ongoing tradition as a science that is closely involved with political processes and narratives. The way that archaeological monuments and finds are claimed to illustrate, interpret and consolidate national history and further political ambitions began as early as the 19th century. Master narratives, significant places of remembrance or of our cultural memory are based on a tradition that is inscribed in texts, images, sites and rites. Those are the determinants that define our conception of history; regardless of whether it was intended or not, archaeological excavations and findings are an integral part of that concept. It is debatable whether ethical principles are always as respected as they should be. Such archaeological sites or finds can be central places and buildings, even if they have become peripheral with time, such as battlefields and burial sites, places of either victory or defeat, prehistoric monuments as well as memorials of the recent past. When terrorists lay waste to highly significant archaeological monuments, as has recently happened all too often, it must be understood as the intentional destruction of places of common remembrance and cultural identity (see Chapter 13).

Contemporary archaeology of the 20th century demands a special sensibility and unambiguously responsible actions regarding the observance of ethical and legal principles, in particular when the investigations deal with dark heritage like dictatorship, terror and death. The conflicts, wars and events of the 20th century are still contemporary for survivors and those who are the living generations of these moments, as well as the bereaved and extended families and communities. It is inevitable that such acute memory and association will fade over time, but archaeologists in general apply a strict ethical code to all sites regardless of time period, just as the remains of humanity's earliest ancestors must always be respected and cherished.

ARCHAEOLOGISTS, STAKEHOLDERS AND LOCAL COMMUNITIES

The most effective approach to defining good ethical principles is to act in communion with the various stakeholder groups and address their interests and moral values with respect. It means that each stakeholder community might influence the archaeological investigations in different ways. In places where human lives were lost through violence and murder, the primary stakeholders are the bereaved in the first instance. Local and inter-regional stakeholders are often involved as well, and may come from religious communities, ethnic groups

Fig. 2.1. Sachsenhausen, boxes filled with human ash during the excavation in the area of the crematoria (© Johannes Weishaupt).

and social and political parties. The representatives of such grassroot organisations must be included in the dialogue while local, national and international interests must be equally taken into account. Archaeologists need to know what is regarded as ethically correct behaviour by and between the various stakeholders, who might not share the archaeologist's perspective. We are obliged to establish a dialogue with each party, to consider their concerns carefully and integrate them into our work.

The principal motivation of all the parties involved may be similar, but the individual interests of the stakeholders are not always identical or even in accordance. While many of the surviving relatives would want the mortal remains to be exhumed and returned home, others may prefer to leave them to rest eternally at their original place of death. In the case of the Katyn massacre (1940), where thousands of Polish officers and other members of the Polish Intelligentsia were murdered and buried in mass graves in Katyn, Mednoje near Twer (both Russia), and in Piatykhatky in the vicinity of Charkiw and Bykiwnja in the vicinity of Kiev (both Ukraine), arrangements were made to have the personal items of the victims put on display at the Katyn museum in Warsaw while their physical remains stayed in the places of their demise, and these mass grave sites were turned into memorials. The places are in a region that is present-day Russia, but Polish archaeologists are conducting the excavations (see Chapter 9).

It is a policy of the government of the United States of America to locate and recover the remains of soldiers who have died in battles abroad to bring them home. The notion is usually shared by the bereaved, who are mobilised around the DPAA (Defense POW/ MIA Accounting Agency) based in Washington D.C. (USA), which is tasked with searching across the world for missing American soldiers from all wars since the 19th century. Actual crash sites from the Second World War are excavated by archaeologists and forensic anthropologists to rescue the bodies or what remains of them, and to collect personal belongings and return them to the U. S. (see Chapter 9).

Wars and battles are not the only catastrophes that result in thousands of deaths; those who oppose totalitarian or dictatorial regimes, who rise up against oppression and exploitation, are always in danger of being killed and buried in mass graves. Exhumations and archaeological investigations that are initiated by either local authorities or other stakeholder groups are usually driven by various interests and do not necessarily result in a full disclosure of the objective factual circumstances surrounding these offences.

Former concentration camp sites are principally also burial sites. Even in places were mass graves and ash dumps are not primarily investigated, the remains of other bodies must always be expected to be concealed in the ground. When a programme of augering was started

at the site of the former German extermination camp of Bełżec in today's Poland to refine the location of hidden mass graves, other archaeologists were indignant at these methods because it was said that Jewish religious standards were being violated, which determine that the peace of the dead must not be disturbed under any circumstances. Augering was also applied in Mauthausen (Austria) to identify the locations of ash dumps, but in that case the measures were sanctioned by the Mauthausen committee prior to excavation. The augering was meant to determinate the exact dimension of the ash spread there. Large piles of ash were also discovered repeatedly during excavations that accompanied the remodelling at the Sachsenhausen memorial site in Germany (see Fig. 2.1). The Jewish religious community had agreed to have the collected ash reburied immediately after the construction work was completed (see Fig. 2.2).

The International Criminal Court at The Hague (The Netherlands) is tasked with gathering evidence for the investigation of war crimes, genocide and crimes against humanity. There are other courts that are pursuing a similar objective to bring the perpetrators to justice. The genocidal mass murder committed by the Khmer Rouge in Cambodia during the late 1970s, the attacks of Hutu against Tutsi in Rwanda in 1994, or the Srebrenica massacre in 1995, are only a few of the examples that are still fresh in our memories (see Chapter 9). It has become almost impossible to punish the original perpetrators of earlier crimes, mass murder or genocides or even the Holocaust, but the forensic methods that are applied by archaeologists nevertheless rarely fail to turn up new information that helps to solve older so-called cold cases, and complements the historiographical records.

While the precise ethical approach will vary widely depending on the different groups and motivations, in most cases the victims will be put centre-stage – a notion that can only be fully supported. A deep-felt responsibility towards the victims is one of the main motivating factors that drove me, personally, towards developing a particular interest in the archaeology of former concentration camps and sites of 20th-century crimes. To act in an ethical manner means to help uncover the crimes against the victims, to inform their surviving relatives, provide answers and to call public attention to such atrocity against humanity. Those crimes are often subject to national or international laws where specific rules apply and must be followed accordingly. There is also a potential for the conflict of loyalties. Archaeologists in these situations find themselves walking a fine line, but one that they are trained for and are fully capable of walking well.

Chapter 3

SOURCES AND METHODOLOGY

INTRODUCTION

The way we interact with our environment is integral to how we perceive ourselves through words, pictures, and objects but also through sounds, fragrances and haptics. We use a wide range of objects in everyday life; we talk to each other, take notes of thoughts and events, take photos of people, places and items or picture them by other forms of images. Normally we retain memories of all kinds of experiences as pictures in our mind. We work and act through objects, words, be they written or spoken, and through images. Our fellow human beings, who may share our cultural upbringing or come from similar backgrounds, can usually understand our messages partially or, ideally, fully if we use objects in a way that is familiar, if we talk and write or if we use images. For current societies we have access to such sources through empirical studies, but such options are often not applicable when studying the more distant past, where the evidence is frequently rather sketchy or fragmentary. This applies most especially to sound and smell in the past, which for the most part escape us today, but which would most certainly have mattered to people in their time.

Material remains are the most important source for archaeological research. When archaeology is dealing with past non-literate cultures, such material remains are usually the only evidence available for reconstructing the way of life and living conditions. In some instances, of course, there are also figurative representations which may amplify the results. The earliest tools discovered in Palaeolithic contexts present the earliest evidence. Over time, the spectrum of tools and objects broadened and differentiated. Even studies from such recent periods as the Middle Ages and the early modern period are often strongly based on the analysis of objects. The potential of other and complementary sources, such as picture- or word-based sources and audio-visual recordings is receiving more and more attention today. This concerns archaeologists, but also historians and art historians who now include material remains as integral components of their own investigations.

THE MULTIPLICITY OF SOURCES

The concept of Historical Archaeology is based on a research framework that is inclusive of all sources, where texts, images, monuments and artefacts hold equal importance and must be studied together. Since the post-medieval era, and especially in modern times, the various sources become more and more numerous, so we also speak of a densely documented era. All the components

Sources to do with hearing

As explained in this chapter, research into our history is largely founded on word-based, object-based and image-based sources. In historical archaeology in particular we are accustomed to analysing written sources, the reports of contemporary witnesses and pictorial sources alongside artefacts. However, other senses and perceptions play an important role in our human actions and behaviour, even if they are difficult to perceive from the distance of time. This is in part because there are today few if any possibilities for grasping the different perceptions provided by smell, hearing or touch in the past. We depend on reports to tell us about, for example, the extreme and unpleasant smells at sites where the dead were left to decay or were burned. The texture of the surface of objects may give us an impression how things feel when touched. With this, perhaps we can understand another sense. Since Thomas Alva Edison invented the phonograph in 1877, we are able to listen to surviving voices and sounds, even if they are distorted in the original recording devices. One example can serve to illustrate how objects too can convey a sense of context and sound: namely, the shoe irons that are often found as artefacts in the camps. These irons shod the soles of the guards' shoes and boots in the concentration

Shoe irons are common finds in former internment camps: this was found in the Mauthausen concentration camp (© Claudia Theune).

and detention camps. Their sound could be heard loudly and clearly on paved or asphalted roads, indicating the footsteps of the SS guards and in this way were a constant source of threat to the prisoners.

that create the evidence of human creativity, actions and communication are considered together, as one. This concept was inspired by the Historical Archaeology already established in the U.S. and Australia; studies there focused mainly on the period after the arrival of the first Europeans, and this approach has had a strong influence. Not all remains have the same ability to provide information, and the information available from different sources does not necessarily correlate closely with each other. Indeed, where the evidence obtained from different sources leads to divergent results, then it is principally not a contradiction but merely proof of their significantly different potential and inherent perspective.

Cultural historical research of the present and the current epistemological approach emphasise all the aspects given above: written sources of various kinds as well as contemporary witness reports are usually created from a specific and individual perspective, and

are subjective. The same applies to images in general, although they can capture the moment in a way that written and oral records cannot. This principle also applies to objects.

It has been emphasised for some time now that verbal sources, and equally pictures, cannot be trusted to provide an objective testimony of past realities because of the narrator's or artist's particular point of view. One and the same event can and will be experienced and reflected differently by different persons. The realisation prompted the so-called 'Cultural turns' (*e.g.* Linguistic turn, Iconic turn, Spatial turn, Material turn, etc.), which triggered a change of paradigm in many fields within the humanities that focus on the study of material culture.

Each single word, be it spoken or written, and equally each drawn or painted picture or photograph, whether large or small in size, is made or ordered to serve a specific intention. We must consider the possibility

Fig. 3.1. Mauthausen, cemetery in the foreground and the infirmary camp in the background after the liberation. Only one row of the barracks is still standing; the kitchen building with its chimneys can be seen on the left-hand side; and the barracks at the rear are already missing (©KZ-Gedenkstätte Mauthausen Sign. 4.7.22, Sammlung Pierre Serge Choumoff, photograph François Lachenal, June 1945).

that the person, or the customer who ordered the final product, would express the intended message differently in words than they would, for instance, through an image. Objects, in turn, provide even more options to pass the message on. Whatever the individual intention or intentions, the multi-disciplinary approach is necessary to generate meaning. Listeners, partners in dialogue, viewers and users would generally be expected to be able to perceive the motivation as well as the message. However, possible misperceptions or misunderstandings can also be intended. The reasons can lie in different perceptions of the messages sent, or perceptions that are conveyed by specific sources. A different use of objects can also be wilfully employed.

Whether one source provides an accurate description of past events and structures down to the smallest detail is of minor importance, nor is it important that other sources may be wrong or right. A verification or falsification is of little relevance in this context; instead it is of greater interest to identify the reasons and motives that lead to significantly different representations of one and the same event or comparable events. It is necessary to consult as many of the available sources as possible to obtain the most comprehensive answers appropriate to the historical context.

An excellent example is that of the parents of Martin Luther, the founder of the Reformation. During so-called dinner speeches, which were reported by guests, Martin Luther always portrayed his parents as modest people from simple backgrounds. Other sources such as tax statements or portraits of Hans and Margarethe Luther make it quite clear that Luther's parents were part of

Fig. 3.2. Mauthausen, infirmary camp, excavation of Barrack 6; foundation of the barrack with nails from the barrack construction and some traces of burning (© Claudia Theune).

the wealthy upper class. Archaeological excavations in his birthplace in Mansfeld (Saxony-Anhalt, Germany) have also uncovered sufficient evidence of a privileged lifestyle, among which are fragments of exquisite tablewares or culinary delicacies of their time.

Another example concerns one part of the former concentration camp Mauthausen (Austria). In written sources recorded by the U.S. liberators it is stated that the so-called infirmary camp was burned down. The archaeological excavation of one of the barracks showed only a small burned layer that could not support the reported record entirely (see Fig. 3.2, see Chapter 6). A photo from June 1945 shows that some barracks are still standing while others are missing (see Fig. 3.1). The U.S. soldiers probably only burned down some of the barracks and not all of them. Furthermore the site was probably levelled after

tearing down all remaining barracks, and traces of the fire were removed.

Each type of source is affected by its inherent capacities or shortcomings. While facts that may appear banal at first and receive little or no attention, such as the various steps required to build a house or manufacture appliances, ranging from the distinctive raw materials required and the different techniques employed, written and depictive sources and the objects themselves can provide a fount of good information when studied in detail. This is where archaeology's real strength lies. Features and objects offer enormous potential to investigate everyday items or daily conditions from a long-term perspective. They are, of course, less useful when approaching the study from the perspective of specific historical moments, unless the study is of a specific site known to exist at the particular historical moment. In wider terms, archaeological material represents the records of daily life and focuses on different matters. This is in contrast to, for example, merchants' books, which are more likely to have entries on contacts, intermediaries, purchases and sales margins, or indeed testimonies that might describe the way supplies (wares) were handled.

Time also exerts an influence on sources. Secondary influences or later interpretations affect the primary sources and can change them. The process is referred to as 'second life'. Whenever something is added, taken away or overwritten it renders older surfaces and layers invisible. We can consider this in the present day by looking at how digitization of text can reveal the different moments when a text was edited or developed. Older versions can be identified by their saving dates, which virtually reveals the older layers. The same principle applies to older material, such as historic buildings that have witnessed major renovations, overhauls and extensions. Paintings are also subject to modifications and can be painted over, and sculptures can be changed as well. Landscapes and the environment we live in are dynamic and in a state of constant change and transformation. The sum of the material cultural heritage therefore retains a palimpsest nature or intricate layering, each of which can be temporal and cultural, and ultimately a means for revealing the important insights being sought.

Archaeological objects allow us to access many aspects of the applied techniques, of traditional craftsmanship and industrial innovations and materials. Typological study helps to deduce their former function based on their shapes and designs and offers significant clues that help to date their origin. Vestiges (traces) of how they were used in the past, be it superficially or embedded in the material, hint at specific production technologies; such traces are indicators of the intensity, duration and type of use. The spatial pattern of how and where certain types of objects occur can illuminate issues associated with distributions, and this in turn can indicate possible areas of origin, patterns of trade and exchange or regions of traditional usage. Even wider insight can be obtained when the items are understood as a means by which past societies used to communicate. The meaning and symbolism of specific acts and objects for people within their social environments is common

knowledge and well-established. Within the Christian-influenced culture in Europe or the Western World in general we have no difficulties in acknowledging and understanding the meaning of most objects that originate within our zone of shared virtues and values. However, more in-depth approaches to cultural history through the study of objects can only be successful when emphasis is applied to that shared background. If we do not separate the items from their contexts, i. e. our living environment, but instead focus on the close relationship between the object and its producer or owner, then the concept of use or the status that is signified by the presence of an item within a group becomes possible to study. In short, we begin to outline the biography or the itinerary of an object.

The written sources that first deal with Central Europe in the late Iron Age were not composed by the indigenous people, but are accounts prepared by foreigners (*i.e.* the Romans) and are for the most part focused on extraordinary events rather than on mundane aspects of daily life. This pattern remained in place until the most recent and post-medieval period.

The oldest art works of mankind, normally fashioned either as paintings on or engravings in stone, but in some cases also as more three-dimensional objects such as figurines and sculptures in stone, clay, bone or wood, date back to the Palaeolithic and they are the earliest known images. Finds of stele or *situlae*, richly decorated vessels, that originated in the (late Bronze Age and early Iron Age) Hallstatt culture, provide more elaborate and detailed depictions of scenes of ritual feasting at that time. It was not before the Roman period, however, that imagery became more consistent and common even in mundane contexts. Religiously inspired scenes prevailed during the medieval period, particularly book illuminations or frescoes in churches and monasteries. Allegories like the Four Seasons, for example, and related motifs occurred only at a later stage of the Middle Ages. But that scenario changed dramatically at the transition from the late medieval to the early modern period when depictions of persons or landscape became extremely popular. Famous examples of that new style are the oil paintings created by Flemish artists of the 16th and 17th centuries, who recorded even small objects of daily use with amazing accuracy.

THE SIGNIFICANCE OF OBJECTS

Objects of all kinds are fixed installations of our daily routine that we can hardly live without. We are using everyday items incessantly, always and everywhere, be it clothing, jewellery, tools, furniture or means of transportation. Far too often we tend to focus our sights on their functionality alone: clothing offers protection from both high and low temperatures; dishes and cutlery are required to prepare and consume our meals; shoes, skates, sleds, small and bigger boats, carts drawn by oxen or carriages drawn by horse, bicycles, trains or cars help us to travel distances. Equipped with tools and appliances we master the daily struggle for survival, no matter whether it is in the professional field or in our spare time. Pieces of jewellery and precious objects are used for personal adornment, while weaponry can bring harm to others. Besides such smaller portable objects, there are bigger immobile ones. Buildings of various kinds also fall into the category of objects; they provide shelter but can also lock us in. Walkways and streets, taking us from one point to another, must be mentioned in this context as well. However, what remains of prehistoric buildings are basically only their contours, foundations and so-called 'negative structures' in the soil. Postholes, for instance, attest to the position of their primary structures, while foundations can provide an idea of the layout of ground- or basement-level rooms. In a category of their own, so-called pit-houses often allow the accessing of their former function as crafts-shop or living area based on the smaller objects and other traces preserved underneath the backfill of the pit. From the medieval and even more so from the modern periods there are a number of standing homes, estates, castles and others that have seen significant alterations over time; they are all historical objects.

Some objects can be very different despite similarities. There are clearly, for instance, many variations of buildings based on their size and features alone, but equally so by criteria of construction or their intended purpose. In the same way, we must expect items of daily use to differ significantly; this could be based on different materials used to make them, whether simple and cheap material or expensive and precious metals, thereby making the production process equally costly or less so. The appreciation of the owner must also be recognised and assessed and may not be influenced by the material value alone, but can be a factor of perception in the face of historical perspective. Even minor objects can attain a certain appreciation through the perception of generations.

Most of the items we choose to surround ourselves with are characterised by our aesthetic perception. The way we value or dismiss trinkets or how we appreciate a tool or not is often a factor of individual taste as well as habit and is strongly affected by common standards, conventions and traditions. We would hardly use objects that do not appear to be handy, and it is equally unlikely that we would choose an accessory that is not appealing to us.

Research on archaeological materials usually begins with a chrono-typological classification and extends to various aspects from production technique, shape, functionality to chronology. Important indicators can be deduced from the exact context of the finds, and clusters in the pattern of their distribution can suggest places of production or use.

An exact dating is often not easy to achieve. As stated above, the internment camps did not only exist during the National Socialist period but also after the end of World War II. Many camps were also in use after the end of the Second World War. Even if the objects found there are recent, their specifics cannot always be clearly assigned to one phase or another. It can be assumed that objects still were in use after the end of the war.

Current trends in the cultural-anthropological and related fields have inspired new approaches during recent years that focus mainly on the relationship between quality, value and distinctive social groups to access social systems and cultural behaviour.

However, the objects that survive can only depict a segment of the past. Objects made from organic materials do not survive well. It was common practice to dispose of objects in the past or to recycle them in a way that renders the traces of their primary use invisible. Items made from glass or metals are prime examples of this, as they can be re-smelted and turned into new and entirely different objects. Within the borders of abandoned settlements, for instance, only those items that were either lost or intentionally discarded are left to be discovered, while graves or deposits can be expected to contain assemblages of choice. Archaeologists are familiar with working with these challenges.

Fig. 3.3. A toothbrush produced in Hungary found in Mauthausen, probably brought there by a Hungarian prisoner (© Claudia Theune).

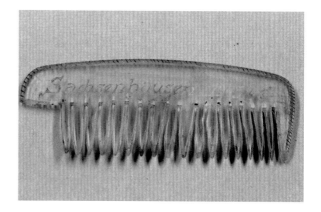

Fig. 3.4. A self-made comb with uneven teeth from the Soviet Special Camp Sachsenhausen (Germany), recollecting the years 1945/46 (© Anne Kathrin Müller).

Examples serve to further illustrate the potential of contemporary archaeology. Objects that are not industrially-manufactured but are hand-made by prisoners using the simplest of tools are often found at former concentration camp sites (see also Chapter 10). Sometimes prisoners would turn a broken handle of a spoon or a knife into a new spoon by pounding the material until it took on a ladle-like form once again, and by twisting the rest to form a new dipper arm. The inmates produced such items themselves and ensured their survival on a day-to-day basis, to have the tools to eat their soup as people do. Self-made knifes are also recovered frequently, despite the fact that the possession of cutting tools was strictly prohibited. To make a knife in secret entailed enormous risk. Those objects are important reminders that even the most basic items like cutlery were not provided in sufficient numbers by the camp's administration. Toiletries like toothbrushes or combs are further examples of items that were not sufficiently available. Inscriptions of trade marks identified on toothbrushes in various languages show their owners came from many different countries from all over Europe (see Fig. 3.3). It was not prohibited to bring a toothbrush into the camp, but they must have been prized possessions. In contrast to a prisoner's striped clothing and shoes that were issued by the camp administration at registration, items of personal hygiene were not supplied. The imprisoned also tried to dress as best as they could; they kept repairing the damaged clothes. The modified fragments of combs and simple plastic pieces that served

as combs by having teeth sawn out of the material represent one example, testifying to a prisoner's need to maintain a minimum standard of grooming (see Fig. 3.4). Personal hygiene is one of our most basic needs. Human well-being is directly affected by the lack of it; and this in turn affects the will and the human desire to survive. Where people are denied the most basic levels of bodily hygiene it does not take long for them to lose any sense of self-worth. The discovery of such objects, therefore, provides strong and tangible evidence of the strategies employed by the imprisoned to maintain their humanity and survive (see Chapter 9).

SPOKEN AND WRITTEN WORDS

Written or oral records are normally the first sources we look for to access the less distant past. The medieval period produced considerable numbers of textual sources. The introduction of the printing press in the 15th century transformed the accessibility of written sources by enabling widespread distribution and numerous copies, and also facilitated a significant increase in the number of administrative regulatory documents, records and registers. Subsequently, the development of the telegram in the middle of the 19th century, as emails and text messages today, made the written word a profuse resource.

These data fall into two primary groups, official administrative documents and personal notes. Historians repeatedly caution against expecting objectivity in personal notes, as they merely reflect the subjective perspective of the author or a client. The same, of course, is true of official documents, as all documents regardless of type are created with particular and specific purposes in mind, and it is the researcher's job to be able to know these limitations because this permits the identification of the objective element that lies ultimately in most documents.

The Registers of Death ('Totenbuch') of the former concentration camps, for example, have countless entries of victims who died from exhaustion, terror or were just killed. The true circumstances of their deaths, however, are withheld. The official entries in the Mauthausen death book mention strokes, myocardial insufficiency, influenza or pneumonia as a cause of death. In several cases it is particularly suspicious that the entries were edited several times (see Fig. 3.5). In one instance, the entry initially stated 'cerebral apoplexy' as the cause of death but was changed to 'suicide, falling from the quarry wall' and then again to 'suicide, jump into quarry'. The entries were made by clerks working for the Chief SS doctor ('SS-Standortarzt'). Survivors reported that they had clear instructions to avoid recording unnatural causes of death, because unnatural death involving a member of the SS-guards was meant to be reported to the police court in Vienna. Contemporary witnesses confirm furthermore that the SS threw prisoners down into the quarry to kill them.

Another source from this era are the letters written by the imprisoned. Once a month the inmates were allowed to write letters and send them to family, relatives and friends. The letters were monitored by the camp officials, and sometimes the inmates had to use predetermined words because no one was allowed to mention anything of the actual circumstances of camp life.

Events of major importance rarely fail to make a lasting impression and imprint themselves onto our

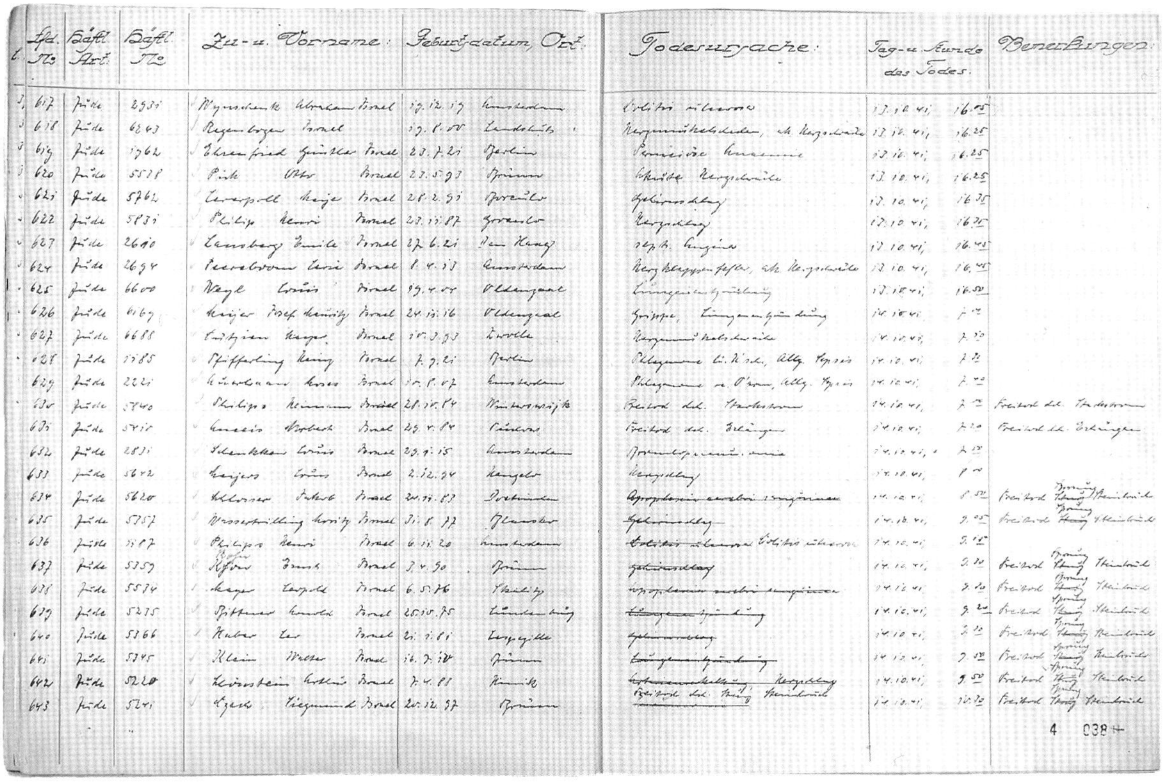

Fig. 3.5. Excerpt from the Registers of Death ('Totenbuch') from Mauthausen with causes of death overwritten several times (© 08/10/1940–03/26/1942, National Archives Collection of World War II War Crimes Records, 1933–1949, Record Group 238, online version available through the Archival Research Catalogue (ARC identifier 305268) at www.archives.gov; May 26th, 2014).

Fig. 3.6. A French forced labourer expresses his patriotism with the motto 'Vive la France'. (© Ute Bauer, Erinnerungsort Flakturm. Der ehemalige Leitturm im Wiener Arenbergpark, Phoibos Verlag Wien, 2010. if-ag.org, photo: Stephan Matyus).

memories. It takes specific situations or questions to evoke those memories. Contemporary history and contemporary archaeology use witness accounts as a major source of information. Witnesses are sharing their memories of the event, while historians can sometimes ask questions of the witness to get further or more detailed information. There is always the possibility that the interviewer influences the witness by the way questions are phrased. It is also the case that memories tend to fade with time and some of them – be it intentionally or involuntarily – are either suppressed or become lost altogether. The shorter the temporal distance between experience and interview, the more vivid and detailed the account, even if some of the details are missing. Memories of the distant past usually become blurred recollections only, as smaller details fade and the course of events is reduced to the main story line. Memories can also be altered later on, for example through the influence of reports from other parties. Consequently, oral sources only reflect the chain of events as the contemporary witness has experienced and remembered them; they do not make any claim to being either objective or complete.

Recently, more and more graffiti is also a source in contemporary archaeology. Short messages, words, names, data, but also drawings and sketches can be found on numerous walls or other materials. It can be said that people wanted to assert themselves openly or secretly. We also receive information about the producers, *e.g.* a name, a date or a worldview (see Fig. 3.6).

IMAGES

Neurological studies tell us that our memory is based predominantly on vision. We do not memorize words to the same extent as images, places or scenes. Intentionally created images, regardless of whether they are two-dimensional photographs, drawings, paintings or three-dimensional objects such as sculptures, capture scenes and impressions that can be reviewed in the future.

The interpretation of these sources requires the same careful consideration as contemporary witness accounts, written records and objects. Paintings and sculptures will often depict fictional scenes. In common with drawings and other image types, their subjectivity lies in the fact that they show us a scene through the artist's eyes and thus reflect the artist's point of view first and foremost, highlighting what is deemed to be important through a personal perspective, while details of minor importance fade into the background or are left out altogether. There is also always the possibility that more than one temporal or spatial dimension is coming together in one image. The way that the artist has chosen to depict the scene is what consolidates its value and usefulness as an historical source.

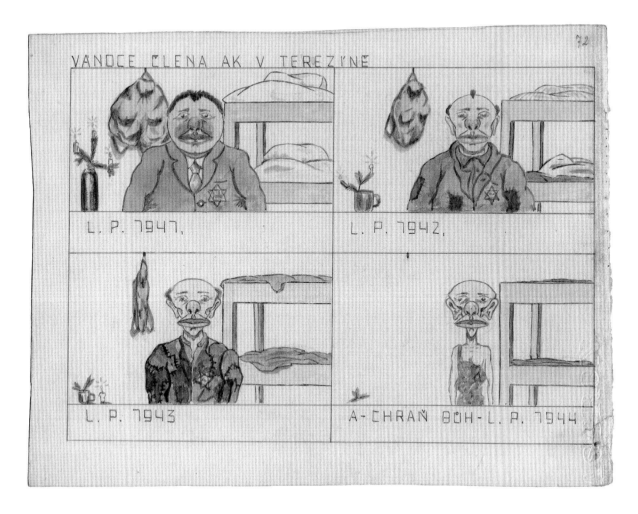

Fig. 3.7. Pavel Fantl, imprisoned in Terezín (Theresienstadt, today Czech Republic) made a drawing entitled 'VANOCE CLENA AK V TEREZÍNE' (Christmas of a member of Terezín). It shows clearly the massive emaciation, the thinning blanket and the fading light. Below the fourth picture he wrote: A-CHRAŇ BŮH-L.P. 1944 (and God willing in the year 1944). P. Fantl was killed in January 1945 on a death march (© Yad Vashem 2147-A-083).

Within the concentration camps, the captives were forced to draw or paint pictures to give them to the guards, while others were created in secret and under perilous conditions. Some of the pictures are realistic illustrations of daily camp life, depicting situations or individuals, while others feature scenarios of the landscape, flowers or similarly pleasant motifs that were impressions of a dream world beyond their reach. In a category of their own are cartoons that satirize daily scenes and allow the artists to put some distance between themselves and the events (see Fig. 3.7). Death, however, the ever-present reality of the camps, is only rarely captured. Its absence is poignant, while the choice of images that are captured reveal the different strategies devised to deal with an extreme situation under the greatest duress in an endless struggle to survive.

Formal technical drawings fall into two groups: the blueprint captures the vision of the architect and engineer, while the layout plans record what was actually constructed and the stages of that building. When featured in documents, these images can help the researcher to understand the narrative being argued; whether it is one that is fuelled by propaganda or one that seeks to be more objective. Equally, when dealing with the raw drawings in isolation, they provide a useful means for scrutinizing individual locations. Even in the as-built plans, there can be omissions and gaps, and this is where archaeological site work can assist in verifying and questioning such recordings.

Photographs and documentaries are equally challenging, despite the fact that they capture actual images and landscapes; it is always necessary to ask about the motivations behind the camera. Photographs are often staged scenarios, the scene carefully arranged; people are taking up rehearsed positions, the scenery highlighted by a section of the landscape that fits best with a specific desire in mind. The scope of the picture shown can be modified, too, long before the days of image-processing software, and it is usually smaller than the natural range of the human eye.

We know that photographs can reconstruct or even construct previous events. This was known from the early days of photography. Images of battlefields were often taken after the engagement because the shutter speeds of the cameras were longer and could not capture the detail of an active battle other than as an immense blur. It was also the case that the classic photo that captures the cutting of the Iron Curtain between Austria and Hungary was taken a few days after the first attempts to bring the fence down (see Fig. 3.8).

The snapshot is a different category. The shutter-release is pressed regardless of the risk that the picture might be blurred, as it seeks to capture the scene spontaneously and no concessions to style and artistic expression are made. As a result, snapshots can be expected to possess more objective qualities than other pictures.

VARIETY OF METHODS IN CONTEMPORARY ARCHAEOLOGY

Archaeological investigation principally requires a specific research question. The questions vary significantly, ranging from those that are related to the revelation and visualization of hidden structures to those that are targeting past economic or social relationships and conditions; they can help to uncover crimes, they can address survival strategies, the reasons behind and the patterns of migration and they can also investigate the awareness and accessibility of public or non-public places. And so much more. Archaeological, historical and art historical methods should be equally chosen with careful regard to the specific question guiding the research. The exceptionally wide range of sources of the early modern and modern periods and especially of the 20th century demands thorough inter- and multi-disciplinary research and comprehensive processing of the available data that does not stop on the threshold to adjacent disciplines.

Contemporary archaeology frequently deals with extensive sites and larger objects. Mass graves or battlefields cover areas of several hectares (see Chapters 4, 5 and 9).

Fig. 3.8. The Hungarian Foreign Minister Gyula Horn and Austrian Foreign Minister Alfred Mock cut the border fence near Sopron on Lake Neusiedl on June 27, 1989. The dismantling of the border fortifications had already begun a few days earlier (© Robert Jäger / APA-Archiv / picturedesk.com).

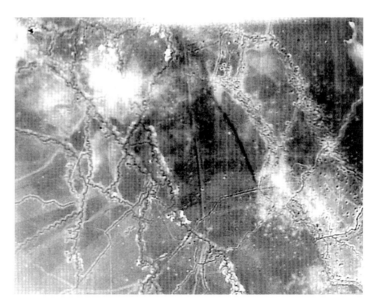

Fig. 3.9. Aerial photograph of the Western Front with endless trenches. Photo by No. 4 Squadron RFC. (© CC0).

Fig. 3.10. Aerial photograph of Mauthausen 2nd April 1945 at its greatest extent, with the main camp and attached eastern camps 2 and 3, the infirmary camp in the southwest, the quarry in the west and the tent camp in the north (© Luftbilddatenbank Dr. Carls GmbH / HES).

The comprehensive research must include records such as contemporary witness accounts, other reports, maps and aerial views, as well as previous archaeological data. Contemporary archaeology must therefore always take into account an enormous volume of different sources. It presents great opportunities for detailed and diverse investigations, but also a great challenge in terms of subtle analysis.

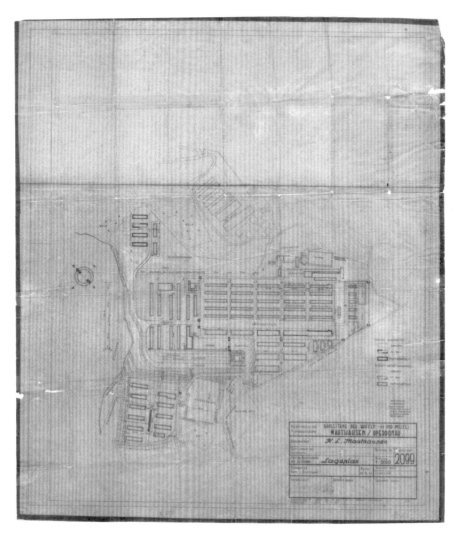

Fig. 3.11. Map of the Mauthausen concentration camp with latest additions in January 1944, with the main camp and attached eastern camps 2 and 3, the infirmary camp in the southwest, the quarry in the west and the tent camp in the north (© Sammlung Mauthausen Memorial, Sign. A/02/02).

Documents and other word-based records provide vital background information and clues for placing the findings in the correct spatial and temporal settings. They help us to access questions regarding the construction process, renovations and modifications, or to identify suppliers and enterprises involved with the construction. Contemporary witness accounts and personal documents (self-testimonies such as letters or diaries) can provide detailed and complementary descriptions of the events from a personal point of view. They can also serve as a means of reasserting one's own identity.

Accounts recorded after the event usually only reflect a limited perspective as they are based on long-term memory, which is not as accurate. Some messages are even passed along on objects such as makers' marks, graffiti or names and owner's marks in general.

The tremendous number of visual sources of the 20th century is overwhelming. Blueprints, maps, movies and videos, usually dated, provide visual impressions of the moment.

When aircraft became increasingly important at the end of World War I, aerial photography was introduced as a new visual resource, and this has been complemented most recently by satellite pictures and LiDAR. All are successfully employed to access archaeological monuments of the 20th century. They are particularly useful for detecting the various constructional changes at concentration camps and other internment camps (see Fig. 3.10–3.14), as well as helping to trace how border fortifications, ramparts and bunkers or factories were constructed. An exemplary investigation of the dimensions of trench systems along the Western Front of

Fig. 3.12. Geophysics Mauthausen, infirmary camp (© Archaeo Prospections®).

the First World War, for instance, relied heavily on dated areal views (see Fig. 3.9). Structures that are preserved only beneath ground level can be similarly well investigated through aerial photography, since they change the way that plants grow within their immediate vicinity. Furthermore, shipwrecks and sunken submarines can be detected in shallow water.

LiDAR is one of the newest techniques in this fast-developing technology area that can be used to acquire aerial imagery (see Fig. 3.14). It can create digital elevation models that allow observations of remains that are hidden beneath vegetation (*e.g.* forests). With these sources we also can get an insight into the wider surrounding landscape in which the internment camps, the battlefield and other sites are embedded.

Another way to assess structures that lie hidden in the ground or under water is through geophysical prospection (see Fig. 3.12) as it is done for other epochs. Different methods exist to detect the traces of stone, metal and

earthen structures. Much of the data is displayed without any temporal differentiation, however, but there are certain devices that can make such inferences under the right circumstances.

In preparation for excavation it also makes sense to employ more traditional archaeological approaches, including field surveys and field walking. The careful and extensive exploration of the terrain of a prospective location prior to excavation helps to build a better understanding of the historical site. The information gathered can suggest initial ideas as to the exact dimensions and topographical characteristics of how a place is situated within the surrounding landscape and its local or regional context.

Augering is an additional means of attaining further information that, though only small-scale and very localised, usually returns excellent results in conjunction with topographical surveys. The cores are spaced regularly and in accordance with a predefined grid system. The

Fig. 3.13. Mauthausen memorial today; many parts of the camp no longer exist (© Bundesamt für Eich- und Vermessungswesen, EGA 2144364).

Fig. 3.14. LiDAR scan of the Mauthausen concentration camp, not only the site of the memorial, but also other parts lying beneath the grass such as the infirmary camp are visible (© Digitales Oberösterreichisches Rauminformationssystem).

cores can be carried out manually and aim to sample the buried soil horizons, both to determine their natural stratigraphy, and to identify cultural heritage indicators, such as brick fragments, mortar, ceramics, glass, metal, or human bone, or ash. The observations are mapped all over the site and help to create an initial ground plan of the monument. Where the soils are too hard for augering, test-pit excavations are an alternative low impact method.

Such preliminary investigative work informs the larger study and helps to pin-point where larger-scale investigation should take place. This can be through excavation, buildings survey or underwater work, depending on the nature of the feature being examined. The size of many of the monuments alone makes it difficult to justify full areal excavation. The challenge becomes apparent when faced with the vast expanses of internment camps, whole battlefields and linear frontier lines that can run for many kilometres. It is more usual to devise a targeted excavation campaign, aimed at investigating only certain areas in detail. The determination is based on what appears to be most significant with regard to a specific research question. As is the case with every type of archaeological investigation, this requires meticulous and illustrated technical documentation. The exposed remains of buildings that are scheduled to be part of a concept for a memorial site demand even more special consideration. To make and keep those structures visible above ground level requires a sustainable conservation treatment since they will otherwise deteriorate quickly, fall down and disappear. To do all this work requires, first and foremost, a firm and sensible financial plan to ensure that the necessary resources exist and will be provided in full and in a long-term perspective.

The existing building stock of the 20th century is still very great. Archaeological examination of building structures is a very necessary method. Seams, damage and additional walls are indicators of construction phases, fixtures and refurbishments, but they can also point to damage by heavy fighting or the former location of killing zones that may have imprinted themselves on the building structure (see Fig. 3.15). Multiple applications of plaster or overpainted sections of the walls, ceilings and floors also provide clues to the stratigraphic context and integrity of a building.

The principal guidelines for excavations of contemporary sites are the same as those that archaeologists

Fig. 3.15. Mauthausen, shooting facility: the mark left by the bullet trap can be seen in the floor. (© Claudia Theune).

apply to work on older monuments. It is of course necessary to abide by the national legislation governing archaeological interventions in the country of work, although most jurisdictions seek to achieve a similar high standard.

Contemporary and forensic archaeology are sometimes mentioned in the same breath. The term 'forensics', often also referred to as 'forensic science', applies to several combined methods of scientific knowledge founded on medicine, biology, chemistry, physics and geology that are used alongside detailed investigation of crime scenes to secure and preserve the evidence. Forensic investigations are performed whenever a body is found and the cause of death is not sufficiently clear and requires further examination. A forensic anthropologist should be part of the archaeological team for work on 20th-century sites. The bodies of those who died on an historic battlefield and were left behind without a proper burial are usually found either as individual graves where they died, or as part of mass graves at or near the site, where the dead were later brought. Mass graves are also a feature of places of genocide (see Chapter 9). In such cases it is particularly important that excavations are conducted with strict regard to the most detailed forensic aspects, not only to investigate the committed crimes properly, but also to provide evidence to the courts and to obtain justice for the victims in the end. A principal main objective of such work is to identify the individual injuries and determine the exact circumstances that finally led to death, but also to identify how the bodies ended up in those graves. Since the body itself is never the only source of evidence on a site, the surrounding context must be examined in detail with special regard to the exact position of the body and the dimensions and positions of the grave pits. It is also important to see whether any attempt at a cover-up took place or not. The presence or absence of certain insects, chrysalises, plant seeds or other biological remains provide further insight, and may indicate the time of year or season when death and/or burial occurred. The work can reveal whether a body was left exposed and, if so, for how long, or if and when it was covered. These are only a few examples of how anthropological and forensic methods can be applied successfully to contemporary archaeology.

Archaeological finds can be classified in chronological order, their spatial origin can be determined, we can see whether they are industrial or handmade, we can analyse traces of use, alterations and reworking. We know their function and often assign them to certain groups of people. Further technological and other sciences provide other information. A large number of available methods, in particular the methods of material culture studies, such as object biographies or actor-network analyses among others, supply us with numerous instruments to gain further insights and learn about the people who used these objects.

The huge numbers of archaeological objects from the 20th century is a very challenging task in terms of curation and preservation. Fragments of ceramics and porcelain, buckles, jewellery and also smaller weapons are normally recovered and restored without problem. However, larger objects such as tanks, submarines, aircraft, railway lines, foundations of barracks and similar objects that go beyond the common scope of archaeology are an entirely different matter. Such recovery operations

are more demanding and can require engineering expertise. There is also the challenge of storing these objects, either as part of museum displays or for long-term storage. The sheer quantity of material is not to be under-estimated. Thousands of nails that belonged to the prisoner's barracks in any one camp remain, along with hundreds of complete or fragmented glass bottles, window panes, porcelain, buttons, countless enamel dishes and billycans, door and window hinges, to name only a few of the range of small items. State offices for the preservation of historical monuments and museums have often exhausted their storage capacities decades ago. The situation has triggered an ongoing discussion on how to resolve the problem.

Should all findings that bear evidence of such crimes be kept? What is their value, their significance? How can we judge, or should we judge between their material value and the meaning they had for their former owner, for the visitors of memorials and museums or for our culture of remembrance? Such discussions concern the objects recovered already, just as they do to projects that will recover even more. Which emplacement on a battlefield is more deserving of protection than others? During the National Socialist regime more than 40,000 detention camps existed spread across Europe – how many of them should be protected as National Heritage? That question certainly does not arise for the approximately 25 main concentration camps and six extermination camps, but how does society deal with the approximately 1,200 sub-camps? And what should become of the several thousand prisoner-of-war camps in Europe, the Atlantic Wall that extends in a length of 2,700 kilometres or the Iron Curtain that runs for over 10,000 kilometres? How can a stretch of land that is riddled with trenches and emplacements like Verdun and its vicinity or the Somme region be best handled from the perspective of the preservation of historic monuments? Increasingly, there is an argument suggesting that those monuments should be left partially exposed to natural decay and without any conservation. Other reflections give suggestions according to which criteria objects can be preserved or disposed of. At the moment there is no commonly accepted solution, but we will have to deal with this issue. Probably we will not be able to preserve all crime scenes and sites of suffering.

Chapter 4

SITES AND MONUMENTS OF THE TWO WORLD WARS

INTRODUCTION

The two world wars in the first half of the 20th century remain among the most destructive and widespread moments of human aggression ever to be unleashed globally. The industrial scale of these wars and their catastrophic impacts on urban and rural settlements and economic areas remains an unforgettable and tragic history. The Cold War era (1946/47–1991) in the second half of the century with the so-called Iron Curtain as a dividing line across Berlin, Germany and Europe (see Chapter 8) ushered in a kind of peace between the major powers, though innumerable 'surrogate' or 'proxy wars' were taking place. The East-West conflict created the Cold War, while a new problem took root that was linked to the decolonisation process of Africa, and eventually grew to become the North-South Divide that triggered further armed conflicts. The fragility of the peace across Europe was revealed shortly after the fall of the Iron Curtain (1989), when a series of wars erupted in southeast Europe across the former Yugoslavian territories (1991–1995 and 1999).

The nature of warfare changed during the 20th century. Battles of larger military units on land, sea and in the air became less common. What used to be referred to as 'symmetrical warfare' has lost a lot of its relevance while 'asymmetric warfare' has become more common. It is no longer a matter of conflict between aggressors with similar overall military power, strategy and resources. Rather, war often involves at least one party pursuing guerrilla or partisan tactics, or resistance or underground movements striking fast and using surprise attacks to weaken or even beat a seemingly more powerful opponent. Warfare is no longer limited to armed conflicts between states and nations. Now non-state organisations also attack states or even transnational groups and societies. A popular early 20th-century example – and one that is revealed through archaeological enquiry – are the methods employed by Lawrence of Arabia, who targeted transport and supply lines of the Ottoman army during the First World War. In the digital age that we now live in, these same strategies are used and referred to by nations under threat from 'cyber warfare'.

It is not always possible to distinguish clearly between sites of wars, civil wars and other conflicts (see Chapters 5–7). However, the sites of the two world wars will take centre stage in this chapter. Sites of internment, of terror and genocide that are without any doubt also connected to the world wars will be discussed in other chapters (see Chapters 6, 9).

Combat actions are sometimes referred to as 'armed conflicts' but it is the case that warfare is also something of a rhetorical question, where the precise terminology is a question of semantics. Warfare does not necessarily start with an open proclamation of war, nor does it require a capitulation or a peace treaty to end. It is often almost impossible to determine when exactly a war started or ended.

Archaeological observations are also affected by such questions. What is the spatial area of the combat operation? Which kinds of material remains should count as sites of war? What kind of challenges and questions arise from declaring them war remains? How did the combat operations affect the landscape? Is this impact still relevant today? Research into battlefield archaeology of the 20th century naturally tends to put the overall focus on the two world wars. Apart from aspects of monument preservation, it is the notion of remembrance of the killed soldiers, of national commemoration that inspires such investigations (see Chapter 9). This becomes evident in the example of Australian colleagues (*e.g.* University of Melbourne) who have recently been investigating sites of

battles where Australian units were involved and suffered fatalities. For its part, asymmetric warfare leaves less clear archaeological traces than epic battles, which tended to take place in large but defined areas. Cyber warfare, in turn, is even less likely to leave any material traces behind.

Battlefields carry the likeness of the battle and, in a more abstract sense, they are mapping the course of the battle. That is perhaps why investigations of individual battlefields are often understood as a means to acquire new insight into the chain of processes that governed the entire conflict. Epic battles could last a day or they could develop into a long-standing positional conflict with little to no movement, and might extend over years. A classic example is the Western Front during the First World War. Such sites occupied enormously large areas with borders that can be extremely diffuse and almost impossible to determine. Remains of such conflicts usually scatter over very large areas. Only large-scale non-invasive methods can help to determine the exact range, while actual excavations can be focused on certain sections. The

Lost at Sea

Battles have been fought at sea since the ancient period. Warships, large or small, and submarines, since the First World War, have been used to attack and sink targets on land and afloat. As a result, countless wrecks lie at the bottom of the sea, whether close to the coast or in the depths of the ocean. National monuments agencies have been paying increased attention to this category of war remains in recent years. Great efforts are being made to catalogue wrecks in national waters, to establish their condition by survey and to record the history of the vessels and their crews with the help of the written sources and witness reports available. The extensive project 'Unknown Marine Assets & Landscapes. Strategic Assessment of Submarines in English Waters' for English Heritage, and the UNESCO Underwater Cultural Heritage Projects dealing with World War I are exemplary here.

These projects primarily record wrecks lying in shallow waters. They involve a long list of ships and submarines of very different types and of different origins.

Large numbers of sailors and crews died in the ships and submarines. The vessels are therefore also the last resting places of those personnel and are regarded as war graves.

German submarine from World War I near the coast of Kent, England (© English Heritage).

Centre for Battlefield Archaeology at the University of Glasgow undertakes many such investigations.

Consequently, it is often only possible to access smaller sections of the much larger overall structure. Systematic surveys that use metal detectors and take measurements of the exact positions of objects can help to illustrate troop movements and even visualize the progress of the battle. The continued improvement and development of the arms industries' products dictate that the strategies and the extent of such traceability are equally changing.

Remains of war are not limited to battlefields. The term extends to several more categories of conflict. Trenches, posts, bunkers, tank traps and similar installations provide additional insight, although they sometimes are part of the larger context of a battlefield. The barracks that had housed the soldiers must also be included. The same goes for places where the armaments industries were located. It may be beneficial, too, to analyse the impact on the civil population close by, by studying their settlements. It is important, though, to include some additional aspects here. Barracks, but also bunkers and other defensive installations, were seldomly used during only one conflict. The Atlantic Wall may serve as an example in this regard: despite the fact that this line of defence was constructed during World War II, its remains are still ever-present even 70 years later. The massive structures built from concrete will last through several lifetimes and can occasionally experience various cycles of reuse.

THE FIRST WORLD WAR: BATTLEFIELDS OF THE WEST

The First World War positional warfare in Belgium and northern France has left numerous and deep scars embedded in the landscape. Memory of the war is still particularly present here. Today, the ever-reducing numbers of veterans still return, and going forward it will inevitably be their suriving family members who visit, along with the many tourists, to commemorate and learn about the events that lie 100 years in the past. The many war cemeteries filled with white crosses greet each visitor, and they are clearly visible from significant distances, testifying to the massive number of deaths. Many memorials remember the victims, victories and defeats alike. Several museums and open-air installations, some among them operated by private organisations, provide information on the local battle stories. Sometimes they present a real hotchpotch of remains, such as excavated trenches (see Fig. 4.1), shelters and posts accompanied by all possible kinds of finds. However, extensive in-depth information on either the objects or the emplacements is rarely seen. The enormous diversity of objects alone appears to provide sufficient documentation.

Archaeological excavations on sites of the First World War began approximately 25 years ago. French officials were motivated to document all the discoveries regardless of their period of origin. The high-speed rail project between Paris and Calais built in in the early 1990s adopted this comprehensive approach, as did the massive development project of the commercial zone at Arras (France). Contemporary remains of the First World War received special attention in that context. Similar work was done in Belgium, where a dedicated department tasked with the sole purpose of leading investigations on the First World War sites was created (Department of First World War Archaeology). It became an international initiative, extending to cooperate with English colleagues in the investigation of British positions and trenches.

Australian archaeologists (*e.g.* University of Melbourne) are also involved in investigating sites across Europe where larger units of their countrymen served as, for example, in the Gallipoli Campaign of 1915 where some 100,000 died, 10% of whom were from Australia and New Zealand. Another site of Australian interest and archaeological activity was the battlefield of Fromelles (1916) (see Chapter 9). A nation's commitment to investigate and understand the fatal destinies of its own soldiers becomes a feature of this new archaeology, regardless of where the deaths occurred abroad.

The archaeological work began with intensive research in written and visual archives and records, including contemporary aerial photography and contemporary witness accounts. Present-day aerial survey and satellite imagery help to locate the exact positions of trenches and other anomalies or changes in the ground, while geophysical surveys can reveal detailed insights into the buried surfaces.

The satellite imagery in particular, while revealing the zigzag lines of the trenches and related front lines, also shows how complex the task is to unpick individual lines of defence and offence because there is so much overlapping of features; it is not a simple picture (see Fig. 3.9). The whole region is one huge archaeological landscape, a battlefield with countless long angular trenches at the forefront, supported by positions, sheltered posts and communication trenches further back. All the units in this landscape are interrelated. The old structures are still visible in today's aerial photographs and show that the landscape preserves old structures like a palimpsest.

Many timber elements were recovered from the trenches that were once used to dress the trench walls in planks, or to cover the ground in certain sections. The timber elements provided an even ground level and helped to prevent soldiers from being stuck in the mud during rainy periods. In some sections brick fixtures or even whole positions built in brick are known, indicating that these sites were intended for longer-term use. The site of Arras, for example, and as illustrated in old photographs, has evidence for even more advanced installations where a section of light-rail track ran along a trench to help in the delivery of ammunitions by pit cars. In other places, the installations included tunnels, as excavation has revealed at Givenchy-lès-la-Bassée (France). The tunnels provided additional shelter and connected different sections of the system.

The excavation at the Kilianstollen near Carspach (Dep. Haut-Rhin, France) in 2011 attracted special attention. Between 1915 and 1916, the tunnel was dug up to 6 m deep into the ground. In March 1918 it was brought to collapse by grenade hits over a length of 60 m. The 21 soldiers who were killed and declared missing have now been recovered and the majority of them identified.

Given the enormous lengths of these features and the extent to which they reach across landscapes, it was not difficult for their study to fit well with the emerging sub-discipline of Landscape Archaeology. It is a classic study in how landscape can be transformed, and this was done by soldiers for soldiers' use. The landscapes of several regions across Northern France and Belgium are thus, through the soldiers' doings, forever marked by war in the most literal sense of the meaning.

Challenges have emerged around the issues of visualisation and commemoration, about how many of these features can be preserved and displayed, and to what extent can the modern tourist have access to these sites of death and tragedy. In some instances, the response has been to recreate copies and permit access to these locations for the experiential exercise. In other instances, and fewer cases, the original installations are exposed to demonstrate more directly the nature of front-line and trench warfare to a broader public.

OTHER FIRST WORLD WAR SITES

The most popular sites of the First World War are clearly located all along the Western Front. However, military

Fig. 4.2. Positions and tunnels from the First World War can be visited in the Dolomites, here on the Paternkofel; hikers obtain information about the battles on the Alpine front from information boards (© Meike Widdig).

Fig. 4.3. Delivery valve of Livens Large Gallery Flame Projector (© Centre for Battlefield Archaeology, Iain Banks).

installations from that era are also present in the Alpine regions (see Fig. 4.2) on both sides, Austrian and Italian alike, and they are receiving increasingly more attention. Favourable conditions when the sites occur under glaciers, for example, have helped to preserve the wooden parts of such stations and sometimes other organic remains.

Many nations took extreme measures to protect their populations by installing bunkers in regions that were prone to attacks by invading enemy forces. Several protective shelters are, for instance, located in southern England and are registered officially as national monuments of World War I, and are duly protected by the local and national authorities. Similar examples exist in Germany. In the North Rhine-Westphalia region, for example, a project is currently underway to create an inventory of archaeological sites from both world wars and the Cold War as well. To a small extent the trenches

and traces of the so-called Christmas battle (January 1917) are also a subject of investigation and heritage southwest of Riga (Latvia).

The enormous demand for weaponry resulted in a massive development of the armaments industries. Remains of the Elisenthal powder mill, founded in 1871 near Windeck in the German Sauerland region, are a monument that served during the First World War, and are considered as such, as is the old firing range in Essen (North Rhine-Westphalia, Germany) where weapons and armaments produced by Krupp industries were once tested. Although Ireland was officially neutral during the Second World War, the Irish state operated munitions facilities in Parkgate, Dublin, where archaeological surveys were carried out to document traces of these facilities. Evidence of newly-invented weaponry from that era was uncovered during excavations in the French area of the Somme (see Fig. 4.3). The Livens Large Gallery Flame Projector, for example, was a flamethrower invented by the British Army captain W. H. Livens. His invention was a reaction to the sinking of 'RMS Lusitania' off the Irish coast in May 1915 with the loss of 1,200 people on board, an event which eventually led to the USA entering World War I. The flamethrowers, however, proved too cumbersome in terms of handling and mobility and were ultimately not very effective. They were used only twice in 1916 during the Battle of the Somme. Recent excavations (Centre for Battlefield Archaeology, University of Glasgow) west of Amiens revealed and extracted parts of one of the flame-throwers, including a tube and fragments of the valves.

Archaeological activities relating to World War I are manifold and reflect a global involvement on many different levels. Another good example is the recent investigation by the University of Bristol into the Arab Revolt of 1916–1918 against the Ottoman Empire, which involved Lawrence of Arabia in what is present-day Jordan. The results are shedding new light on Ottoman defensive strategies and their changes through time. What was linear defence in the earliest stages was abandoned later. In response to ongoing guerrilla warfare, linear defence was replaced by small individual redoubts. While the Ottoman involvement becomes evident through numerous finds and features, their Arab and British attackers left hardly any traces in the archaeological record. Rifle bullets and shrapnel remain the only testimony to the hostilities. Objects that perhaps can be related to Lawrence of Arabia personally were found recently.

BATTLEFIELDS OF THE SECOND WORLD WAR

The exploration of Second World War battlefields in Europe is strongly linked to the Battle of Berlin and the last stands that concluded the war in spring 1945. Nevertheless, the D-Day event in Pointe-du-Hoc, where Allied Forces engaged the Germans on June 6th, 1944, in Normandy (France), and their further advance into the interior of France until they reached the Rhine and onward in the direction of Berlin have been equally investigated. The investigations in Normandy in particular are associated with remembrance and commemoration. The battlefields from the beginning of the war are also beginning to attract attention, as for instance at Grebbeberg near Rhenen (The Netherlands) where Dutch troops tried to stop the invading Germans. Excavations in 2008 succeeded in

targeting casemates, communication trenches and tank traps. Telephone lines were uncovered that ran along the trenches and gave evidence of a military infrastructure far more advanced than previously known. It was also a revelation to discover that tank traps were installed there.

The progress of the Western Allies through the Rhine region and the long continuous battles that accompanied this progress in autumn 1944 are apparent in the archaeological record at Hürtgenwald, a wooded zone west of Aachen (North Rhine-Westphalia, Germany), where several remains of the Western Wall (Siegfried Line) are located. Posts and military equipment of both sides were unearthed there. The progress of the Russian armies on the Eastern Front in Brandenburg is also evident from archaeological investigations. In Klein Görigk (Brandenburg, Germany), for example, archaeologists exposed the bodies of German and Russian soldiers alike.

Crash sites of planes are another important category of archaeological evidence with a global footprint, be it in elevated Alpine regions, at the bottom of the sea, or even in Newfoundland and in Papua New Guinea. This is especially true when human remains of the crew are considered to be still on site (see Chapter 2). Excavations take place to recover and rescue the bodies, identify the victims and transport their remains back to their homelands. Such war remains occur more frequently in remote sparsely populated regions where preservation is better compared to such discoveries in densely populated areas. In Newfoundland, investigations traced the wide scatter pattern or debris field of the wreckage extremely well (see Fig. 4.4). Similar investigations are undertaken concerning sunken vessels and submarines (see box 4) (see Chapter 13).

In regions where the landscape has not changed drastically through building development after the Second World War, it is still possible to detect covered posts – simple structures built from earth alone – hidden by wooded zones and copses.

Second World War battles in Europe were mostly ground combat, while the Pacific War was dominated by naval actions and aerial combat. The Japanese were especially adept, and conquered vast parts of the Pacific including many of the island chains, from the Aleutians to Midway, and extending to the Mariana Islands, Marshall Islands, Samoan Islands, Palou Islands, and Papua New Guinea between North America and Asia

on the southern edge of the North Pacific Bering Sea. By 1942 this advance facilitated a massive military expansion resulting in the construction of numerous airbases. Archaeological surveys and excavations are now taking place on many of the islands. The research focuses on the more strongly fortified Japanese bases, but includes American installations and remains as well. Investigations at Midway are especially important because it was here that Japan suffered the decisive loss of four out of its six aircraft carriers, marking a turning point in the war and heralding the approaching American victory. On Watom Island (Papua New Guinea) the Japanese used American prisoners of war and forced labourers to dig an enormous tunnel system through volcanic rock. Surveys are showing that the tunnels were unexpectedly extensive and had a variety of different functions. These included use as hospitals, stores and industrial plants, alongside submarine and ship pens, and they also housed gun emplacements (see Fig. 4.5). Similar investigations were conducted (by the U.S. military) on the island of Saipan in the western Pacific, where important battles took place between the Japanese and the Americans. The Japanese had conquered the island during the First World War, but it was recaptured by the Americans in June and July 1944 and is now an associated state of the USA. Among other things, caves were investigated in which the population had sought shelter. Underwater archaeological research documents Japanese and U.S. vehicles, shipwrecks and aircraft.

A tragic closing chapter of the Second World War that extended into the Post War and Cold War era took place in the East Tyrol area (Austria) between Oberdrauburg and Lienz. In late April 1945, a camp was situated here of about 25,000 Cossacks who had supported Wehrmacht soldiers on their retreat from Italy and later surrendered to the British forces. Following the Yalta Conference, which decreed that so-called displaced Russians were to be returned to their homeland, the Cossacks were handed over to Soviet authorities, despite the real expectation that they would be treated as National Socialist collaborators. Many of the Cossacks tried to escape or committed suicide, while countless died during the summer. For a long time this tragedy was covered up. Archaeological investigations (University of Innsbruck) have unearthed material remains related to the incident. There are also contemporary witness accounts and written records, and the evidence is now filtering out to the wider public.

Archaeologists working on any period will often find middens and dumps of waste material to be especially instructive. This is also the case with sites from the end of the Second World War. In some cases, the contents have been found to include evidence of the approaching German defeat at the end of the war, and also of the post-war situation. In Stade (Lower Saxony, Germany) for example, archaeologists recovered an index of members of the NSDAP ('Nationalsozialistische Deutsche Arbeiterpartei' /National Socialist German Workers' Party), while in Halberstadt (Saxony-Anhalt, Germany) a bust of Hitler was discovered that had been symbolically executed by a headshot and then dumped (see Fig. 4.6). Pieces of so-called 'degenerate art' ('entartete Kunst') were rediscovered hidden in a house next to the city hall

Fig. 4.6. A bust of Adolf Hitler was found with a bullet hole in its forehead near Halberstadt Cathedral, Germany (© Landesamt für Denkmalpflege und Archäologie SachsenAnhalt, Uwe Fiedler).

of Berlin. In Augsburg (Bavaria, Germany), U.S. forces had occupied the place that previously served as a National Socialist headquarters. Apparently they cleared it out and set fire to some of the furniture and added some objects of undeniable American army provenance. Similar evidence turned up in Landau upon Isar (Bavaria, Germany); the presence of Coca-Cola bottles within the backfill of a dump site points to the U.S. troops as the most likely source.

Sometimes archaeologists find rotten containers with objects which the former owners deliberately buried towards the end of the war but were unable to recover after the liberation. These can be valuable objects, porcelain, cutlery or works of art. If it is still possible to find heirs after the retrieval, the objects are returned.

BUNKER SYSTEMS

Archaeological investigations of large-scale field monuments associated with the European wars are a focus of attention, including large ramparts such as the Western Wall and the Atlantic Wall; tank traps that extend for countless kilometres in the Aachen region (North Rhine-Westphalia, Germany); and bunkers. British and German archaeological investigations and publications that provide systematic inventories of bunkers reflect the fact that both nations acknowledge these as permanent remains of the great wars forming part of their national archaeological heritages. With such large numbers surviving, again questions arise around how many such objects should be preserved, and also which bunker systems, tank traps and linear fortifications should be investigated and documented and even whether some of them should be systematically demolished. The current trend is to list them as National Monuments, and so *de facto* preservation applies. The most obvious examples are concrete structures, but it should not be forgotten that many such features were built of earth and timber, and lie hidden in wooded areas today, waiting to be explored and studied.

Bunkers can have very different functions. They can be used to protect the civilian population or (military) industrial plants from hostile attacks; they are part of military fortifications to protect an area or to impede the enemy's advance. Flak towers were used to ward off air raids. Some of the bunkers combine several of these functions.

The British version of the bunker is epitomised in their pillboxes, the origins of which lie in the First World War. The majority of their World War II pillboxes were built by 1940 in preparation for an expected German invasion (Operation Sea Lion) and represent a ribbon of largely coastal defences. They are often located close to sites of strategic importance such as rivers, bridges and airports. Thousands of pillboxes are still visible today.

Others are part of more complex defence systems. The Western Wall, for example, stretched about 630 kilometres from Kleve on the Dutch border in the Lower Rhine basin (North Rhine-Westphalia, Germany) to Grenzach-Wyhlen on the Swiss border (Baden-Württemberg, Germany). It was built between 1938 and 1940 for the most part. The Atlantic Wall in turn runs for over 2,600 kilometres and was built between the North Cape in Norway, along the coastlines of Denmark, The Netherlands, Belgium and France, and on the Channel Islands between 1942 and 1944 (see Fig. 4.7). It was to serve the National Socialists

Fig. 4.7. Bunker of the Atlantic Wall on the shore of Jersey, Channel Islands, England (© Claudia Theune).

as a defence against Allied invasion. Such monuments are a testimony to the enormous defensive efforts that consumed millions of tons of reinforced concrete. Countless forced labourers, inmates of concentration camps and prisoners of war were required to accomplish the task. The actual defensive effect of these linear works was, however, surprisingly low because the invading Allies did not attack in Norway or at Calais (France), where the English Channel is narrowest. Their efforts were directed south at Normandy, where D-Day began on June 6th, 1944. The Allies targeted the defensive line in a location where it was not as strong as further north and breached the wall within a day. Not only was the wall weak here, but its hinterland lacked the supporting fortifications to impede progress. Within a surprisingly short period of time, the German garrison in Paris was defeated and surrendered the capital to the Allies on August 25th. With the failure of the Atlantic Wall, attention now focused on the Western Wall as the Allies engaged the Germans there.

The bunkers were standardised constructions with only minor variations. The so-called 'Regelbaus' (standard construction) were differentiated by size and the thickness of walls and ceilings. In Germany they have been documented archaeologically at, for example, Pachten near Dillingen (Saar Department), Elmpt near Niederkrüchten and Kahlenbusch near Metternich (both North Rhine-Westphalia) and Korker Waldstellung (Baden-Württemberg).

The individual posts are in varying stages of preservation today. The massive bunkers have walls that are up to 3.5 m thick, so it is not surprising that examples are still standing along the former defensive lines. Some have been demolished and, like tank traps, painstakingly dismantled piece by piece to make room for new construction concepts. Nature has also reclaimed others that are now almost fully concealed by vegetation. The past decades have also seen a selected number of former bunkers being refurbished and turned into documentation centres and museums. It was mandatory in the post-war era to remove all signs and symbols of National Socialism as soon as possible, but some swastikas are still fixed on the walls of bunkers along the Western Wall to this day (see Fig. 4.8).

The rediscovery of some special bunkers in Berlin has attracted considerable media attention, in particular that of the Drivers' Bunker with several examples of SS artwork

Fig. 4.8. All over Europe and beyond there are numerous bunkers. In one bunker built by the National Socialists the swastika was untypically not removed after the war (© Claudia Theune).

that show the First Panzer Division Leibstandarte Adolf Hitler. Some bunkers are isolated separate structures.

Other protective installations were mostly built in urban areas to keep the civil population safe as, for instance, air-raid shelters or the high-rise bunkers known from Mannheim-Käfertal (Baden-Württemberg, Germany) or Emden (Lower Saxony, Germany) and at other places.

Some of the Flak towers in Hamburg, Berlin, Vienna or on the Helgoland Island are among those buildings that were spared destruction after the Second World War; they still exist in varying states of preservation or modification, although they were converted for alternative use. The Flak towers consisted of a combat tower ('Gefechtsturm' or G-tower) that housed batteries of Flak – anti-aircraft-guns – and a lead tower ('Leitturm' or L-tower) where the firing control centres equipped with sensor systems were based. Forced labourers had to build the towers to predetermined designs. The National Socialists had intended to refurbish such plain unadorned buildings

Fig. 4.9. The lead tower in Vienna, Arensberg Park (© Ute Bauer, Erinnerungsort Flakturm. Der ehemalige Leitturm im Wiener Arenbergpark, Phoibos Verlag Wien, 2010. if-ag.org, photograph: Helmut K. Lackner).

completely with richly ornamented façades after the war. Three of the Berlin Flak towers (located in Tiergarten, Volkspark Friedrichshain and Humboldt Hain) were thought to have been successfully demolished by controlled explosions but some remains are still present in Friedrichshain and Humboldthain. In Hamburg, two of the remaining combat towers have undergone massive modifications, one being converted into a media centre, while the other now serves as an energy centre. In Vienna, all three pairs of towers survive and have been partly converted to alternative uses (see Fig. 4.9). Investigations of such buildings are often arduous and difficult because of limited access and because of modifications made to cover over any traces of the National Socialist occupation. Building surveys are useful means of conducting research into these structures.

A combined approach using archaeological methods in conjunction with a study of blueprints, written sources and first-hand accounts has been applied recently to a study of the lead tower of Arenberg Park in Vienna,

and may be considered a model for the archaeological investigation of bunkers. That tower contained nine levels beneath the roof with the ground level being the only storey modified after the war. Numerous details deviate from the original blueprints. A comprehensive and thorough recording of all letters written on the building was made, regardless of whether they represented official signs, graffiti or drawings. The research discovered documents and small finds that had been gathered and deposited in certain places of the interior. Still untouched material such as written documents and various objects from Room 1 on the 5th floor indicates that it originally served as a paramedic station. Other finds include militaria, fragments of clothing, furniture and light fixtures, office supplies, tobacco products, games and tins of various kinds. Many of the 170 pieces of graffiti that are present all over the place related to the forced labourers tasked with the construction. Names, initials and dates ranging from autumn 1944 to spring 1945 occur frequently. They suggest that the workers originated in Italy, France, (the former) Czechoslovakia, Ukraine and Serbia, but Soviet prisoners of war might have been among the group as well. Over 800 written sources help to reconstruct the daily routine of the soldiers who manned the Flak tower, among them personal letters, photographs, diaries or newspapers. The latter provide a vivid insight into contemporary propaganda.

The remains of huge bunkers in the forest of Mühldorf, Bavaria (Germany) or in Bremen (Germany) are impressive examples of bunkers constructed to shelter an entire industrial plant (see Fig. 4.10–4.11). 'Bunker Valentin' is located near Bremen; the construction process began in late 1942/early 1943 on the understanding that a new and more advanced submarine type would be assembled there that would turn the tide in submarine warfare to Germany's advantage. The building was never fully completed and consequently no submarine was ever assembled there. Planned as a defence production unit, it was built mostly by forced labourers, and was enormous in size measuring 426 m long, 97 m wide and 33 m high above ground. The walls were up to 7 m thick. Ultimately, however, the project was a failure and the building was not finished by the end of the war. Recent excavations (University of Bremen, Landesdenkmalamt Bremen) involving many local young people have revealed the bases of

Fig. 4.10. Near Mühldorf am Inn, a semi-subterranean armament bunker for the production of the Messerschmitt Me 262 was built by forced labourers during the Second World War. The bunker measured 33 m wide and 400 m long with eight floors under twelve huge concrete arches. Only seven of the sections were completed. After the war, six of the arches were blown up (© Walter Irlinger).

the concrete-mixing plant. The collaboration of young people and professional archaeologists is recognised as achieving an educational goal to further an awareness and understanding of WWII through archaeological project work. The project is also driven by the desire to commemorate the victims of the war in the Bremen area.

CONCLUSIONS

These are a few examples of monuments from the world wars. The trenches provide countless small objects, many among them trampled into the mud and dirt. They reveal a lot about the situation facing soldiers living in the trenches (see Chapter 10). Numerous remains of ammunition are present there, especially bullet casings of various calibres, along with other pieces of military equipment and personal items like dishware, cutlery, writing utensils, along with items of personal hygiene, crucifixes, rosaries, small figurines of the Virgin Mary or other religious figurines. Objects of so-called trench art also occur in large numbers. Made from various kinds of militaria, a vast range shows the different stages of their production and the tools used to fashion them, and are clear evidence for the making of these objects in the trenches themselves. Such objects often attract commercial interest today, where the market for these pieces appears to be insatiable.

Alongside the small objects, there are the very large and bulky artillery pieces and all kinds of vehicles, including First World War tanks. A recent excavation near Cambrai (France) exposed the wreck of a British tank that German soldiers had buried under tons of soil (see Fig. 4.12). Planes that came down and crashed left remains scattered over large areas. The rescue and especially the sustainable conservation of such large objects presents an enormous challenge for archaeologists and national heritage bodies. Conventional conservation is challenged to deal with them, so special means are required, and it remains the case that museums must also wrestle with having the capacity to display such pieces in sufficiently sheltered spaces.

Investigations on the grounds of larger garrisons are rare occurrences because many of these locations are still in use for military purposes. However, archaeological excavations carried out at the Edinburgh Mortonhall Army Camp (Scotland) have revealed the bases of several former barracks. Various phases became evident as was expected because occupation of the camp goes back to the First World War and was expanded during the Second World War.

This chapter would be incomplete without mentioning the victims of these wars (see Chapter 9). They

include countless soldiers from the various armies as well as the undocumented numbers of civilian casualties. War victims are constantly being discovered, be they lying unburied on the battlefield or hurriedly interred in mass graves. In some cases, especially in relation to plane crashes, archaeological and anthropological methods are employed to search for missing soldiers. It has become of paramount importance to identify the dead soldiers. The final decision on how to deal with their mortal remains usually involves an agreement with possible descendants and the war graves commission. One outcome can be to transport the body back to the native country, while another option is to bury the remains in the local war cemetery.

Chapter 5

LOCAL WARS, TOTALITARIANISM AND RESISTANCE AGAINST STATE AUTHORITIES

INTRODUCTION

Global diplomacy based on the threat of 'mutually assured destruction' (MAD) during the Cold War era prevented our world from further destruction by another war on a global scale. Nevertheless, even after the capitulation of Germany and Japan countless armed conflicts occurring around the world saw the (global) superpowers face each other. The physical engagement of the superpowers in these conflicts was either indirect (arms supply) or relatively small-scale direct intervention (sending in small numbers of troops and/or 'military advisors'. Nevertheless the resulting suffering could be huge. This strategy gave its name to a new form of warfare, namely, proxy wars, and these conflicts tend to be asymmetric warfare.

Colonialism is a root cause behind these unrests. Both the attitudes of the coloniser and the fight for liberation by the colonised create the dynamic. Civil war is a common outcome. Other armed conflicts such as uprisings and resistance against state authorities cannot be ignored in this context either. International terrorism is another form of violence against a nation or a community of nations. Terrorists frequently consider their attacks as full-on wars, waged against one or several states. The majority of such conflicts, especially where hostilities over strategically important matters are concerned, are characterised by their global scope that outweighs local or regional interests, and is clearly evidenced by archaeological research.

In this chapter the conflicts that affect more regional aspects will be addressed. A closer inspection of archaeological activities related to sites of wars and armed action against state authorities again confirms that national and local commemoration is one of the key drivers for surveys and excavations. On many occasions, an upcoming commemorative year has inspired archaeological commitment. The resulting excavations are a part of the overall marking of events that lie 10, 50 or 100 years in the past. It is of little consequence whether the conflict is an ancient one or has just ended; the commemoration feeds into a process of how history is perceived and how a regional or national identity is developed (see Chapter 13).

Archaeology has a special relevance in the search for and location of mass graves (see Chapter 9), and has proved useful in the aftermaths of, for example, the Ugandan Bush War (1981–1986) and the Ugandan Northern War (1986–2006); the Killing Fields of Cambodia (1975–1979); on sites of the civil war in Rwanda and the genocide of the Tutsi in 1994, as well as the Yugoslav Wars (1991–2001). Srebrenica in particular

Rwandan Civil War

Civil wars have long been the subjects of archaeological investigations and among these are several cases related to Africa. Within the context of the Rwandan Civil War (1990–1994) and the resulting mass genocide, for instance, archaeological projects began to investigate key sites and mass graves almost immediately after the official end of the conflict in 1995. The conflict left countless material traces behind, including bullet holes in the walls of the house of parliament in Kigali (Rwanda). Other related remains are on display at the Presidential Palace Museum. There are currently plans for future projects aimed at extending the archaeological scope to include farmsteads and villages destroyed during the fighting that often led to civilian fatalities. The latter refers to another important aspect of the archaeology of civil wars, and that is to focus on the suffering of the general population rather than to further investigations of the decisive battles and places alone. It widens the scope and understanding of these events.

At the parliament in Kigali (Rwanda) the bullet holes from the fighting can still be seen (© John Daniel Giblin).

has become sadly famous for the mass murder of 8,000 Muslim Bosniaks in 1995. The mass burials of the victims of the Armenian Genocide that cost about 1.5 million lives between 1915 and 1916 are only now being discovered in Armenia and Syria. As long as the Republic of Turkey does not officially recognise the Genocide, it remains very unlikely that excavations will be sanctioned there. The list would be incomplete without including those who 'disappeared' during the Fascist reign and the civil war in Spain (1936–1939); in Guatemala (1960–1996); Ethiopia (1974–1991); Iraq (2003–2011); and the victims of dictatorship across much of South America, in Argentina (1976–1983); Chile (1973–1990); Uruguay (1973–1985); and many other parts of the world. Spain has begun to address past conflicts and injustice, along with Greece (military dictatorship 1967–1974) and Poland (time of martial law 1981–1983).

One of the most cruel proxy wars was the Vietnam War (1955–1975), where archaeological and cultural anthropological research has just started. The first investigations deal with the recovering of missing American soldiers. Again, the efforts tend to focus on the search for and recovery of victims, their appreciation and commemoration.

Archaeologists are members of committees and boards that plan how to install new memorials for the victims of mass murder or how to maintain the archaeological remains and results. The process of a public memorialization usually follows the official narratives (see Chapter 13).

Civil disobedience and resistance against state authorities characterises the conflict around Northern Ireland (The Troubles) during the second half of the 20th century, for example. Such conflicts, often having their roots in a struggle of minor groups against state authorities, are always prone to develop into actual civil wars.

A field where archaeological investigations have proven especially useful deals with reconstructing combat tactics and obtaining information on how the involved parties were actually armed and equipped. The use of different archaeological methods in combination has the potential to provide deeper insight into the individual combat strategies of the various parties involved. The integrated use of field surveys, geophysical prospection, the deployment of metal detectors, detailed mapping, excavations of trenches, posts, bunkers etc. can enable researchers to detect if and how other activities occurred in the wake of the battles. For instance, where the number of shells on a site is remarkably low, this can suggest that the party who prevailed collected them later with the intention of recycling them. The conditions for the preservation of findings vary greatly, especially where the impacted areas are extensive, depending on the nature and intensity of land use. Arid zones or rocky and elevated areas are, for example, clearly more favourable for both preservation and the possible scale of investigations, compared to more densely populated areas.

Excavations or surveys, regardless of their location or objective, can almost always be trusted to draw increased public attention, and offer good opportunities to address hitherto unresolved topics with regard to regional or national history, to provide new perspectives beyond conventional patterns. To uncover the past – in a literal sense of the word – that has been shrouded, intentionally concealed, or just randomly or not at all addressed by the authorities, often excites public discussion with reference to interpretations or competitive commemoration. Regardless of anything else, they will always help with the recognition of the victims, of crimes, conflicts and wars, and the awareness of 'unwanted history'. It is essential that archaeologists are at all times aware that theirs is an active socio-politically-charged role that they are playing in the larger scheme of regional, national or international history. Archaeological and historical research is often affected to a certain extent by the prevalent political climate of a region or nation. A repressive environment is very unlikely to allow such investigations since a certain degree of openness – especially if there is potential for an uncomfortable truth – is required. Under such conditions, it seems that such work is often focused on events of the more distant past rather than targeting sites of conflicts that are still fresh memories. Some selected cases will be discussed in different chapters.

CONFLICTS AND MYTHS OF THE PERIOD OF COLONIALISM

Vast parts of the African continent were claimed by European colonial powers into the mid-20th century. The division of the continent, especially during the 18th and 19th centuries, depended on the economic interests of the Great Powers alone, without any regard for existing ethnic or other social structures. According to *longue durée* research, places that are related to uprisings and the resulting violence between native populations and colonial powers at the end of the 19th and early 20th centuries are sites of particular archaeological interest, since they have the potential to reflect historical conflicts whose impacts are felt even today. A good example is that of a South African fort that played a major role over a century ago in the Anglo-Zulu War (1879) in South Africa. Several different archaeological methods were applied in the course of those investigations. The material remains confirm the presence of both of the parties involved in the battle, but there is also evidence for a subsequent use by the Zulu.

Investigations of a battlefield in the Kallaya saltpan in the Sirtica Desert, south of the Bu Njem oasis, conducted by the Centre for Battlefield Archaeology (Glasgow, Scotland), have revealed complex patterns that can only be understood against the background of the equally complex history of Libya under the colonial power Italy.

Sirtica is the desert area between Tripoli and Cyrenaica (Libya), which was of strategic importance in the early 20th century. The battlefield, near the so-called Kallaya salt pit, is about 20 km south of the Bu Njem oasis, where important traffic routes cross. The saltpan is located in a north-south valley bordered by longitudinal outcrops of rocks. The salt was essential for the tribes living there.

Archaeologists commenced their surveys assuming they would come across remains of a minor battle between Italians and Mujahideen, who had fought as a part of a Holy War (jihad) against the invading Italian forces since 1911. One of the combatants was the father of Colonel Muammar Mohamed Abdul Salam Hameed

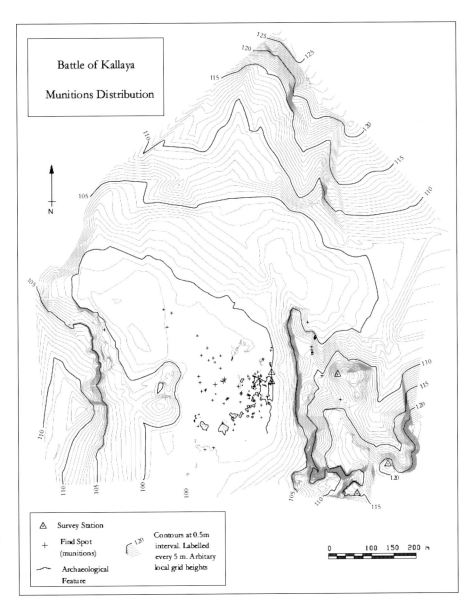

Fig. 5.1. *Map of the distribution of munitions at the site of the Kallaya battlefield (© Iain Banks).*

Abu Menyar al Gaddafi, who was injured in the battle. Gaddafi mentioned the battle himself and drew public attention to it, which increased recent awareness of the event. Gaddafi's family was affiliated with the local Alghus tribe and is from Sirte in the Sirtica Dessert. Ironically, while his father fought in a battle against the Senussi under the command of Sayyid Idris, the later King of Libya (1943–1969) in 1918, it was Gaddafi himself who would overthrow King Idris I in 1969 and become the ruler of Libya. However, the Senussi order was rather influential during the first decades of the 20th century. After the decline of the Ottoman Empire's

rule over Libya in 1912 and the Italian invasion, the influence of the Sufi order of the Senussi increased until they became the strongest power structure in Cyrenaica, and never stopped trying to extend their control over local tribes and families.

What the archaeological surveys revealed was the evidence of a skirmish between two small units of unequal opponents. The recovered remains of weaponry are remarkably heterogeneous in their provenance, with many items being of Italian origin. Since Italian arms and ammunition occurred on both sides it appeared unlikely that Italian forces were involved themselves. After the results were diligently mapped and measured, the resulting pattern clearly demonstrated that European parties had supplied both opposing sides. The detailed investigation also provided further insight into the battle. Apparently, the bigger of the warring parties had taken up positions on the hilly outcrops that rise in the east over the salt pit and were firing down on the outnumbered group. As the battle continued, they must have left their strategically superior position at some point and advanced down towards the saltpan.

Even after the fieldwork was completed the identity of the two hostile parties who engaged in the Kallaya skirmish remained unclear. Only through a careful consideration of textual sources in the Arabic language was it eventually possible to attain a comprehensive, consistent result.

The testimonies report that at the end of 1918 a group of about 300 Senussi and a small group (30–40 persons) of local families, including members of the Gadafa Alghus family and the Alpattata family, came to Kallaya. The Senussi refused them access to the saltpan; instead, they opened fire. The Senussi were on the strategically better mountain ridge on the eastern side of the Kallaya Pit, overlooking the saltpan and with a clear view of the Alpattata and Alghus groups. The Senussi were far superior, but both sides suffered losses. The Alpattata and Alghus groups withdrew to the north-west, and the Senussi made the mistake of abandoning their strategic position on higher ground, probably storming down the slope towards the saltpan to pursue the retreating men. By doing so, they lost their cover and had to accept heavy losses.

A large number of artefacts were left behind when the combatants abandoned the battlefield, and the environmental conditions of the Kallaya saltpan acted in favour of their preservation. The archaeologists have documented and mapped all the militaria detected, which were scattered widely, but decided against recovering them (see Fig. 5.1). Those items will remain *in situ*, buried by the sand of the Sirtica Dessert.

The sensible and integrated use of archaeological sources, of oral traditions and textual sources of different origin creates an added value as long as a variety of different sources is consulted with due regard to source criticism, and contextualised accordingly. Only when

the archaeological material is fully considered, and the results are projected against the background provided by oral and written sources can we hope to unravel the complex history of a site such as Kallaya. The difference in narratives, constructs and the perception of the past is reflected in the conflicts, and confirms the prerogative of interpretation.

The Kallaya battle was a skirmish that had nothing to do with the big events that have taken place elsewhere in the world. This struggle is not related to the colonisation of Libya through Italy. It was a fight at a local level between locals about access to a landscape resource, namely, salt.

Extensive investigations have also been carried out by the Spanish archaeologist Alfredo González-Ruibal in Ethiopia, especially on the Ethiopian-Sudanese border. Despite great attempts by the European powers to colonise the country, Ethiopia was able to defend itself until the 1930s. In 1896 Ethiopia won an important battle against the Italians at Adwa. The Italian dictator Mussolini, in particular, tried to bring the country under his control in the 1930s. In 1936 Emperor Haile Selassie went into exile in Britain, but the Italians never achieved complete control of the country. Archaeological investigations have been carried out in the border areas to Sudan. Surveys and excavations were conducted at three sites: Was' i (Asosa), a small outpost on the border; Afodo, another, larger outpost on the border; and Gubba, a residence of the local Funj dynasty that included a palace, which the Italians used as their headquarters. The presence of Italian units was documented at all locations. However, those sites that were located far from central places were finally abandoned in favour of military bases in the centre.

THE EASTER RISING IN IRELAND

Some archaeological projects were initiated through the celebration of the Centenary of the Easter Rising in Ireland. The uprising in April 1916 was one of the significant events within the process of ending British rule over Ireland. Although the uprising went on for only a few days, losses were equally high on both sides, causing considerable destruction in some Dublin districts and culminating in the almost instant execution of the leaders in May. Such ruthless punishments along with the brutal intervention against civilians led to further protests, resulting in the declaration of independence in January 1919 and eventually in the outbreak of the Irish War of Independence (1919–1921). After a truce in June 1921 and ensuing peace negotiations that precipitated the Anglo-Irish Treaty in December of the same year, the path to independence was open. Furthered by the treaty, the proclamation of the Irish Free State followed in 1922. It included all Irish counties except six counties within the old northern province of Ulster (now becoming Northern Ireland), which remained a part of the British Empire. This provoked conflicts among the ruling political forces of Ireland that soon consumed the civil population and became the Irish Civil War (1922–1923). However, the Easter Rising of 1916 was without doubt the trigger event that sparked the struggle for independence – a factor that was recognised and publicly honoured 100 years later by a series of public events along with the institution of several memorial sites. Archaeological surveys and excavations

took place before the installation of memorials at major sites of the conflict.

During the Rising the rebels took over the main post office in Sackville Street, central Dublin (today O'Connell Street) along with a number of surrounding buildings. The superior British units (which ironically included Irish soldiers serving in the British units during WWI) used armed force against well-armed rebels and civilians alike, bombarding both buildings still held by the Irish but also those already abandoned and causing fires to break out in many places. The archaeological investigations focused on those buildings and parts of Dublin which the rebels had reportedly occupied during one of the bloodiest battles of the conflict. They focused further on evidence of how the Irish revolutionaries retreated from the post office while it went up in flames on the last day of the rebellion and also on their last known headquarters in Moore Street and neighbouring houses. Many of the early

Fig. 5.2. Wall breakthrough through the interior walls of the house at No. 17 Moore Street to No. 16 Moore Street, Dublin, Ireland (© Frank Myles, Archaeology and Built Heritage, 2012).

20th-century buildings have survived to the present day, some retaining the scars from the actions of both sides prior to or during the rebel withdrawal. The carefully documented evidence comprises mainly of bullet holes and breakthroughs in the walls to the neighbouring houses, and clearly show how the rebels managed their escape from No. 17 Moore Street to No. 16 Moore Street. The precise nature of the archaeological work indicates that the event lasted only about 24 hours, and so creates an example of how short-term violence can imprint onto the archaeological record (see Fig. 5.2).

Another focal point was to investigate some of the internment camps related to the Easter Rising, including Frongoch (Wales), Spike Island outside Cork City (Ireland), and the Curragh (Co. Kildare, Ireland). These were the places where members of the Irish Republican Army (IRA) were taken, both in the aftermath of the revolt and also subsequently in the course of ensuing conflicts. Although some of the foundations of former barracks are still visible, the archaeologists focused on small finds from these camps. It was one of the prisoners' pastimes to produce little personal items. The predominantly male inmates produced mostly adornments and accessories for women, some of them even with personal dedications. It was a means of staying socially and emotionally attached to the world outside the prison walls. The motifs vary but some carry a clear nationalist narrative, and include harps, round towers or copies of the Tara Brooch (see Chapter 10).

'THE TROUBLES' IN IRELAND

The long-lasting hostilities between what eventually became the Republic of Ireland in 1948/1949 and Great Britain and Northern Ireland never truly ceased, smoldering on until they escalated once again to become a violent conflict in 1968, known as 'The Troubles' or 'The Northern Ireland Conflict'. The Troubles ebbed and flowed, and continued until 1998, involving two opposing factions that can be divided

Fig. 5.3. Large paintings in the streets of Belfast serve political positioning; here portraits of the Irish hunger strikers of 1981 (© Hajotthu, CC BY-SA 3.0, commons.wikimedia.org).

by economic, ethnic, social and religious aspects. It took a long and difficult process to re-establish peace but eventually the majority of the factions accepted a peace treaty and signed the Good Friday Agreement of 1998. Peace remains fragile, as is clearly demonstrated by reoccurring conflicts and acts of violence.

Material remains from the period of The Troubles are still present in many places, especially in the cities of Derry and Belfast. Many houses are embellished with politically-inspired wall murals that show graphic representations of political ideas, symbols or popular political activists, and in some cases also the victims (see Fig. 5.3). The murals exist to communicate, to encourage political commitment and to commemorate. Some of the houses have bullet holes that riddle the walls as a physical proof of recurring violence. In Belfast, the so-called Peace Lines, also known as Peace Walls (see also Chapter 8), are significant reminders of the riotous past as they cannot be missed with their towering height up to eight metres and stretching from a few hundred metres in length to several kilometres. Such walls separate and divide without any doubt and act as a barrier; perhaps they should protect, but they form liminal zones, have gates and are insurmountable.

The prisons where about 25,000 members of the IRA (Irish Republican Army) were held captive have also become a focus for archaeologists. Her Majesty's Prison Maze, also known as Long Kesh Detention Centre, is located near Lisburn, south-west of Belfast, and is where the detainees went on hunger strike after escalating conflicts between the IRA and the British government in 1981, resulting in the death of ten internees (see also Chapter 6). The prison was closed in 2000. Several written records, some viewed from a government perspective while others are descriptions from the detainees' point of view, provide two very different narratives. After new cellblocks with the distinct shape of an 'H' were added during the 1970s, the prison became colloquially known as the 'H-Blocks'. Viewed through the eyes of archaeologists, it represents a building structure with extensive interior fittings and a plethora of different features. The building aside, it is particularly the prison equipment, such as the bedsteads of the hunger-striking and deceased prisoners, that draws attention. An object as simple as a prison bed is charged with symbolic meaning as soon as it is put in a

context with historical events; it then becomes part of the personal history of the victim.

Many items related to The Troubles are kept by local museums. Clothing with bullet holes and the dried blood of the victims on them, for instance in the Museum of Free Derry, can create a direct confrontation and cause highly emotional reactions from the visitors to those exhibitions (see Chapter 13). Again, the narratives, presented to visitors by exhibitions in various museums, differ from one another.

The archaeological investigations of Irish sites related to conflicts of the 20th century are excellent examples of how the results have increased public awareness. It is no surprise that the events of a century ago inspire less controversy and can be more readily integrated into national commemoration, in contrast to those events of the Northern Ireland conflict, which remain active in the conscious memory of society north and south of the border.

THE ARCHAEOLOGY AT PLACES OF THE SPANISH CIVIL WAR

The difficult process of reappraising national history is illustrated by the archaeological activities at sites that staged significant events of the Spanish Civil War (1936–1939) and the ensuing fascist dictatorship (1939–1975). When around the turn of the new millennium mass graves were first opened to search for missing persons, the revelations inspired a broad public discussion about the more recent history of Spain. Archaeological field schools that allow students and citizens with an interest to partake in ongoing excavations have added further to the public awareness. The reappraisal is not yet finished, but has been helped by archaeology and forensic archaeology for more than a decade, and the Spanish population is finally addressing that chapter of their less distant national past.

Although archaeologists have been involved in the opening of mass graves from the periods of both the civil war and the Fascist dictatorship (see Chapter 9), they have also conducted surveys and excavations of bunkers, posts and trenches, on the battlefields, of internment camps and prisons. Their highly significant finds are numerous and different in types and size, among them personal items that once belonged to combatants of both parties,

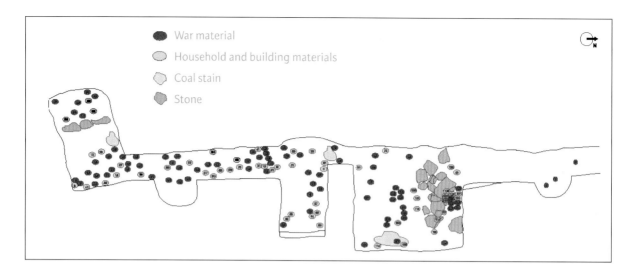

Fig. 5.4. Map of the distribution of militaria from the Spanish Civil War in Oviedo (© A Fanjul Peraza 2014).

and their arms, which are distinct enough to make the individual groups involved identifiable. It is of particular importance that Spanish colleagues are looking carefully into what remains of the positions of both sides – the Republicans who were eventually defeated, as well as the victorious Nationalists under fascist dictator Franco.

Excavations on Spanish battlefields, most clearly characterised by findings of posts and trenches, have increased in number lately. A site of special significance is Oviedo. The Siege of Oviedo (July 19th–October 16th, 1936) was a key event in the civil war. The still visible positions of the extensive trench system as well as of the bunkers in and around Oviedo allow the engagements and battle lines to be followed easily enough. Pico Paisano, the highest peak of Monte Naranco in the north of Oviedo, had major strategic importance in that region, and was equally important with regard to ordnance. At this site, a long-standing combat was settled between the Republicans and the Nationalist forces from Spanish Morocco, trying to gain control over Oviedo and the surroundings. The Nationalists' trenches encompassed the mountain almost like cobwebs, as recently demonstrated by excavation (by the School of Archaeology, Oviedo, Spain). Integrated into the defensive system were shelters and gun emplacements. The soldiers would take cover behind parapets made from stone and sandbags. Personal items and militaria of both parties, defenders as well as attackers, emerged in larger quantities from the bottom of trenches or shelters

(see Fig. 5.4) and indicate that the attackers, for instance, were joined by supporters from various parts of Mexico, from the former Czechoslovakia, but also from France, Poland and Austria.

Two more sites deserve consideration in this context: the first one is the Campus de Moncloa at the Ciudad de Universidad Complutense de Madrid, and the second is the battlefield of Guadalajara near Abánades, south of Madrid. Excavations have recently taken place at both sites. In 1936, one of the fierce battles of the civil war was fought on today's university campus. The excavations revealed remains of the trenches and bunkers of the Republicans, and once again finds and small finds give testimony to the international origins of many of their supporters. However, typical militaria such as shell casings that normally occur in abundance at combat sites are surprisingly rare in this case. Textual sources suggest that the casings were retrieved to be recycled to compensate for a material shortage.

Archaeologists (from the Spanish National Research Council) who excavated another civil war-site at Mount El Castillo, near Abánades, also found trenches, shelters, bunkers and other concrete elements of defensive structures installed there, by the Nationalists this time. Not unlike the evidence from Monte Naranco, the individual defensive elements extend around the hill. Communication trenches connected the individual posts. The first line of trenches was dug directly into

the bedrock or the soil; they were quite narrow (0.8 m), though, and measured 1.2 – 1.6 m in depth, while parapets built from sandbags offered additional cover. Some sections of the trenches had been reinforced using concrete and asbestos. Evenly-spaced gaps in parapets and trench walls, so-called loopholes, facilitated the discharge of defensive fire on the enemy. The pillboxes remained above ground level and were not sunk into the ground, while the gun emplacements had polygonal shapes. Sheltered posts turned out to be located in front of the trenches although without any direct connection. The latter shows that the defensive system of El Castillo was outdated even at the time of the civil war because more advanced fortifications already offered covered passages between shelters and trench systems.

Archaeological investigations (Spanish National Research Council, University of Barcelona and Barcelona Supercomputing Centre) into the Battle of the Ebro, for instance at Fatarella Ridge (Catalan Central Depression), are using an integrated methodology to map the features and finds based on spatial analysis of a larger area supported by GIS (Geographic information systems). That particular battle in July 1938 was the decisive one that brought about the turning point in the civil war and the inevitable victory of the Nationalists some months later.

Based on the position of a defensive trench, several bunkers in strategically important posts and the spatial analysis of further war remains in conjunction with textual and visual sources revealed striking new facts concerning the progress of the battle and how the Nationalists eventually emerged as the winning party. Visual field analysis is vital to the project since the lines of sight from specific posts and bunkers reveal how much of the area could be controlled from them (see Fig. 5.5). The deployment of the combined methods achieved a result that clearly showed that the Republican forces were initially in a very good position. Well-coordinated attacks from the air and from the ground by tanks and concentrated heavy artillery fire eventually razed the Republicans bunkers and trenches. Despite massive enemy fire, the Republicans nevertheless managed to hold their lines until the defeated troops had retreated beyond the Ebro.

The overall conclusion is that the results obtained by the archaeological excavations hint at distinct changes in battle strategy during the course of the civil war. At the early stage from 1936–1937 the pattern of extensive defensive trench systems including occasional bunkers still followed those of the Western Front during the First World War. The victory of the Francoist nationalists in the Battle of the Ebro shows the good strategic positioning of the Republicans, but in the end they were overwhelmed by the combined operation of different military forces. This new strategy was in the end successful, a strategy that was common in the Second World War, too.

THE FINNISH CIVIL WAR

The Finnish Civil War preceded the previously mentioned events by two decades, breaking out in 1918 and lasting five months. It was born from a power vacuum after the fall of the Russian Emperor and turned into a struggle for leadership between Democrats and Socialists after the declaration of independence. Germany supported the democratic so-called White Guard party, while the Russians backed the opposing socialist so-called Red Guards. It appears that both forces were ill trained and poorly equipped for a military engagement. Finnish archaeologists (University of Helsinki) have recently investigated the site of the battle of Ahvola, northeast of Vyborg (Karelia) in a territory that is now Russia. The survey aimed to provide new insight into one of the decisive battles that resulted in a turning point in favour of the democratic White Guards that repulsed the Red Guards and paved the way for Finland to become a part of the Western World. Between 1918 and 1940/1944 Ahvola had been within the boundaries of Finland but it became incorporated into the Soviet Union after the ceasefire agreement between both states. During the time of the civil war in 1918, that particular stretch of land was strategically important because of the railway line to Saint Petersburg. The surveys revealed the locations of several fortified structures, trenches and emplacements of both sides. It appears that the posts of the White Guards were better constructed. This might have been because they had a few leaders with basic combat training and military experience. Even today, the region remains sparsely populated – a fact that has worked in favour of the state of preservation of the battle remains.

THE NEW CHALLENGE: INTERNATIONAL TERRORISM

It is a question of definition and semantics as to whether officials will classify a violent attack as a terrorist outrage or not. Archaeology has only recently begun to approach sites of terrorism. In doing so, archaeologists create another opportunity to commit themselves to socio-political agendas. The archaeological approach must be mindful of certain specifics. The most distinctive feature is that terrorist incidents are always one-sided. The deadly strikes happen without advance warning; offenders target public and private places alike. The archaeologist is able to study the footprint of the attack, whose imprint might be left on buildings and the surrounding terrain. In contrast to open combat, or even to guerrilla warfare, the archaeologist is less able to see the response of the official forces, as the terrorist has struck by surprise. It remains to be seen whether archaeologists come to understand and study the locations of official response, which may be more muted or quite invisible since the response could be a series of arrests and sentences, for instance. Archaeological investigations and documentation should always record the obvious traces, although the ultimate challenge does not end there and demands that we look far beyond the scene. The latest investigations at Ground Zero in New York provide a good example of where archaeology should be heading with regard to an archaeology of international terrorism. As governments increasingly respond to the terror threat by deploying rapid-response units, the material available to the archaeologist for study will also undoubtedly change.

Chapter 6
CONCENTRATION CAMPS AND INTERNMENT CAMPS

INTRODUCTION

Respect for and the protection of human dignity, personal freedom and liberty are fundamental human rights; so are the freedoms of thought, conscience, religion and opinion, and the freedoms of movement and residence. Yet human beings all over the world are far too often deprived of their dignity and freedom because of their ideology and opinions, of their social status, religion, ethnicity or their political stance against the authorities. Many end up held in concentration or internment camps, mostly without trial and judicial process. To deprive human beings of their dignity and freedom by putting them behind walls and barbed wire is a fundamental punishment, a severe abuse of civil and human rights. Such sites of detention are a particularly popular method which dictatorships and other totalitarian regimes use to oppress and control those who are secretly or openly in opposition to the government, who offer resistance against state authorities or official national interests.

The world of camps and hence the methods of repression are highly complex. The internment camps of the 20th century have become widely associated with concentration camps and Auschwitz (in point of fact Auschwitz-Birkenau), making the term synonymous with the Holocaust and the extermination camps. The camps of the National Socialists represent the mass murder of the Jewish people; these camps embody the cultural memory of the biggest atrocity within forcible detention camps of the 20th century.

A United States Holocaust Memorial Museum (USHMM) study reveals that about 42,500 forcible detention camps of different categories once existed. The first concentration camp opened in 1933 in Dachau only three weeks after the National Socialists seized power in Germany. Those deported suffered forcible detention, humiliation and degradation, were deprived of rights, forced into slave labour, exploited, tortured and killed. In addition to the six death- or extermination camps Auschwitz-Birkenau (Auschwitz II, not to be confused with the concentration camp Auschwitz I), Majdanek (also known as Lublin), Bełżec, Sobibór, Treblinka and Kulmhof-Chełmno, where ca. 3,000,000 people were murdered, there were 20–25 main concentration camps and an estimated 1,200 sub-camps (see Fig. 6.1). The number of sub-camps per main camp varied significantly from three (Bergen-Belsen) to 200 (Dachau). Six euthanasia centres should also be mentioned, operated specifically for the targeted elimination of captives. There were also over 1,000 ghettos, at least 25,000 forced-labour camps, some 150 prisoner camps, 200 workers' educational camps, 100 police prison camps, several juvenile concentration

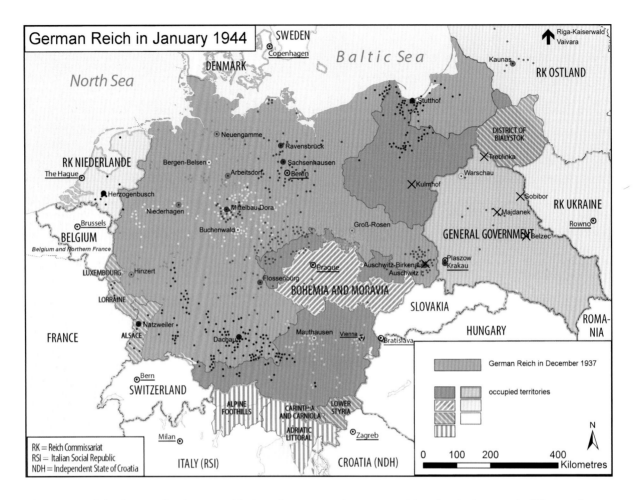

Fig. 6.1. Map of the six extermination camps (x), the main concentration camps and the related sub-camps in different colours (© Peter Hinterndorfer).

camps, so-called birthing centres (for foreign workers), several thousand prisoner-of-war camps as well as many smaller and bigger internment camps. The numbers vary or might be inaccurate at times since many camps existed only for a couple of weeks or months. Their functions often changed repeatedly during their existence and the National Socialists never established an official registry of camps. Despite the large number of camps, there are only a few where relics or constructional remains have survived. The National Socialists themselves levelled several sites to cover up the traces of their atrocities. Most of the standardised barracks of the Reich Labour Service (Reichsarbeitsdienst RAD) were wooden constructions, which after the war became a valuable resource and the buildings were transferred to different places. Many sites have literally disappeared beneath turf and tarmac

and have been forgotten for decades. The main camps have tended to be remembered and they are marked by monuments and memorials. The number of such memorials has also grown significantly (see Chapter 13).

The individual types of camps served a multitude of different functions. Their general purpose was to exercise control, to exploit human labour or to re-educate the inmates according to the state ideology. Concentration camps and their sub-camps in particular served to acquire forced labourers for strategic industries, such as at the Western Wall (Hintzert – Rhineland-Palatinate, Germany) or near the so-called Friesenwall (Schwesing – Schleswig-Holstein, Germany); to work in stone quarries as at Flossenbürg (Bavaria, Germany), Mauthausen and Gusen (both Upper Austria, Austria), and Natzweiler-Struthof (today France); or in brick factories like Sachsenhausen

Work sites

Archaeological research and the museum presentations of former internment camps usually focus on the areas within the camp fences. These are the spaces where the prisoners had their quarters in the barracks, and include the killing areas, the roll-call square and sometimes even the fences themselves. The places where the inmates of the concentration camps, the forced-labour camps, the prisoner-of-war camps or of the prisons were set to work are less often the subject of scientific investigation or memorial presentation. The prisoners were considered as cheap forced labourers, available to the armaments industry in huge numbers, especially during the Second World War. It is usual that hardly anything has survived or is known of the former facilities. However, a precise search of a site will help to find a number of foundations or buildings. In Mauthausen, and in the large sub-camp at Gusen, there are still large stone crushers only a few steps away from the quarries in which granite was extracted for Adolf Hitler's buildings in Linz and elsewhere. These are the concrete shells of formerly massive buildings. In addition, there are the foundations of armament-production halls and various other facilities necessary for the operation of the quarry.

The work in the quarries was considered to be very hard and many of the prisoners lost their lives there. The detention conditions in the internment camps, where the detainees were deliberately not called on to work, were also regarded as being particularly hard. Boredom is seen as a particularly severe aspect of being held in detention.

Not far from the Gusen Memorial and the quarry is the stone crusher in which the granite was processed; in the background is the quarry (© Bertrand Perz).

north of Berlin (Brandenburg, Germany) or Neuengamme (Hamburg, Germany).

Many of those held in labour camps had to work in the armaments industry. Forced labourers were also used to build defence installations such as the Atlantic Wall from Norway to France, the Flak towers in Vienna (Austria), Berlin and Hamburg (Germany) or the giant Valentin submarine bunker near Bremen (Germany), all of whose remains testify to the monstrous scale of the forced labour. The horrific conditions in many of the camps led to high mortality rates, while the unpredictable arbitrary will of the camp staff posed an additional deadly threat. In addition, East Europeans were treated much worse in comparison to forced labourers from Western Europe. Those deported to the extermination camps had no chance. They ended up being either shot or murdered by carbon monoxide gas or Cyclone B.

The history of concentrating and detaining human beings in camps did not begin with the National Socialists. The term 'concentration camp' first occurs around 1900 and is used to describe camps installed by the British forces during the Second Boer War (1899–1902). The Boers had the broad support of the white farming population. By detaining the farmers in so-called 'concentration camps', the British made sure that the Boers' support withered away. As epidemics and malnourishment caused the death of many of the internees, a wave of public outrage swept across Great Britain, and the ensuing debate drew wider attention to the idea of concentration camps. Around the same time, some colonial powers began building camps to detain reported insurgents as, for example, in Spanish Cuba and the Philippines where the Americans constructed such sites, or in South West Africa (Namibia) where the Germans were responsible. A whole network of camps spread throughout many parts of the world during the First World War to detain prisoners of war as well as refugees, resisters and protesters classified as public enemies. After the Easter Rising in 1916 in Ireland, the British installed several camps in Ireland and Wales where insurgents of the Irish Republicans, the predecessor organisation of the IRA, were detained (see Chapter 5). In the period between the world wars other nations under totalitarian rule, regardless of being communist or fascist, began to build such camps. Italy, for instance, built several camps in Libya to intern the native population while the country was an Italian colony during the Mussolini era from 1922 to 1943. When Franco took over power in Spain, he had followers of the Republican opposition detained in prisoner-of-war camps from 1936, and later built specifically designated prison or repression camps. In post-revolution Soviet Russia, it was a common practice to deport political opponents to the designated concentration camps. The Gulag camp system of the Stalinist era reportedly cost the lives of about 2.5 million people who were committed to forced labour, malnourishment and punishments. After the Japanese invaded China in the 1930s, they also installed and operated camps which were notorious for their brutal and inhuman conditions.

Throughout World War II, every army maintained their own prisoner-of-war camps in their homelands and in their colonies. Enemy aliens, for example Jewish refugees from Germany or Austria, were detained on the so-called British Five Islands (today Trinidad) and other camps in the Caribbean, while Japanese people were interned in camps in the United States.

It remained a common practice in countries run by dictators, as in Argentina or Chile, to detain opposition-party members in camps even after the end of the Second World War. Forcible detention camps continue to exist in many parts of the world.

The building structure has always been subject to change and development in the course of a camp's life. Concentration camps would be extended again and again to keep more people imprisoned. The plans and aerial photographs from the last days of the Second World War only reflect the latest and final constructions in the National Socialist camps.

Liberation of the internees does not necessarily mean that such camps ceased to function as such. After the end of World War II, Allied Forces continued to use many of the former National Socialist camps as internment camps, some of them as so-called Soviet Special Camps, where National Socialist perpetrators were imprisoned; while others served as temporary refugee camps or penal institutions.

The issue of reuse is more frequently addressed in this book. Various other possibilities are conceivable and well known. Some of the former camps were completely demolished and the area was used in a very different way. In other cases, some buildings were dismantled and reused elsewhere. Or, as mentioned, the infrastructure and the buildings remained in use, whether as a prison or as private houses. It is also the case that memorials erected on such sites can be changed and altered over time and these also become part of a camp's archaeological narrative (see Chapter 13).

Systematic violation of international law as well as the disrespect of fundamental human rights are what characterised the routine in all internment camps. The way individuals and whole groups of people were locked up often only because of being different, along with how they were deprived of food and medical care, exploited and forced into labour, subjected to control, repression, terror, re-education, punishment, torture and murder denotes those camps. The nature of prisoner accommodation is another characteristic that sets internment or forcible detention camps apart from prisons, for instance. While more or less weather-resistant, barracks and even tents were the common accommodation of the camps, and traditional prisoners were usually housed in individual or group cells.

The ongoing debate regarding the camps, be it from the archaeological or the historical perspective, will only be productive as long as state and national authorities allow an open dialogue with the past even if it means facing and accepting uncomfortable truths. A number of examples will be discussed below, but there are many more nations where people were and are held forcefully in camps. Archaeological and historical research that is contrary to an official state's policy is often met with little or no tolerance. There is however a constructive movement to become aware of these travesties, and states like Spain, Greece, Argentina and Chile, for example, are showing initial signs of movement in the right direction. There is also useful research being done on the former Soviet Gulag system, but it is still the National Socialist camps and the prisoner-of-war camps of both world wars that attract the most attention and inspire the most outward-looking results.

The camps are never hermetically sealed areas, even if the prisoners had and have no chance of being released. They are part of a larger landscape with its hamlets, villages and towns. The work places were usually located outside the camp's walls. The camps were supplied with goods of all kinds by a variety of local merchants. The camps and prisons were a significant economic factor, especially for the local region. The administration of the camp cooperated with the local administration. This aspect is still a gap in research.

THE ARCHAEOLOGY OF NATIONAL SOCIALIST DETENTION CAMPS

Archaeological investigations of concentration and internment camps, especially those that the National Socialists first set up in Germany and then later extended throughout most of the territories occupied by the German Reich, play a prominent role within the field of 20th-century archaeology. It is why these examples are discussed before others.

A major paradigm shift swept across Germany in the mid-1980s with regard to its National Socialist past, and this was followed by a new perception of its history. On 8th May 1985 the former federal president Richard von Weizsäcker gave his much-noticed speech in commemoration of the end of the World War II in Europe. He stated that the 8th May did not mark a defeat for Germany, but a day of relief. His speech opened a completely new outlook on a difficult past. The acceptance of responsibility for the Holocaust and war crimes in much of Europe and attributing the day of the surrender as the day of relief marked the beginnings of a new culture of acceptance that no longer denied, withheld, or played down the National Socialist past, and embraced the commemoration of the victims as its main concern.

There followed a period of intensified research into the National Socialist past that eventually inspired excavations of the concentration camps. The first investigation was at Witten-Annen (North Rhine-Westphalia, Germany) in 1990/91, a sub-camp of Buchenwald (Thuringia, Germany), and from there work shifted to Buchenwald itself and then Sachsenhausen (Brandenburg, Germany). That direct approach to the terrors of the concentration camps was another step towards a critical examination of Germany's own history. Interestingly, there was an earlier excavation at the extermination camp in Kulmhof-Chełmno (modern-day Poland) in the late 1980s and before the political change in Poland, a country that was particularly affected by the National Socialists and World War II. Research intensified during the late 1990s. Polish archaeologists were seeking proof of the crimes perpetrated against their people. The primary focus of their activities was to confront the National Socialist crimes against the Polish and Polish-Jewish populations during the occupation as well as those committed during the Stalinist era. Too few memorials existed at that time to commemorate the victims, regardless of whether they were Poles or foreigners. In other European countries where National Socialist camps once existed archaeological operations have taken root since the turn of the millennium.

Young people and local people are often involved in the excavations. It is part and parcel of a political education that celebrates democratic values and tolerance over those of former dictatorships.

Exposing the outlines of barracks, gates, fences and all traces of the killing machine constitutes a fundamental part of those excavations in former camps. The places of captivity and oppression are coming back to light. It appears that the renewed visualisation is necessary for many people to help them contemplate and comprehend the horrors of the past as well as to commemorate the victims. For the survivors, contemporary witnesses and their descendants, and also for tourists, it is very important to visit the former camps and the memorials to remember, commemorate and mourn. The idea of setting up memorials cuts across all divides and is a feature of local as well as national and international initiatives. Archaeologists are becoming involved in the task by exposing the remaining structures or, in cases where concentration and extermination camps are concerned, helping to locate critical sections, such as the gas chambers or crematoria. Items that once belonged to either victims or perpetrators are frequently dug up during fieldwork too. The remains of the camps and any finds or personal effects related to internees or guards (see Chapter 10) are an important resource to complement or even expand the picture created by written, vocal or visual sources. This only highlights the fact that archaeology plays a key role in commemoration projects and (museum) visualisations of historical structures alike (see Chapter 13).

EXCAVATIONS AT EXTERMINATION CAMP SITES OF THE FORMER GENERAL GOVERNMENT FOR THE OCCUPIED POLISH AREAS, THE 'REICHSGAU WARTHELAND' AND 'REGIERUNGSBEZIRK KATTOWITZ'

Historical and archaeological research of the extermination camps provide essential material for Holocaust studies. The installation of the camps at Bełżec, Sobibór and Treblinka was part of operation 'Aktion Reinhardt', the sole objective of which was to systematically kill Jews and Roma. The SS supervised those camps. Another camp in Kulmhof-Chełmno was also operated by the SS, while the camps of Auschwitz-Birkenau and Majdanek were set up as concentration camps and fell under the responsibility of the Concentration Camps Inspectorate (IKL), or the SS Main Economic and Administrative Office (SS-WVHA). Some of the camps lasted for only a short time. Bełżec, for instance, operated only for nine months, from March to

December 1942. Nevertheless, more than 400,000 people were killed there. The camp of Sobibór, located further north at the Russian border, was built around the same time. Estimates regarding the number of victims vary from 150,000 up to 250,000. Around 900,000 people were murdered in Treblinka from July 1942 to November 1943. The National Socialists eventually disbanded and closed those three camps and established farms on top of the remains to cover their traces. Kulmhof-Chełmno was already operative in December 1941 and the killings began immediately. Some 150,000 people were killed there before the camp was closed by the National Socialists.

Unlike the other four death camps, the new arrivals in Majdanek and Auschwitz were sorted into those who were fit or unfit to work. The weak and fragile were herded straight into the gas chambers. About 80,000 victims died in Majdanek and nearly 1,100,000 perished in Auschwitz-Birkenau.

Investigations into these sites faced the almost unimaginably high numbers of victims. They led to the early installation of a memorial in Majdanek in November 1944, shortly after the Red Army arrived there (in July 1944). In Auschwitz a memorial site and museum was set up in summer 1947. No other site in the world embodies the Holocaust more than Auschwitz-Birkenau. Consequently, UNESCO recognised the place as a World Heritage site in 1979, and since 2007 under the name 'Auschwitz Birkenau German National Socialist Concentration and Extermination Camp (1940–1945)'. After the political turnaround in Eastern Europe, it became evident that more memorials were needed in other places too.

Plans for the installation of new or the renovation of existing memorials are strong drivers for archaeological research today. After archaeologists (University of Toruń) completed their investigations of Bełżec in 2004, a new memorial followed shortly afterwards. Likewise, modifications to the Sobibór memorial were triggered by the results of excavations carried out by an international team coordinated by the Foundation for Polish-German Reconciliation. Without archaeology and archaeological research, our knowledge of the concentration camps would be far less detailed.

The efforts of the archaeologist are vital because many of the crime scenes left no visible traces above ground, and documents, contemporary witness reports, maps and photographs are rare. At Bełżec, only three former

Fig. 6.2. Railway lines and railway carriages are one of the most impressive symbols of concentration and extermination camps and are often an important part of the presentation in memorials – here the memorial in Auschwitz-Birkenau (© Claudia Theune)

prisoners are known to have survived. A citizen who lived nearby sketched a site plan from memory, but only after the war was over. Another sketch was made by one of the survivors – also from memory some time after the liberation. The plans reflect the memories, perceptions and perspectives of the drawers. They have arranged the buildings and paths in the drawing and placed them spatially in the way that corresponds to their memory and what was important for them at that moment. This personal view becomes particularly obvious, as the archaeological investigations revealed a different location of the structures.

Among the earliest sites excavated was Chełmno, with an initial field season in 1986/87 that continued in 1997 and the years after. Bełżec followed in 1997, Sobibór in 2000, Majdanek in 2005 and eventually Treblinka in 2007. In Auschwitz and Auschwitz-Birkenau archaeologists are accompanying the latest construction activities. The focus has been not only to locate the gas chambers but also to discover any later modifications. Equally important has been locating the cremation chambers that were often later additions and the mass graves, too. There is always the expectation that the archaeologists can help obtain information about the exact dimensions of the camp as a whole or about specific areas. Archaeologists are expected to provide details concerning individual barracks, connecting roads, gates, fences or the position of those functional buildings that were formerly occupied by the SS. Railways and their platforms are also part of the

extended camp infrastructure. The famous pictures of the rails leading into Auschwitz-Birkenau (see Fig. 6.2) are iconic, but the railroads that ended in Bełżec, Treblinka, Sobibór and the terminals there as well as in other concentration camps cannot be neglected either. Those trains were the means for deporting many thousands into the death camps.

Archaeological surveys employ both invasive and non-invasive methods. The right choice of methods is of utmost importance if the discovery of human remains is anticipated. According to Jewish belief and traditions, the dead should not be disturbed. The situation demands consultation with the local Jewish organisations prior to the actual fieldwork, and supra-regional stakeholders should be likewise included. It is one of the main reasons that geophysical surveys are employed to locate mass graves, barracks and the gas chambers in Treblinka. A different approach was taken in Bełżec, where augering was applied to locate the mass graves and determine their exact dimensions and also to establish the outlines of several buildings. Extensive excavations were required to reveal hitherto unknown parts of the camp and to expose the remains of the killing facilities.

After the victims arrived at the Kulmhof-Chełmno site, they had to move through the manor house (see Fig. 6.3) before being herded onto waiting lorries where they were suffocated by exhaust fumes. During excavations at the mansion, the rooms that the victims had to cross were exposed. The surrounding area was filled with

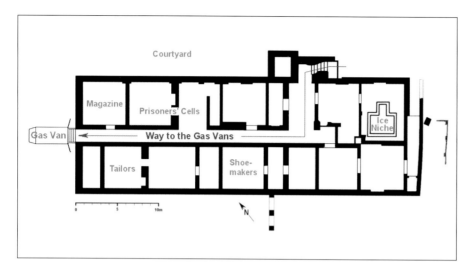

Fig. 6.3. Kulmhof-Chełmno, manor house. Route of the prisoners to the gas vans (© Zdzisław Lorek).

Fig. 6.4. The exposed gas chambers at Sobibór (© Ivar Schute).

items that had Hebrew inscriptions or displayed Jewish symbols. At first, the dead were kept in lorries and were then transported into the nearby Rzuchów forest to be buried there in mass graves. In summer 1942 crematoria were eventually built. The archaeologists located the remains of four of the crematoria and four field ovens. What remained of the crematoria were the bricks and fragmentary piping of the ovens.

Archaeological surveys at the site of the former extermination camp Bełżec began in 1997 and initially comprised mainly of augering and occasional excavations to determine the extent of preserved structures in the ground. They revealed several well-preserved building structures and also showed the location of several mass graves. By the time the camp was nearly completed and already operating (1942), extensive remodeling had occurred, allowing two distinct phases to be differentiated. The complex building structures in the centre of the site indicate that the original gas chambers were located there, but they seem to have then been relocated further to the north. It should be noted, however, that this interpretation remains uncertain because the above-ground structures

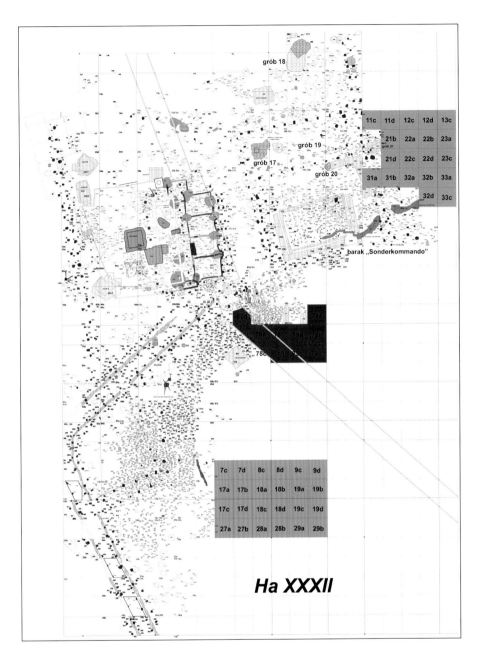

grób 18

grób 19
grób 17
grób 20

11c	11d	12c	12d	13c
21b	22a	22b	23a
21d	22c	22d	23c
31a	31b	32a	32b	33a
		32d	33c

barak „Sonderkommando"

7c	7d	8c	8d	9c	9d
17a	17b	18a	18b	19a	19b
17c	17d	18c	18d	19c	19d
27a	27b	28a	28b	29a	29b

Ha XXXII

Fig. 6.5. Map of the gas
chambers at Sobibór
(© Ivar Schute).

■ Barrack area
▨ East area of the barracks
▩ Area of grave 21 and escape tunnel

are completely gone, with only foundations remaining. The few drawings of the site are too vague in that regard, making the interpretation extremely difficult. The augering surveys identified thirty-three mass graves, spaced irregularly through the compound.

The remains of the corpses were found in the lower layers and the cremation remains in the upper layers. It appears that during the initial phase the bodies of the victims were buried without further manipulation and that over time only cremated remains were dumped

Fig. 6.6. Sobibór: the tunnel during the excavation (© Ivar Schute).

on top. As no crematorium is known to have existed in Bełżec, it had previously been assumed that bodies were only incinerated but not actually cremated.

When the investigations at the site of Sobibór started out in 2000, augering was the first method applied there. An international team of archaeologists (under leadership of Yoram Haimi, Wojciech Mazurek and Ivar Schute) has been working there for some years now, and they have surveyed large areas of the former extermination camp. Geophysical prospection was used to obtain better insight into the general camp structure, which had comprised five sub-areas. The so-called Vorlager (outer camp) included the living quarters of the SS staff and the now newly exposed ramp to the railway, while Camp I housed the Jewish labourers who worked in the warehouses of Camp II sorting through the belongings of the victims. The so-called 'Road to Heaven' was the barbed wire fenced path that the doomed had to take to get to Camp III where the gas chambers awaited them, and that further connected to Camp IV where the housing of the special unit was located. Sections of the path are being re-exposed, including the three steps at its end that led into the gas chambers. Camp III, the place of demise and extermination, is of special interest. In 2014, the archaeologists eventually succeeded in locating four of the gas chambers, and subsequent excavations brought their foundations back to light (see Fig. 6.4-6.5), but these remains had already been partially destroyed when the memorial for the victims was built back during the 1960s. Each of the gas chambers measured 4 x 5 m

and could contain a maximum of 100 people at a time. Showerheads are among the finds from this particular area, and confirm and demonstrate that the purpose of those chambers was camouflaged to make them appear to be shower rooms. The archaeologists also successfully determined the locations of mass graves and crematoria. Out of respect for Jewish beliefs, the mass graves remain untouched and were not excavated.

When an escape tunnel (see Fig. 6.6) was detected at the Sobibór extermination camp it was of particular interest. The inmates had intended to use that tunnel as their escape route in 1943. A revolt and ensuing mass escape ended in a hail of bullets. The project was abandoned and the tunnel remained unfinished.

The National Socialists dismantled the extermination camp of Treblinka at the end of 1943, leaving almost nothing intact. The principal aims of research were focused on locating the remains of the former barracks, gas chambers and crematoria. Surprisingly, more than 100 well-preserved structures were located, far more than initially expected (see Fig. 6.7). Geophysical and field-walking surveys were the principal archaeological methods used, while excavations were kept to a minimum. The dimensions of the former camp far exceeded the grounds outlined by the present-day memorial. The fake infirmary called the 'Lazarett' was identified. It was a place hidden by high earth ridges where the old, invalided and sick were herded directly upon arrival and forced to wait at the edge of a wide trench to be executed. It is also highly likely that other structures recorded are

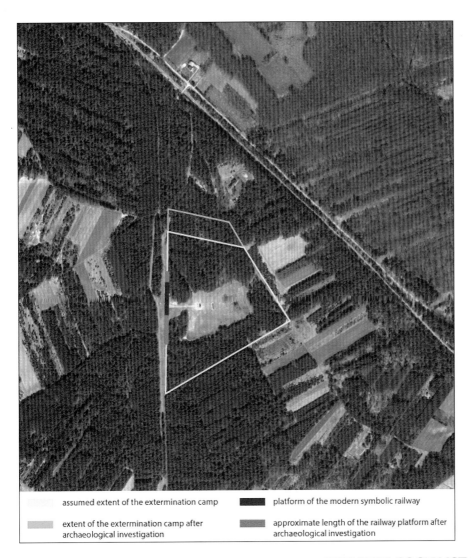

	assumed extent of the extermination camp		platform of the modern symbolic railway
	extent of the extermination camp after archaeological investigation		approximate length of the railway platform after archaeological investigation

Fig. 6.7. The archaeological investigation showed that the extermination camp of Treblinka had larger dimensions than assumed (© Graphic: Iris Winkelbauer after information from Caroline Sturdy Colls).

the remains of (older) gas chambers. Test trenches and detailed documentary research identified the older gas chambers without a doubt. The location of the mass graves was also confirmed, and probing showed that the victims were originally buried without incineration. It was only at a later stage that the bodies were incinerated, but the state of the preserved bone fragments indicates that this happened at lower temperatures at first. Finds of teeth and dental prosthetics occur close to the death chambers. Witness accounts mention how other inmates had to collect the dental gold from the victims after they were killed. Other teeth occasionally broke free and fell to the ground in that process. The human remains recovered and rescued from the site of Treblinka as well as elsewhere were later reburied.

NATIONAL SOCIALIST CONCENTRATION CAMPS IN GERMANY AND AUSTRIA

Excavations at Witten-Annen, located in the southern Ruhr area (North Rhine-Westphalia, Germany), were the first archaeological investigations of a former concentration camp on German territory. Buchenwald, Mittelbau-Dora (both Thuringia, Germany), Sachsenhausen, Ravensbrück (both Brandenburg, Germany), Bergen-Belsen (Lower Saxony, Germany) and Dachau (Bavaria, Germany) soon followed, while sites like Mauthausen (Upper Austria, Austria), Neuengamme (Hamburg, Germany), Flossenbürg (Bavaria, Germany) and several of the sub-camps were considered later.

Witten-Annen was a sub-camp that had been forgotten and was brought back to public attention in the late 1980s.

Between September 1944 and the liberation in late March 1945, the imprisoned worked in the nearby cast-steel plant in the district of Annen. The camp consisted of four barracks, several buildings with other functions and the infirmary. A second camp located close by was reserved for Russian forced labourers (the so-called Russian camp). After the war, the camp was swiftly dismantled and new living quarters were erected above most of the remaining structures. Only a small area remained where some of the barracks remained in use after the end of the war before being dismantled. The site came to wider attention when students of a local school visited the Dachau memorial during the mid-1980s and noticed the name of their home town on one of the information boards as listed among Buchenwald's external and sub-camps. The site had been almost forgotten, but now local initiative was followed by communal officials who contacted the Westphalian Office for the Preservation of Historical Monuments with a request to conduct excavations to locate the remains in the ground and make them visible again. Archaeological surveys in 1990/91 became the pioneer campaign for Germany. Extensive archival research prior to site work led to the discovery of a contemporary site map made in 1941, while several written records provided clues to how the camp was structured. Nevertheless, a plethora of questions remained even after the archival work was concluded so that the excavations were faced by high expectations. Several foundations were well preserved and accessible as well as the concrete posts of the wire fence that once surrounded the camp. Ensuing excavations exposed the foundations of the barracks formerly occupied by the camp guards complete with boiler room and coal store. Numerous small finds recovered from the soil illustrate various details of the daily camp routine. A dump site was uncovered where various items from the barracks were disposed of at the end of the war. Today the place has become a memorial site. A commemorative stone reminds visitors of what the victims had to endure, while concrete fence posts mark the boundaries, and the locations of some of the buildings are highlighted by floor slabs set into the ground. The whole ensemble is protected as a national heritage monument, although no signs point to it, and it remains a difficult place to find.

Buchenwald concentration camp

Buchenwald concentration camp was established on Ettersberg Hill near Weimar (Thuringia, Germany) in 1937. It was composed of three separate zones: the main camp, the 'Little Camp' where a quarantine station existed since 1942, and the 'tent camp'. During the final stage, the quarantine station in particular served as a death camp. Those incarcerated in Buchenwald were forced into labour either in a nearby quarry or in the

Fig. 6.8. Excavated toilet facilities in the former concentration camp Buchenwald; before the latrine was built, a fence, marked by concrete pillars, separated the area (© Claudia Theune).

local armaments factories. Soon after the liberation the camp was reused by the Soviet occupation authorities as an internment camp, known as NKVD special camp number 2, 1945–1950, and it became a National GDR Memorial complex, in 1958. At the time of the great change in Germany during the early 1990s, the site witnessed a new chapter. Excavation and the recovery of finds accompanied the construction work (see Fig. 6.8). Special focus was given to the 'Little Camp', where structural remains of several barracks emerged from the soil, along with a dumping pit that has been examined in detail since 1996. Those pits within the camp boundaries were vast in size. Some 4,000 buttons plus 2,500 other items were recovered alone from a strip measuring only 4 x 8 m in size. Although the inmates would normally arrive with only a few personal items, such a concentration of small finds testifies to the level of overcrowding.

Concentration camp Sachsenhausen

Sachsenhausen was set up in 1936 north of Berlin, where the Olympic Games were hosted that year. Its floor plan was designed with a distinctive triangular shape. Nothing obstructed the view of the barracks arranged in a semi-circle from the gate and watchtower A, situated at the base of the triangle; it conveyed a sense of total control, a Panopticon. Building extensions are not easy when keeping to the triangular shape, so other concentration camps did not copy the layout of Sachsenhausen, instead favouring the more conventional rectangular ground plan. Even when Sachsenhausen itself was expanded two years after the initial set-up, the new additions were not integrated into the original layout. Separated from the main camp in the industrial area at the west side was Station Z, the execution zone: this included a shooting range, gas chambers and a crematorium. It is no coincidence that the National Socialists marked the watchtower near the entrance gate with an 'A', signaling the prisoners initial stage of their 'journey', while the killing zone was termed Station Z, the final and terminal stage.

The camp was liberated on April 22nd/23rd 1945. Like Buchenwald, Sachenhausen became a Soviet Special Camp for a couple of years, starting in August 1945. The Russian occupation excluded only the former Station Z. From 1950, the Nationale Volksarmee (NVA) (National People's Army) of the German Democratic Republic (GDR) took partial occupancy of the camp, but large areas became unoccupied and deteriorated while Station Z was blown up and destroyed. In 1961, the

Fig. 6.9. Ash bin next to the crematoria in the concentration camp Sachsenhausen (© Johannes Weishaupt).

Fig. 6.10. Mauthausen, former concentration camp during the construction works at the so-called Russian Camp / Infirmary Camp; view from south (© MHC Fons Amical de Mauthausen).

site became a National Commemoration Monument of the GDR. Over time, the camp experienced multiple makeovers and several buildings were demolished. Since 1993, it has housed the memorial and Museum Sachsenhausen. The main objective of the museum is to provide an introduction to all aspects of the National Socialist concentration camp, as well as the Soviet Special Camp and the GDR national memorial site.

Archaeological investigation was completed as part of the museum works. Station Z has been investigated. A crematorium existed there since at least 1939. Winter 1941/42 saw the setting up of the shooting range and a new crematorium, while the gas chamber was an addition in 1943. A cobbled-path entrance that led into the gas chamber has been exposed. Prosthetic teeth and other small items were discovered between individual cobbles. Archaeologists also discovered traces of a path that had once surrounded the crematorium that was thought to include the ashes of the victims. The oven was cleared regularly of ash and the remains deposited in a huge bin attached to the outside wall but accessible from the interior (see Fig. 6.9). As soon as that bin had filled, the ash was transferred into large pits nearby. A vast quantity of cremated remains has been exposed. Photographs taken in the aftermath of the liberation already showed huge piles of ash there. The new investigations have marked these locations and made them visible, while the human remains have been reburied with proper ceremony in a graveyard that forms part of the recent memorial (see also Figs. 2.1 and 2.2).

Concentration camp Mauthausen

The planned reform of both the memorial and the exhibition at Mauthausen made historical and archaeological surveys necessary. The concentration

camp was founded in summer 1938, and the internees used as forced labourers in a nearby granite quarry. In its latest stage, Mauthausen comprised a main camp (Camp I) with 20 prisoner barracks and the special camp, Camp II, as an extension within the walled core area. Some functional buildings including the kitchen, laundry and infirmary lay inside the walls, along with the detention block, gas chamber and several crematoria in the basement. To the south-west lay the so-called 'Infirmary Camp' (also known as the Russian Camp, see Fig. 6.10; see also Figs. 3.1 and 3.12) with another ten prisoner barracks plus a kitchen and the sanitary building. To the south-east was Camp III; a tent camp with six large tents and a number of smaller ones lay to the north. The SS barracks (sleeping quarters and workshops) were situated to the west of the main camp. The walls of concentration camp Mauthausen towards the Danube valley had a special significance. High walls built of granite with integrated towers surrounded the whole complex at the top of an elevated area. The result is a striking resemblance to historical strongholds, and fits with other examples of monumental and government architecture from that era, reflecting the intentions the SS builders. This design narrative was not lost on the inmates either, who refer to Mauthausen as 'The Fortress'.

The area that had once housed the SS workshops was turned into a visitor centre during the early 2000s. Geophysical surveys were carried out at the 'Infirmary Camp', the tent camp and some SS workshops to assess the extent to which remains were preserved under the ground surface. The results pinpointed the exact positions of the individual barracks and other buildings, of the tents and the workshops in the northern part. The partial remains of one of the infirmary barracks were exposed. The standardised barracks were 55 m long and 9.5 m wide, and are similar to buildings from other concentration camps. They were mainly built from timber. The main structures including their stone foundations were very well preserved. A carefully constructed brick-paved doorway led into the building in the middle. Roof posts divided the interior into three sections, and the foundations of an oven were found. The Mauthausen barracks had been built on solid foundations.

Written documents seem to imply that the Americans burned the Infirmary Camp after liberation because they feared the spread of disease. However, the archaeologists found little evidence to support that theory. Although traces of charring occurred in some areas, they were by no means strong enough to be indicative of a fire that consumed the whole camp. Likewise, some of the photographs taken shortly after the liberation show that some of the barracks were indeed missing at that stage while others appear to be still intact (see Figs. 3.1 and 3.2). We may conclude that the contemporary reports merely stated intentions rather than recounting what actually occurred.

As the camp became massively overcrowded by autumn 1944 – as in many of the camps located in the

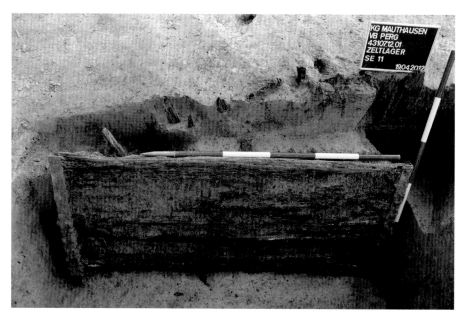

Fig. 6.12. Mauthausen, excavation at the site of the tent camp with boarding *in situ* (© Claudia Theune).

west, because of the military advance of the Red Army – the authorities decided to use tents to accommodate the increasing numbers of inmates. Sanitary facilities were absent; the bases of the tents had no firm ground and offered no insulation from the cold earth beneath, while flysheets covered only the roofs and the sidewalls. Nutrition was catastrophically poor. In search of evidence for those horrific conditions, geophysical surveys clearly showed anomalies that occurred along the sides of where the tents once stood. It is very likely that these anomalies mark the former positions of the tent poles. No such anomalies occurred within the interiors. Excavation went on to show that the ground was adapted to create platforms on which the tents were set. There is no indication of this above ground today due to erosion. The excavations revealed indications of small ditch features running parallel to the tents, which are interpreted as features dug by the inmates to direct rainwater away from the tents. Numerous items were recovered in this earth, including a little mirror, a shoe, and toothbrushes with Hungarian inscriptions (see Fig. 3.3), a necklace (see Fig. 6.11) and other personal effects. Several wooden boards embedded in the soil hint at how the inmates tried to improve their accommodations; the boards may have served to create separate areas inside the large tent which would provide a little bit of privacy (see Fig. 6.12).

Archaeological survey of each building has produced detailed records for the killing zone,

Fig. 6.13. Mauthausen, camp brothel: the door has no lock, but instead an observation slit (© Claudia Theune).

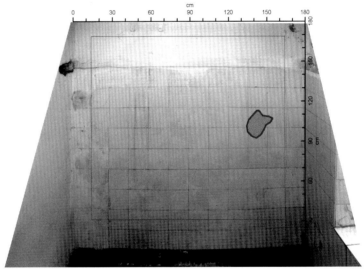

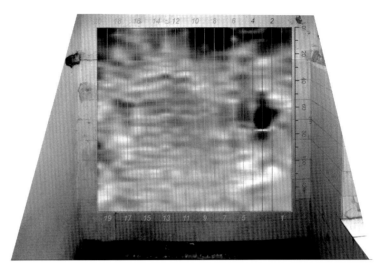

Fig. 6.14. Mauthausen, antechamber of the gas chamber where the apparatus was installed, through which the gas was fed into the gas chamber (© Archeo Prospections ®).

including the execution sites 2 and 3, the gas chamber and crematoria, as well as the kitchens and barrack 1, which housed the camp brothel. Remains from the execution zone 1 were subsequently destroyed and replaced by a post-war fire-fighting tank. The evidence overall indicates that several buildings were adapted and refurbished to the extent that ceilings and walls received fresh paint in light colours such as white, light green and yellow. The wall murals and once colourful patterns that dated back to the National Socialist era disappeared completely beneath coats of fresh paint.

Almost all main concentration camps had a camp brothel. Female inmates of the concentration camp for women in Ravensbrück were transferred to Mauthausen and forced into prostitution. Prisoner functionaries (see also Chapter 10) were allowed to visit the brothel. The small individual rooms that served as sex cabins had no locks but small rectangular peepholes, guaranteeing control at all times (see Fig. 6.13). Buildings archaeology revealed fragments of colourful painted lines that had once framed walls and ceilings in an attempt to make those cabins look a bit more cheerful.

In the former kitchen area, the pits that accommodated a series of huge cauldrons used to prepare the meals are still visible, especially from phase 2, which saw the total raised to 23 cauldrons, replacing the previous sixteen. The well-documented cellars underneath the kitchen floors give an idea of where and how the supplies were stored.

The evidence for redesign and improvement is also seen in the structural surveys conducted in the areas that had housed the infirmary and the laundry. The majority of toilet stalls in the laundry area lacked any evidence for dividing walls or doors and provided little to no privacy. Only one of the stalls appears to have been equipped with both. It seems likely that only one or more so-called functional inmates with certain privileges were entitled to use that particular booth.

Within the area of the former killing zone the evidence allows for the identification of three successive shooting installations. The first one, located north of the camp, was later dismantled before being turned into a water reservoir for the fire-fighting pond, as mentioned. The excavations failed to locate any intact structural remains there. All traces of a second killing apparatus were lost when a cremation chamber was built at that point. A small semicircular recess preserved at floor level marked the location of a third one. Comparative analysis identified it as a bullet trap (see Fig. 3.15). The victims were shot from the front while being led to believe that a photo was to be taken of them.

The sum of the evidence reveals the multiplicity of ways in which these places were used to kill. The evidence combines the results of geophysical surveys with a careful typological classification of the wall tiles inside the gas chamber and in a small antechamber with an outlet that channeled the gas into the chamber (see Fig. 6.14). The tiles vary according to the intensity of their colour and the accuracy of how their edges are aligned. Maker's stamps on their reverse show that they are the products of different workshops. Images obtained by ground penetrating radar help to pinpoint the exact location of the gas outlet in the wall. A picture taken in 1945 shows the outlet exposed and framed by nine damaged tiles that stand out because they vary in colour against the surrounding wall. Today, there are 16 tiles that do not fit in with the others surrounding the gas channel. When all available evidence is taken into consideration, the following picture emerges: shortly before the Allies arrived in Mauthausen, the National Socialists removed the gas-injecting machine and covered the breach in the wall with nine tiles. When the liberators arrived, they had the camouflaging tiles removed. Several of the original tiles were damaged in the process; consequently 16 new tiles had to be applied to repair the damage. This is a good example of how a careful analysis of all available sources allows the reconstruction of even the smallest of details.

Further examples of excavations in former concentration camps

The archaeological surveys at Buchenwald, Sachsenhausen and Mauthausen are representative of

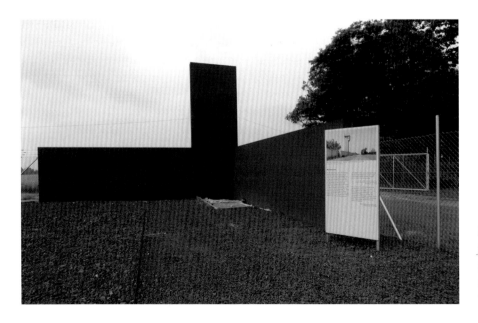

Fig. 6.15. Esterwegen, feature of the excavation next to the wall, fence and watchtower (© Claudia Theune).

larger scale efforts. Other examples are available, such as the former concentration – and then prisoner – camp Esterwegen (Lower Saxony, Germany), or the concentration camps Neuengamme (Hamburg, Germany), Bergen-Belsen (Lower Saxony, Germany), Dachau (Bavaria, Germany), and Flossenbürg (Bavaria, Germany). There is also the women's concentration camp Ravensbrück (Brandenburg, Germany), where excavations and geophysical surveys have been conducted. Published information is not always easy to come by, but many of these sites are open to visitors. In most cases, the structures of buildings are partly exposed and made visible again, while other visual elements such as models and information panels provide further details. One of the key motives that trigger excavations of such sites is the desire to once again make visible the locations and layouts of barracks, watchtowers and other structures of significance (see Fig. 6.15). The introduction of new state-of-the-art presentation techniques that often include landscape design make ground impacts unavoidable and so require archaeological assessment, prospection, investigation and documentation.

As previously stated, most of these former camps are subject to constant change and massive deterioration. It is a situation witnessed at many sites, including Witten-Annen, where many of the features were severely damaged and buildings reused and reshaped or even demolished and built over. It often takes contemporary areal photographs and other visual sources to get an idea of how densely the barracks and other buildings were situated. It is important that current visitors get an understanding of the dimensions of the former barracks, the location of the fences, watchtowers or other significant structures. Excavated foundations and cellars can help.

At Bergen-Belsen a memorial was established immediately after the end of World War II. During the 1990s, surveys took place in Bergen-Belsen with the aim of investigating the structural remains preserved below ground level. The small as well as big delousing barracks, prisoners' quarters, a water reservoir, latrine blocks, sewer systems and storage chambers were exposed and marked for visitors and complemented by models.

Esterwegen, located in the Emsland district of Lower Saxony, was the place where the 'Peat Bog Soldiers' were forced into moorland labour, cultivating the wetlands equipped with nothing more but a spade. It belonged to a group of 15 so-called Emsland camps and several outposts. Here prisoners wrote the song 'die Moorsoldaten' (the moor-soldiers). The excavations recovered parts of the fence and the wall, focusing on the border between camp and outer world (see Fig. 6.15).

Among the most recent memorials is one located at the site of the former concentration camp Flossenbürg. That site had experienced multiple phases of reuse, which eventually led to larger-scale construction over the site and the establishment of dense vegetation cover. The first archaeological approaches were initiated a year after the memorial was established, in 1999. The initial field campaign started out in search of preserved remains of barracks, lanes, fences and sewer systems. Aerial photography, artefact collection and geophysical prospections combined to offer striking insight into the underground structures. The exposure of those structures was a priority because they held special meaning, such as the 'Death Ramp'. Corpses were carried over that particular ramp and through a tunnel into the basement crematorium. Its access channel was poorly preserved and required intense conservation, and has now become an integral part of the current permanent exhibition.

Research into sub-camps

Research into the sub-camps has become more common lately to complement the studies of the main concentration camps. The same range of issues that prompt archaeological work exist, once development and memorial plans get under way. However, contemporary written and visual sources are normally scarcer when it comes to those smaller camps.

Rathenow is a small town in Brandenburg (Germany) that housed a sub-camp of Sachsenhausen that was set up as late as 1944 to provide forced labour to the ARADO aircraft plant nearby. During the early 2000s, development plans for an industrial park threatened the site. Rescue excavations took place and determined that large parts of the former camp had already been disturbed and were incomplete. The barracks had been designed to rest on pile foundations while the bathrooms had had strip foundations and remains of the fences were discovered. Today the site is represented above ground by a solitary commemorative plaque.

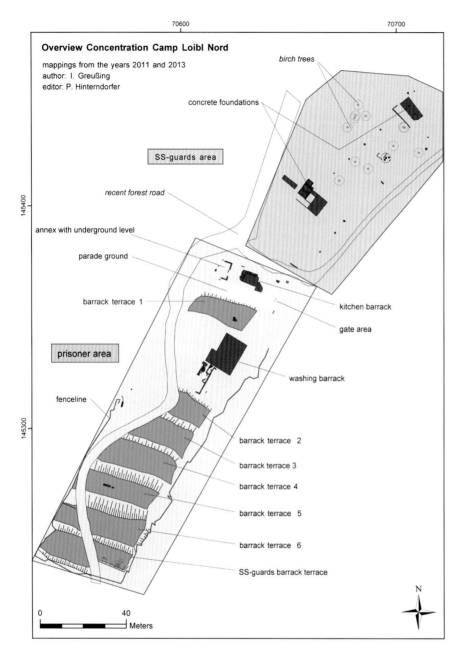

Overview Concentration Camp Loibl Nord

mappings from the years 2011 and 2013
author: I. Greußing
editor: P. Hinterndorfer

birch trees

concrete foundations

SS-guards area

recent forest road

annex with underground level

parade ground

barrack terrace 1

kitchen barrack

gate area

prisoner area

washing barrack

fenceline

barrack terrace 2

barrack terrace 3

barrack terrace 4

barrack terrace 5

barrack terrace 6

SS-guards barrack terrace

70600   70700

145400

145300

0   40
Meters

N

Fig. 6.16. Map of the results of the survey at the sub-camp Loibl-Nord/Loibl-North (© Isabella Greußing and Peter Hinterndorfer).

Other archaeological projects result from forces associated with political education. At Walldorf-Mörfelden (Hesse, Germany), a sub-camp of the concentration camp Natzweiler-Struthof (Alsace, present-day France), operated for only a very short time, from August to November 1944. Jewish internees were forced to work on the first concrete airfield of the Rhein-Main airbase in Frankfurt. As a part of the commemorative work, local youth participated in the archaeological investigations of the former kitchen

barracks alongside descendants of the Jewish families. A similarly inspired project led to excavations in Kaltenkirchen (Schleswig-Holstein, Germany), at a sub-camp of the concentration camp Neuengamme concentration camp. The initial focus was to locate and expose the camp's bathrooms and outhouses. Unfortunately, local authorities are not always in agreement and cooperative. It often requires huge efforts from committed students and other stakeholders to counter the resistance and to overcome wider

Fig. 6.17. Photograph taken shortly after the end of the war from the Loibl-Nord/Loibl-North camp with a simple barbed wire fence and wooden barracks (© Fotografische Sammlung der KZ-Gedenkstätte Mauthausen/Sammlung Janko Tišler / Photo: British Armee, Landry).

resentment to win support in facing the past and to set up a commemorative plaque or even a memorial site.

Further excavations took place in Gablingen (Bavaria, Germany), which once housed a sub-camp of Dachau; in Loibl-Nord (Carinthia, Austria), a sub-camp of Mauthausen; and even in Berlin at the old Tempelhof airfield, where the Columbia Damm camp was one of the earliest small camps, and at several forced-labour camps, as well.

The camp at Gusen (Upper Austria, Austria) used to be almost as large as the main camp in Mauthausen itself. A densely built-up area constrains archaeological fieldwork in this instance. Indeed, a number of the site's original houses are still occupied as domestic homes, including the former camp brothel. Others stand empty and are preserved, such as a former barracks, and while open space for excavation is scarce, it was possible to uncover the former roll-call, and to identify some foundations along with the crematoria that are located in a courtyard and can be visited.

At Loibl Pass south of Klagenfurt (Carinthia, Austria), prisoners from Mauthausen had to dig a tunnel through the Karawanks Mountains. The tunnel was never completed, but it later played a role as retreating troops crossed over the Alps to the north. The tunnel works

began from both sides of the pass simultaneously, and the prisoners were interned in two sub-camps of the Mauthausen concentration camp, one on each side of the pass (Loibl-Süd/Loibl-South, in today's Slowenia and Loibl-Nord/Loibl-North in Austria). While on the Slovenian site a memorial has existed for many years, archaeological surveys took place at the site of Loibl-Nord camp only recently. Excavations produced evidence of a simple wooden gate, located the former roll-call, and revealed the entire line of the barbed wire fences that had once surrounded the compound (see Fig. 6.16). The results make it possible to visualize the former dimensions of the camp and establish several observation points for visitors.

Structural evidence revealed during the excavations at Loibl Pass illustrate the constructional differences that existed between it and the main camp in Mauthausen near Linz. While Mauthausen was designed to inspire the illusion that it was a fortress, the Loibl camp was surrounded by a wooden fence reinforced only with barbed wire and a simple wooden gate (see Fig. 6.17). There is little to compare with the heavy gate in Mauthausen that was also flanked by two massive watchtowers. Mauthausen is situated at the heart of the so-called Ostmark and was meant to be a show of strength and power, while such displays were not required of the sub-camps located in the remote territory of the Carinthian Mountains.

Another aspect of the sub-camps concerns the forced-labour sites to which inmates were sent. The munitions and armament industrial sites became easy targets for the Allied air raids from 1943. The industries were relocated underground for safety, and while large tunnel systems are known, some 170 in all, many are inaccessible today as hazardous sites. Yet they remain important sources of archaeological research as they retain items and remains left behind. Surveys have been possible at only a few such sites, and it remains a new horizon for future research to explore.

The euthanasia killing centres of Hartheim and Brandenburg/Havel

The excavations in Hartheim (Upper Austria) were hugely successful and produced sufficient visual information for later public presentation. Between 1940 and 1944 Hartheim Castle was used as a killing centre in the National Socialist euthanasia programme. Archaeological excavations began when the castle was to be renovated and a memorial and information centre were being planned. An archaeological buildings survey preceded the actual excavations. The backfill of one of the trenches was discovered to hold important finds of the victims along with large amounts of cremated bone. A pit filled with what remained of the personal possessions of the victims was discovered and documented in detail. It was possible to salvage the contents of the pit in a block excavation that is now on display in the newly designed museum (see Fig 10.1).

The archaeological activities that took place in Brandenburg/Havel (Brandenburg, Germany) occurred in a very similar context. It was possible to salvage the remaining building structures in a way that provides enough visual sources and illustrates to visitors the killing process that took place there.

National Socialist camps in The Netherlands, France and Great Britain

The process of confronting the remains of National Socialist camps across Europe eventually triggered more research beyond the German and Polish borders. Concentration camps existed in the German-occupied Netherlands, Norway, France, in the Baltic countries, on the British Channel Islands and even in southern Europe in larger numbers. However, archaeological surveys are still limited to the Dutch, Norwegian and French territories as well as to the Channel Island of Alderney. The Dutch research has focused especially on camps in Westerbork, Amersfort and Herzogenbusch near the city of Hertogenbosch, commonly known as 'Camp Vught'. Westerbork and Amersfort operated as transit camps from where Dutch Jews were deported to the bigger European extermination camps. The internees spent only limited time there. In contrast, Camp Vught was a concentration camp.

Archaeological activities in The Netherlands were once concerned with extensions of the memorials and surveys assessing the state of preservation of remains buried in the ground, as the knowledge concerning the locations of the barracks and other functional buildings had been lost. As was the case with several sites in Germany, the midden pits attracted much attention, and resulted in a detailed record and the recovery of numerous items. The material was handed over to the museum in the memorial for conservation and archiving. All in all, those projects received much public attention, increasing the recognition of such efforts.

Little is known of the concentration camp of Alderney that was called 'Sylt'. It was initially assigned to Sachsenhausen, but later was part of Neuengamme. The internees were used as labour to build several bunkers and other fortifications for the Wehrmacht in many locations on the island that were linked to the Atlantic Wall. Archaeologists are currently making inventories of the remains that are still visible above ground within the boundaries of the former camp, and have found that it was larger than previously thought. Remains of the Atlantic Wall are also to be catalogued and documented (see Chapter 4).

Archaeological research has started at the former concentration camp Natzweiler-Struthof (Alsace, in present-day France) only recently.

Youth concentration camp Uckermark

The youth concentration camp Uckermark is located 100 km north of Berlin. Originally designated as

Fig. 6.18. Excavation of the sanitary facilities at Camp Wick on Jersey, Channel Islands (© Claudia Theune).

a detention camp for juvenile girls, at the end of the war women from Ravensbrück were also sent there for extermination. Archaeological excavation (Brandenburgisches Landesamt für Denkmalpflege und Archäologisches Landesmuseum) took place when road development works were to impact on the site. Little was known about the site layout, and the excavations helped to confirm the locations of the barracks and also provided information relating to the former dimensions of the camp.

FORCED-LABOUR CAMPS

The National Socialists operated about 25,000 labour camps all over Europe. There are estimates suggesting that over 8 million civil workers were brought to Germany during the war under false pretences to work on farms and in private households or were deployed to provide labour to the German war industry. Those who were sent to the armament and related industrial complexes were often

detained behind barbed wire fences. The labour camps varied in size, ranging from small shacks that held only a few labourers to large sites for more than 1,000 people. The importance of forced labour for the essential industries eventually led to improved conditions for the labourers during the course of the war, mainly because Germany relied so heavily on their labour and it became a vital requirement for carrying on with the war. Archaeological studies of the labour camps still lag behind those that have considered extermination and concentration camps. There are a few interesting examples, however, from Berlin and its vicinity, including Kleinmachnow, Berlin-Tempelhof and Mahlow (all Brandenburg, Germany).

The observations gained on the infirmary for forced labourers in Mahlow derive from a research project, while excavations in Kleinmachnow occurred as a result of planning requirements associated with modern land- development proposals. The camp of Kleinmachnow accommodated both prisoners of war and forced labourers from the Soviet Union and from

Western states. It appears that Soviet internees suffered significantly worse conditions than West Europeans. The barracks that housed the West Europeans had solid foundations, indoor bathrooms and occasionally even attached air-raid shelters. East Europeans had to make do with simple timber constructions without attached bathrooms. They had to use the common bathhouse. Archaeological work confirmed this. The discoveries made on sites of lightly built shacks without proper foundations usually revealed personal effects with Cyrillic inscriptions, while markings in Latin script occurred elsewhere on site.

The barracks at the former Tempelhof airport in Berlin were used for forced labour to service the aircraft companies 'Weser Flugzeugbau' and 'Lufthansa'. In both camps, the foundations of the barracks as well as an anti-splinter trench were detected. Many personal belongings were uncovered in the trench, which reveal the origins of the workers. Several forced-labour camps in Austria were used for the construction of hydropower plants, such as in Kirchbichl (Tyrol) or Suggadin (Vorarlberg).

Other sites that might repay further study include an air-ammunitions factory in the forest next to Xanten (North Rhine-Westphalia, Germany), which contained more than 100 buildings for ammunition- and ignition-storage depots, and the ammunitions facility at Horgau in Bavaria (Germany). Xanten was blown up after the war.

Camp Wick on Jersey (Channel Islands, Great Britain) was operated as a forced-labour camp between 1942 and 1944, when many West European inmates had to work on the Atlantic Wall. Attention has focused on the nine wooden barracks sites and the concrete foundations of the kitchen and the sanitary facilities (see Fig. 6.18). Many finds provide insight into the living conditions within the camp.

PRISONER-OF-WAR CAMPS

Every war inevitably results in the captivity of soldiers in prisoner-of-war camps. As established by The Hague Regulations in 1907, affirmed by the Geneva Convention on prisoners of war in 1929, supplemented in 1949, prisoners of war must be treated with humanity with regard to provisions, accommodations and clothing. Only Japan and the Soviet Union refrained from signing the treaty. Regardless, the National Socialists denied captured Polish soldiers their prisoners-of-war status, and the way they handled Russian soldiers was even less in accordance with the Geneva Conventions.

Exemplary among the archaeological excavations of World War I camps is that of Quedlinburg (Saxony-Anhalt, Germany), which was excavated (Landesamt für Denkmalpflege und Archäologie Sachsen-Anhalt) on a large scale in 2004 (see Fig. 6.19). It was followed closely by investigations at Dülmen (North Rhine-

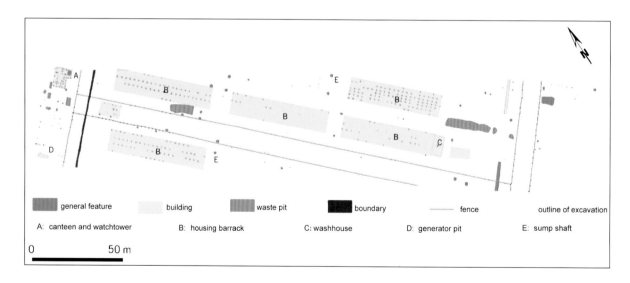

Fig. 6.19. Map of the excavations in the prisoner-of-war camp Quedlinburg with floor plans of the building, a waste pit and the fencing (© Landesamt für Denkmalpflege und Archäologie Sachsen-Anhalt, graphic: K. Ulrich).

Westphalia, Germany). In the German Reich alone, 175 camps reportedly existed that held up to 2.5 million soldiers. During road construction near Quedlinburg, an excavation began to reveal series of occupation levels ranging from the prehistoric past to medieval and early modern times. It also included a stratum from World War I, which related to the prisoner-of-war camp. Not many captives were held there during the initial stages of the war and evidence indicates that not all of the barracks were even occupied then. However, during the final stages of the war the camp was filling up swiftly until it was finally severely overpopulated. At the end of the war, Quedlinburg was not instantly disbanded, and the last of the Russian/Soviet inmates left it only three years later.

The camp comprised 48 barracks, each with a floor space measuring 50 m long by 15–20 m wide. Five of the barracks were excavated. Discoloured traces in the ground marked the places were the barbed wire perimeter fences once stood. Based on contemporary written records, it is even possible to define the former functions of the individual barracks. While the prison barracks were built mostly from timber, leaving the usual postholes behind for the archaeologists to find, other buildings had brick-built foundations. It is very likely that the brick-built structures belonged to one of the watchtowers. A stone-built house served as wash-house, while at another building a great many fragments of glasses, bottles, dishes and also cutlery were found, indicating that it was the former cook-house.

Plenty of the so-called STALAGs ('Stammlager'/main camp) and STALAGs Luft ('Stammlager der Luftwaffe'/main camp of the air force), which the National Socialists operated during World War II, are either investigated through excavations or can be located through aerial scanning combined with 3D-modelling (see Fig. 6.20). These are managed in a suitable manner by national heritage authorities. During investigations of STALAG Luft III, located in Zagan (Poland), archaeologists succeeded in locating one of the escape tunnels that the captives built in secret.

Similar investigations are under way in other parts of Europe, including Norway, Finland, France and Austria, and they are extending beyond the European borders to the United States and Canada. The activities in Norway and Finland are carried out as part of an effort to understand their national positions within the wider global political context during World War II. In the USA and Canada, the idea of preventing those almost forgotten places from falling into complete oblivion is a strong motive, as is the desire to draw public attention to them.

The Germans operated about 500 prisoner-of-war camps in Norway during the occupation period (1940–1945), mainly to incarcerate Soviet captives. Research (Norwegian University of Science and

Fig. 6.20. The entire STALAG XVII B at Krems-Gneixendorf is still visible in the LiDAR scan. (© NÖGIS).

Fig. 6.21. In the wilderness of Finnish Lapland some wooden barracks of the prisoner-of-war-camp at Inari Hyljelahti are still standing, more or less (© Oula Seitsonen).

Fig. 6.22. The deepened areas show the areas of the sunken houses in the forest camp in the outskirts of Berlin. (© Brandenburgisches Landesamt für Denkmalpflege und archäologisches Museum, Thomas Kersting).

Technology) into them started with the SS prison camp in Falstad near Trondheim. Installed in 1941, it became the second largest prisoner-of-war camp on Norwegian territory and from 1942 it turned into the place where most of the deported Norwegian Jews were also sent. Recent geophysical surveys have returned data on the foundations of the former barracks, indicating that some are partially preserved beneath present-day ground level.

Of special importance, however, is the fact that the Falstad SS punitive camp was linked to the Atlantic Wall, as many more camps in other locations were. Future research should consider that detail further and expand the focus accordingly. Prisoners of war from numerous camps were the forced labourers who had to construct the bunkers of the Atlantic Wall (see Chapter 4) along with connecting roads and much more of the related infrastructure. That circumstance connects the monuments of the wall in a way that should be given far more attention by researchers. However, because of their huge number, only a selected few can be researched in detail to obtain the vital information that will help to understand others as well. Since the labourers originated mostly from the former Soviet Union, one possible research objective could be to investigate how the Soviets were treated and how their imprisonment conditions and chances of survival compared with captives from other nations.

The most recent research on German camps in Finland reveals that almost 100 sites existed there, although only one camp, STALAG 309, in Salla (Lapland) was ever made official (see Fig. 6.21). Contemporary information is extremely scarce on the unofficial sites, but even for Salla records are in very short supply. Through archaeological surveys and documentation (by the Universities of Helsinki and Oulu) the camp was located. One of the advantages of a territory as sparsely populated as Finland is that the World War remains were not built upon, and this allows for more extensive surveys although the process is still in its initial stages. Early results from Peltojoki (Lapland), where a camp existed next to a military base, demonstrate how the Soviet prisoners of war lived in self-built huts, and wore clothing and had utensils that were much better adapted to the climatic conditions of Finnish Lapland than those of the Wehrmacht soldiers (see Fig. 6.21). The barracks

and functional buildings were not arranged in a strict rectangle but followed the topographical layout of the site. Without archaeology it would be impossible to write a comprehensive history of the Deutsche Wehrmacht and their treatment of prisoners of war.

In the U.S. and Canada, there is currently a new trend to recognize the long-forgotten sites of the Home Front. This refers to the places that lie outside actual battlefields, including armaments factories and also detention camps. The issues and considerations are almost identical to those dealing with combat operations in Europe. Various sites were recently excavated, most of them camps for Germans (e.g. Canada: Whitewater, Manitoba; U.S.: Camp Trinidad, Colorado; Bexar County and Ford Hood, Texas; Indianola, Nebraska); but some also for Japanese captives (e.g. Manzanar, California; Amache, Colorado; Honouliuli, Hawaii; Kooskia and Minidoka, both Idaho; Heart Mountain, Wyoming).

Recent surveys in the vicinity of Berlin as well as north of Vienna (Austria) have revealed an unknown type of camp that existed to hold Red Army soldiers until their return to the Soviet Union. The spatial organisation of these camps is very distinctive. Their most obvious features are pit-houses, log lodges and dugouts. The pit-houses of the Berlin camp had diameters of 3 x 4 m (see Figs. 6.22-6.23), while the houses of the Austrian Weinviertel region were considerably more spacious.

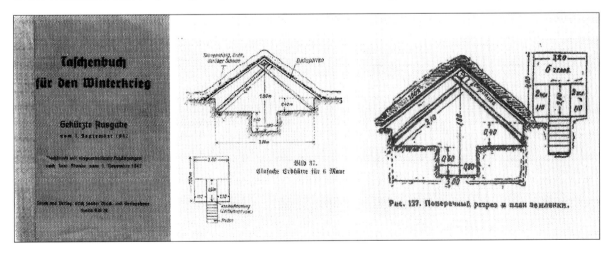

Fig. 6.23. Comparable building instructions for earth huts from the Soviet military manual a 'Спутник партизана' (Companion for Partisans) from 1943 and the manual for the Winter War of the German Wehrmacht from 1942 (© Erich Zander Druck- und Verlagshaus Berlin, edition 1942 – reprint YOYO Media from Спутник партизана 1943).

FORMER SOVIET SPECIAL CAMPS

During excavations in former concentration camps where it is mandatory to record all the individual layers, the period of the Cold War is often included by default. At the end of the war, Allied Forces quickly established camps in all of the occupied zones to detain war criminals or potentially dangerous National Socialists and functionaries. The Soviet Military Administration used some of the former concentration camps in the same way and turned them into Special Camps as, for example, at Sachsenhausen (Brandenburg, Germany), Buchenwald (Thuringia, Germany) and Jamlitz, a sub-camp of Sachsenhausen located southwest of Frankfurt/Oder (Brandenburg, Germany). Initially under the jurisdiction of the Military Administration, they were later run by the Camp Administration Department of the Soviet Ministry of Internal Affairs from summer 1948. Ten of those camps existed within the Soviet occupied zone. Buchenwald, also known as Special Camp No. 2, was active from August 1945 until February 1950. Special Camp No. 7 (later renamed No. 1) – Sachsenhausen – was also set up in August 1945 but remained active a while longer and closed in March 1950. About 60,000 prisoners were held captive in Sachsenhausen while about 28,000 were imprisoned in Buchenwald.

The Soviet Special Camp of Sachsenhausen occupied the distinctly triangular-shaped inner courtyard on the grounds of the former concentration camp and extended to the northeast as well as further south the industrial facilities located to the west. Guard units and the camp leadership occupied the zone at the base of the triangular structure. About 60 barracks accommodated the prisoners. The camp kitchen, laundry and the detention cells kept their former function, and some other barracks served as hospitals. Contrary to the earlier situation when Sachsenhausen was still a concentration camp, the prisoners were not forced into slave labour. Several contemporary witness accounts mention long periods of demoralising inactivity and idleness. Poor medical care, frequent illnesses, low food rations, and other forms of repression led to a significantly increased death rate. Board games and similar pastime activities were only allowed from 1948 onwards (see Chapter 10). Even after Buchenwald was officially closed and first ideas to transform it into a national GDR memorial were current, Sachsenhausen remained partially occupied by the Nationale Volksarmee (NVA). It was during this period that several of the original buildings in the camp area were demolished and dismantled. Station Z, the extermination site of the former concentration camp, was blown up in 1952/53. Other areas of the extended site deteriorated during this period and ended up partly dismantled or ransacked. However, at the end of the 1950s plans eventually formed to turn Sachsenhausen into a second national memorial site. The opening ceremony took place in April 1961, but the site had undergone fundamental changes by then with the majority of its old buildings removed and the addition of a new memorial centre. It was not until after the political change of 1989 that the possibility of modifications presented itself. Some of the structures were rebuilt or reconstructed with the objective to finally make all the many temporal layers of the site re-visible. The political u-turn brought about new perspectives for historians too and led to an intensified research into the special camps, which had languished in the shadows for too long. The concept for Sachsenhausen went beyond a mere documentation centre and aimed to include and commemorate the victims, so a new museum was built at the head of the triangular-shaped structure to keep their memory alive.

INTERNMENT CAMPS FOR ENEMY ALIENS

In wartime foreigners could always become enemy aliens as soon as their home nation entered the war. The status of refugees and other foreigners in a country could change to their becoming potential enemies abruptly, regardless of how long they may have resided there. After the Japanese attack of December 7th, 1941, on Pearl Harbour all people of Japanese origin in the United States were viewed as potential enemies. Many of them ended up in one of ten so-called relocation camps, and worked as forced labourers until being set free in October 1945. Excavations were conducted at several sites. While Kooskia accommodated only several hundred Japanese, about 7,000 were reportedly located in Minidoka and more than 10,000 in Manzanar. The main research objective was to find out how the internees managed to preserve their cultural capital during detainment. It appears that many internees took up gardening during confinement, which is a traditional Japanese pastime. Geophysical methods

were used to uncover and locate traces of gardening. Excavations soon followed to verify that the features identified were actually the remains of the prisoner gardens. Among others at Minidoka and Manzanar memorial sites were set up afterwards (see Fig. 6.24).

Lesser known are internment camps in the Caribbean. Two small internment camps are on Trinidad, on the so-called Five Islands just short of Trinidad's west coast. Islands were often used as internment camps or prisons as there is almost no need to build a fence or wall around the imprisoned. The Five Islands had served as transit camps and as a quarantine facility for migrants from India during the 19th century. German and Austrian Jews were detained there during the 1930s. After Great Britain entered into the war on September 3rd 1939, their status changed from migrants to enemies and led to their imprisonment on two of the smaller islands: male prisoners were held captive on Nelson Island, while women and children went to Caledonia Island (see Fig. 6.25). No new buildings were erected to accommodate the prisoners since existing older structures could be reused. The archaeological project (National Trust of Trinidad and Tobago, the University of the West Indies and the University of Vienna) there is investigating the old buildings and is looking for traces and items left behind by the former prisoners.

PRISONS

Archaeological research is not limited to the study of internment camps. Prisons are also investigated and questions remain regarding the conditions under which arrests happened. The option to investigate is, however, limited to prisons that are no longer operating. One of the first excavations of a prison related to the National Socialist terror took place in 1985 and 1986 at the former GESTAPO and SS headquarters and Reich Security Main Office. (see box 1). Although not carried out as a scientific archaeological excavation, the work nevertheless revealed well-preserved subterranean structures of the north-east wing along with remains of prison cells, demonstrating for the first time how close to the surface the remains of the National Socialist regime are actually buried and how little effort is required to make them visible. Those now exposed structures are a vital part of the 'Topography of Terror' (*Topographie des Terrors*) memorial site in Berlin (see Chapter 13).

Fig. 6.26. Maze Prison (Long Kesh), entrance of compound 19 (© GiollaUidir, CC BY-SA 2.5, commons.wikimedia.org).

There is another former prison in Berlin that has now been turned into a memorial for the victims detained in the German Democratic Republic during the Cold War era: the STASI prison that was operated as a Soviet prison before the German Democratic Republic (GDR). While no archaeological activities have taken place, the material remains are being show-cased as a part of the memorial site and are presented accordingly.

Other archaeological projects have considered the prison complex on Robben Island (South Africa), where Nelson Mandela served the larger part of his prison term from 1964 to 1990, and the Maze Prison (also known as Long Kesh or the H-Blocks) south of Belfast (Northern Ireland), which accommodated convicted Irish Republican Army members during the conflict known as 'The Troubles' (see Chapters 5 and 13). Archaeological activity at both sites consisted mainly of a detailed documentation of their building structures. The Robben Island complex recovered several personal belongings of the former prisoners. The principal focus of the Robben Island project is not exclusively on the period of the apartheid regime, but extends further to include all periods from the 17th century onward. While the whole island is today part of the World Cultural Heritage site, the prison has been turned into a museum and memorial site.

During The Troubles in the 1970s in Ireland, the Maze/Long Kesh was used for the mass internment of Irish Republican prisoners. At one point in 1974, the prisoners set fire to the wooden barracks of the former airbase at Long Kesh. After that incident, a new high-security complex was built, nicknamed the H-Blocks because of the shape of the eight blocks. When the Good Friday Agreement came into effect in 1998, the authorities released many prisoners and eventually closed the prison in 2000 (see Fig. 6.26). That place played a unique role for the Northern Ireland Republicans not only because many of their leaders were imprisoned there, but also because it became synonymous with the hunger strikes of 1981 which led to the death of ten of them. Access to the former prison is limited, but an archaeological investigation was possible (University of Bristol). Its past narrative remains vivid in the presence of artefacts from those incidents and items associated with the hunger strike victims, some of which remain preserved in place.

FURTHER ARCHAEOLOGICAL RESEARCH QUESTIONS REGARDING FORMER CAMPS

The idea behind 20th-century concentration- and internment-camp archaeology is to make structures that are already erased above ground level visible again. It leads to the excavation of the central places of terror and murder, the penitentiary gates and also the barracks and sites of forced-labour operations. The point is to see how the camps can be exposed again and how the remains can be integrated into memorial sites. Depending on future research interests, new research objectives will emerge with respect to the global phenomenon of internment camps.

There are still many open questions regarding the features and architecture or the utilization of the available space. How did the design of the camps change through time? Did the camps vary by design during different phases of the 20th century or in different parts of the world? Are there differences in patterns of the camps closer to central places in comparison to those of the periphery? Did camps with different functions show differences in terms of internal structures? Which part of a camp was the public area and which was the closed-off and secret area? How was the landscape used to create these different narratives? Where were punishments carried out and under what actual conditions? How were enclosures, fences and walls designed?

At first glance, it may appear that the camps were principally fashioned in the way of military bases. It should be noted, however, that places designed as internment camps can never be compared to military compounds where soldiers are barracked, because where people are interned they are being retained forcibly against their will, because of their worldview and ideology, their social or religious background or ethnicity. Internment camps and military camps may share some basic features as, for instance, the regular layout of barracks and functional buildings, but the housing of soldiers hardly compares to the forcible detention of captives. That becomes even more evident when the architecture and standards of features are compared in depth, and with regard to provisions, security and measures of punishment. Such comparative approaches exist, but they are still in their initial stages. Future research should be heading in that direction.

Chapter 7

THE ARCHAEOLOGY OF CIVIL DISOBEDIENCE

INTRODUCTION

While chapters 4 and 5 bring archaeological observation of the world wars and local wars into focus, the present chapter discusses examples where protest, and specifically civil disobedience, has experienced archaeological research. Sites where such protests manifest themselves through the archaeological record were largely ignored in the past, but have now begun to capture the attention of researchers.

Protests sparked by social injustice are in the first instance directed against municipalities and state institutions. The protesters are often a minor group of persons who act against a powerful institution of the state or enterprises. Protest arises among other things from movements to combat military build-ups, (environmental) pollution and industrial exploitation. Strike action is a means of expressing protest in the latter case; in such cases the protest is directed against individual companies.

The borders between different forms of protest and resistance are without doubt blurred. Violence from any side is inevitably an aspect, be it symbolic violence, psychological violence or physical violence. Subtle differences exist, and such protests are generally not directed against the state as a form of government but rather against an acute or chronic despotism of the state and certain practices, principles and objectives.

However, the examples presented here primarily concern protesting against armaments and the nuclear threat in the Cold War era. Certainly other examples could be found; a strike ending in a bloody confrontation from the early 20th century is presented in the box.

In this chapter I will examine a small number of examples and all are from the recent past. Many contemporary witness reports exist and the authors are often still alive to tell the story, making the aural record a particularly important resource. In many respects, the wealth of contemporary visual and media records escalates the archaeological approaches into 3-dimensional space.

MERCURY CITY, NEVADA

Among other well-known archaeological projects are the investigations of the 3,500 km^2 of desert occupied by the Nevada National Security Site. Between 1951 and 1962 there were 119 above-ground nuclear tests conducted here, and an estimated 1,000 subterranean tests. Several airfields, smaller airstrips, helicopter landing pads, 28 separate testing areas, buildings and other infrastructure are located within the area, while

Ludlow, Colorado

The site of the Ludlow Massacre in Colorado (USA, 1914) was one of the earliest protest sites to be investigated by archaeologists. The Rockefeller-owned Ludlow mining company employed mostly migrants who had to labour under inhuman conditions. Their wages were based solely on the quantity of coal that each collier could produce, and the company required the workers to stay in company-owned towns and to buy in stores owned by the company. In September 1913, the miners went on strike to protest against such conditions, supported by their trade union. They quit their company-owned accommodations and built 12 camps with about 200 tents located in the rocky landscape near the exits of the valley to keep strike-breakers out. The company imported professional strike-breakers and set the Colorado National Guard against the miners. They arrested many strikers and shot others. Eventually the situation got out of control and on April 20th 1914 at least 25 people were killed. The army was called in and managed to disband and disarm the crowd – strikers and National Guards alike – and ended the conflict without further bloodshed. The strike continued without violence and without success until December 1914. It had lasted 14 months. A memorial was subsequently built there, but this was later vandalised and needed to be repaired. In the early 2000s, an archaeological survey was carried out where the camp had been located. The overall objective was to test the record of events as provided by contemporary witness accounts and written sources against the evidence obtained by archaeological methods.

The former positions of tents along with pits and cellars were identified and examined. It appears that most of the features were used to store supplies, but some might have served as shelters too. The research was particularly interested to see whether the information could help to understand how food supplies were organised. Canned foods and a high number of whiskey and beer bottles dominated the record, but there were also some indicators of fresh foods. It is quite unlikely that the workers continued to purchase their supplies from the factory stores because that would have weakened the force of their strike. The trade union might have organised for supplies, but local farmers also made contributions. Remains of weapons are also present and provide indications of how the strikers were armed.

Ludlow, drawing of the outlines of a tent with ditches, stakeholes and postholes (© Randall H. McGuire).

the main gate lies near Mercury City. Although the testing site is no longer actively used and vast sections are abandoned, other parts are still restricted areas where access is prohibited.

The first protests began in the late 1950s and became more numerous in the 1970s, generating ever-larger numbers of protesters. When the tests ended, so did the protests. A museum was built 100 km away in Las Vegas, and an on-site Nevada Test Site Guide provides information describing the history of the

compound and the development of the atom bomb from the official perspective; it does not linger too much on the protests.

The anti-nuclear protests focused on the gate near Mercury City, where the protesters established and permanently occupied a camp as early as the late 1950s (see Fig. 7.1). Since the camp existed there for several decades and the scale of the protest movement continued to grow it eventually occupied a vast area, measuring almost 240 ha in size. Archaeological surveys (by the

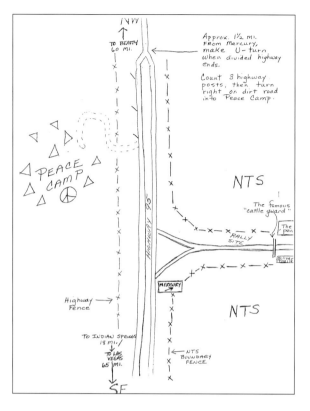

Universities of York and Nevada) have revealed a diversity of complex structures. While certain areas appeared to be completely cleared of rubble and larger stones and may have served as open sleeping spaces, small stone circles and enclosures might indicate the location of campfires and camping sites. Various objects recovered from the soil are indicative of various social groups and they represent different parties of protesters. The observations indicate that the site was kept scrupulously clean and the waste was cleared out regularly to avoid the accumulation of litter. Small sculpted items made from stone were also recovered, and include the peace symbol motif, as well as symbolically deposited figurines of children – so-called Shadow Children (see Fig. 7.2) – along with stone sculptures or graffiti related to the protesters' campaigns.

GREENHAM COMMON, GREAT BRITAIN

Camps in other places linked to the protests against the military build-ups of the Cold War era have also been investigated. The decision of the British government to allow cruise missiles to be based at the Royal Air Force Station of Greenham Common in 1981 sparked a protest movement, with camps being set up next to each of the gates that led into the compound. Organised by women, the camps became exclusive to females. The women

stayed at the camp until 2000, even after the cruise missiles were relocated as a result of the Intermediate-Range Nuclear Forces Treaty in 1991, and their objective changed to become a demand for a memorial site and documentation centre, to keep the memory of the protests alive for future generations. The women eventually disbanded the camps after they achieved that final goal through a judicial decision.

Several of the spectacular actions brought global attention and took place under the careful surveillance of the media. One action was the human chain that the women formed all around the Royal Air Force Station. It happened twice, in April and December 1983 respectively. While the women were repeatedly evicted from nine (smaller) camps that formed the Greenham Common Peace Camp, they always returned a little later. The camps were individually named and referred to the colours of the rainbow, with each camp's inhabitants having specific socio-political objectives and gender preferences. Their campaigns often involved cutting the wire fences around the airbase compound. Actually, many of their actions targeted those fences, to affix banners with political and protest statements, balloons, the peace sign, rainbow depictions and a variety of very different items (see Fig. 7.3). The damage and other traces of the protests are still visible in places in what is left of the former airbase, although the volume of items on the remaining fences has long gone. Future research might consider the detail of the items still present and the narratives that these items retain.

The official website of the Greenham Common Women's Peace Camp - Commemorative and Historic Site/ New Greenham Park presents information on the concept of the Memorial Peace Garden (see Chapter 13). The site represents a camp surrounded by a circle of seven large upright standing boulders with a high flaring symbolic fire at its centre. The whole installation stands for the four elements: earth, fire, water and air. A stone and steel spiral sculpture represents the continuous protest. More brasses and installations will supposedly follow, and not only at Greenham Common itself. However, the existing site receives varied perceptions and interpretations from the media. One reason may be because the memorial site is linked with the death of Helen Thomas, who died there in a tragic accident with a police vehicle in 1989. Her untimely death might

Fig. 7.3. Many objects were fixed on the fence at Greenham Common; today almost nothing is left (© Ceridwen, CC BY-SA 2.0, geograph.org.uk).

suggest that the flame sculpture within the stone circle can also be interpreted as an eternal flame. The different readings illustrate how complex and multi-dimensional interpretations can be, and are based on a wide range of perspectives. After the inauguration of the memorial site in 2002, the site was repeatedly subject to vandalism and wilful damage, with even some of the stones being taken away. Such occurrences are relevant to the archaeological and historical assessment of a site as they reflect its contention by different parties who have different views.

Gender played an important role in this particular context. Men had only limited or no access at times to the camp. During the 1980s, the independent and successful organisation of the protests became a powerful statement for women's emancipation globally. For the archaeologist, such a site offers the unique opportunity to investigate a place where only one gender should have left its signature behind.

The archaeological work (University of York) completed to date has surveyed some of the nine camps, determining their former dimensions and mapping the surviving remains. Evictions, for instance, have clearly left their mark, but later building development to make way for new streets was also apparent. Modifications of the terrain caused by the women are still detectable, and their fireplaces could still be located, along with numerous objects they left behind. The archaeological investigations at Turquoise Gate, a camp that is reported to have housed a group of vegan women, was particularly detailed and

Fig. 7.4. Structures from the huts were found during the excavations at the protest camp in Gorleben, here made with the help of roofing felt (© Attila Dézsi).

produced enough evidence to demonstrate that their diet was not exclusively based on vegan supplies, despite the accounts of former camp inhabitants, clearly highlighting how different sources reflect different perspectives.

GORLEBEN, GERMANY

Gorleben camp became for Germany what the Greenham Common Women's Peace camp was for Great Britain. The Gorleben salt dome is located in the Wendland region (Lower Saxony). Since 1995, it has served as an intermediate storage facility for highly radioactive waste. The existing plans to turn the salt dome into a permanent disposal site for nuclear waste are still in place. When those plans became known in 1970, spontaneous protests broke out and never fully went away because the final disposal site question is still open. The situation led to the installation of an on-site protest camp named 'Republik Freies Wendland' (Republic Free Wendland). About 120

huts housed 2,000 people temporarily. After only one month, the police were ordered to disband the camp forcibly. Geophysical surveys and excavations (by the Universität Hamburg) are currently taking place at the site, where archaeologists deploy aerial photography to determine the actual expanse of the former camp and map the known elements to gather as much information as possible about the daily life of the protesters (see Fig. 7.4). The project work includes extensive archival research and considers textual and audiovisual sources, along with interviews with local residents and contemporary witnesses. The different stakeholder groups are integrated into the project work.

CONCLUSION

Archaeologists have surveyed various sites with strong links to protest movements, such as the places and buildings occupied by squatters as part of their protests against the use of nuclear power. The protesters built camps in those places, where they would live, and would add political and visual pressure to their cause as well as facilitate the organisation of their resistance over a long period. The camps were normally temporary and saw many changes during their existence. However, the finds and findings speak to their life cycle, be it short over several weeks or extended over several years. Quite apart from informing the current political discussion, such sites provide wonderful opportunities for archaeologists to study transient occupation. In addition, it is possible to see how and to what extent space is being occupied (sometimes not legally) and marked.

The examples are tackling issues of public concern and protests where the archaeologists are deliberately taking part in an ongoing socio-political discourse. While the archaeologists involved are acutely aware of their function, that particular role becomes a key driver and motivates them to see the project through. The focus is from the protesters' perspective and helps to bring it to the fore. People who are actively involved with the protests are also often participating in these archaeological projects. The resulting archaeological narrative is certainly not always in tune with the official records. They aim to keep the memory of why the protests exist alive, to point out serious social contradictions and to discuss them in a broad public context through archaeological, historical and cultural-anthropological methods.

Where the study is dealing with events that are concluded, the archaeologist plays a role within the historic dimension, but where the events are active and ongoing, the archaeologist is an active party remaining as objective as possible yet often being drawn into the discussion. Typically, such a pull comes from the side of the protester, and so the archaeological contribution to date has tended to be one that offers an alternative account to those that are presented in the official accounts of the events.

Chapter 8

BORDERS

INTRODUCTION

Ever since the opening of the borders in Berlin, Germany and Europe almost 30 years ago, borders have been a relevant research topic. Different disciplines have focused on space, the perception of space, the actions of people in space and the negotiations of boundaries in a multitude of studies, looking at territorial as well as social spaces. Both spheres are closely connected and cannot be regarded in isolation. Basically, every division of space emanates from people, and spaces are arranged by societies. We create territorial and social spaces as well as borders.

Spaces can provide certainty of orientation with rules and norms indicating a direction within these boundaries, but spaces can also potentially confine people. On this basis, sociology defines the constitution of space as the reciprocity of action and structure, whereas social and location-related factors decisively affect the composition of space.

In addition to the temporal dimension, spaces are essential constants and determinants in life and the coexistence of human beings. In groups or societies, we live, act and operate within spaces at particular times.

If we talk about borders, we do so with territorial space predominantly in mind, imagining boundaries as linear structures. We think about the outline of a room, a house, a camp, a city or a country. We have plans with outlines of the referred structures in mind – lines that separate single units.

Such spaces can be small and may enclose a room, a prison cell, a prisoners' barrack or a parcel of land. They can also be large, comprising a camp, a village, a city or a country. Doors, gates or boom barriers allow us to cross these boundaries, or limit us to move within a defined space. So-called open borders may still constitute informal physical boundaries; nevertheless, some of the formal structures have disappeared. Likewise, communication can be crossing borders or limited within borders. Frontiers can be torn down and dissolved, consequently changing previously existing spaces, just as well as borders can be rebuilt to separate societies.

The development of linear boundaries is frequently associated with the formation of nation states, whereas for more ancient times the existence of borderlands or frontiers between two areas can be assumed. Furthermore, borders are buffer zones, characterised by liminality. Borders are always contact zones between two spaces in which social groups can meet, communicate and interact.

Borders and spaces, both territorial and social, always deal with inside and outside, with inclusion and exclusion. Inclusion conveys the belonging to a group, a 'We-group'. Exclusion, on the other hand, means otherness.

Barbed wire and insulators

Barbed wire consists of two twisted metal wires. Two further wires are then wrapped around these at regular intervals close together, with the four sharp ends left to protrude. This means that the barbed wire itself is a source of injury for anyone who comes into careless contact with it. It is a clear obstacle, a border that cannot be overcome easily.

Barbed wire is not very old as such. It was invented in the second half of the 19th century to fence in herds of cattle in the American west. The need for cowboys consequently diminished to the extent that there was widespread unemployment, while the indigenous population was prevented from moving unhindered across the landscape.

During the First World War, barbed wire was laid out on a huge scale in front of the endless trenches. Here too it was an obstacle that could not be overcome easily, but which had to be cut through and removed with difficulty – sometimes under fire.

Electrification brought a further level of hindrance that was first exploited by the National Socialists, who used it to electrify the perimeter fences of their camps. Now, not only the spines of the barbed wire caused injury, but the whole fence was deadly to come into contact with.

Barbed wire is still commonly used as a deterrent. A 6 m-high barbed wire fence runs between the USA and Mexico.

Barbed wire and electrical insulators are among the most common finds from excavations at former concentration and detention camps. In every case they reflect limitation and the restriction of movement, of imprisonment.

Barbed wire and isolators are often used to reinforce the border of fences and walls (© Peter Hinterndorfer).

Therefore space and borders have identity-establishing functions. Everything within these boundaries can have a consolidating effect on communities. Anyone who is on the other side of the border can be excluded.

For example, boundaries and spaces in a social context may signify the belonging to a family, a social group or class, associations and institutions, a smaller or larger community, or to a nation. Such units provide a structuring of social space. Rules and norms determine the inclusion within or exclusion from a group.

Spaces and boundaries are never static, but are continuously (re)negotiated and processual. It implies a certain permeability of boundaries in general and hence the possibility to overcome them and move into other spaces. Hermetically confined spaces with definite boundaries may be sometimes aimed for, but in fact, they can hardly ever be realised.

War is perhaps the most brutal means of overstepping space and borders and defining new territories. The colonial wars (see Chapter 5) and the two world wars (see Chapter 4) were waged with the aim of conquering new territories and gaining new land for one's own population. In this framework, a social difference between conquerors and the conquered is almost always presumed by the former, the intruders, who usually conceive of themselves as superior and more civilised than the conquered,

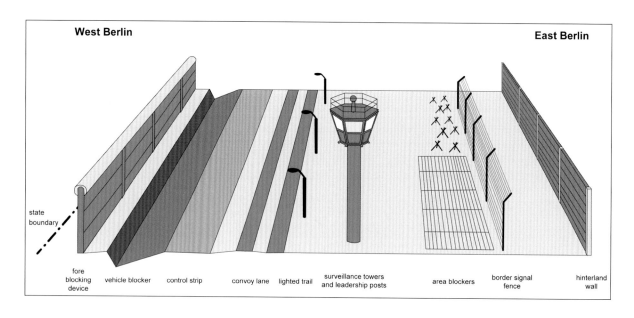

West Berlin — East Berlin

state boundary

fore blocking device | vehicle blocker | control strip | convoy lane | lighted trail | surveillance towers and leadership posts | area blockers | border signal fence | hinterland wall

Fig. 8.1. Structure of Berlin Wall (© Judith Benedix and Peter Hinterndorfer).

who are regarded as barbarians. Attempts to overcome social and territorial boundaries include revolutions, social riots, resistance to state power or protests against institutions and organisations. The Berlin Wall (see Fig. 8.1) or the Iron Curtain as well as electrified perimeter fences of the former concentration camps are often called hermetic borders. Without doubt, these physical borders could hardly be overcome. However, even those harsh frontiers were fitted with gates that enabled their crossing. Furthermore, those closed spaces were dissolved by war and political changes.

ENCLOSED WITH BARBED WIRE

Internment camps, concentration camps, but also prisons are generally enclosed by electrically-charged fences and high walls with barbed wire (see Chapter 6, Figs. 6.8, 6.16 and 6.17). These installations are intended to prevent crossing, but only for certain groups. Guards and wardens can always pass and move relatively freely within the fenced ground. On the contrary, imprisoned people are severely restricted in their liberty of action. Conversely, fences block access to an area. This applies to the internment camps, but also to military facilities, as discussed in Chapter 7 for Greenham Common and the Nevada Test Site.

Numerous locked gates (see Fig. 8.2) and doors, barred windows, inaccessible areas, massively protected entrance areas and a strictly regulated daily routine defined by the authorities illustrate the lack of freedom in different areas. During excavations in former concentration camps, the camps' boundaries are usually easy to recognize in the archaeological record through the discovery of fences, barbed wire or isolators of electric perimeter fences. At Treblinka (Poland), for instance, geophysical measurements revealed the exact outline of the extermination camp, which was larger than previously assumed (see Fig. 6.7).

The Loibl-Nord camp, a sub-camp of the Mauthausen concentration camp in Austria on the border with Slovenia was well concealed within an alpine forest until the area was to be cleared. Surveys identified not only the position of prisoners' barracks, the barrack with washrooms, the kitchen and the roll-call, but also the barbed wire fence enclosing the camp, which was found almost along its entire length on the edge of the forest (see Fig. 6.16). At the Loibl-Nord camp or in Sobibór (Poland), remains of barbed wire are still attached to tree trunks at the edge of the former camps (see Fig. 8.3). Archaeological investigations enable the identification of essential elements that highlight the symbolism of those camps. Postholes of the entrance gate could also be excavated at the Loibl-Pass (see Fig. 6.16). During excavations in Sobibór, the discovery of escape tunnels attests to prisoners' attempts to subvert the enforced boundaries.

Fig. 8.2. Mauthausen Memorial, the closed main gate (© Claudia Theune).

Prisons and internment camps in particular offer the opportunity for archaeological and landscape archaeological studies inspired by the sociology of space. To understand the utilization and functions of different spaces in the camps is crucial in order to reveal structures of power and repression. The spatial planning and logistics of the camps can be examined on a macro level by analysing their location, function, environment and infrastructure. Actor-specific perspectives and perceptions of space in the microcosm of the camp can be explored through detailed spatial analysis.

Of special interest would be further investigations into the structure of areas that were only partly accessible or entirely inaccessible to prisoners, as these would further studies of areas where public or hidden punishments were carried out.

Spatial concepts realised in different types of camps or by different responsible administrative authorities constitute another subject that requires further analyses. In addition, there remain questions about concepts of space that were active at different times during the camps' life. The landscape surrounding the camps should always be taken into consideration. In many cases, prisoners were used for forced labour. In this context, guarded prisoners had to pass through the gates to leave the camp. Although there has been a long history of denial and silence around the civilian population's awareness of camps in their vicinity, it can be assumed that the local population was very much aware of the prisoners, just as the prisoners

Fig. 8.3. Loibl-Nord camp; barbed wire around a tree trunk (© Claudia Theune).

were very much aware of the world outside the camp. Archaeologists have yet to explore whether it is possible to trace the unauthorised and secret means of communication that existed between the outside world and the camps, as some reports of contemporary witnesses suggest.

THE PEACE WALL IN BELFAST

The euphemistically named 'Peace Wall' (also called 'Peace Line') in Belfast was built by British authorities to isolate the opposing Catholic (nationalist) and Protestant (unionist) groups in order to prevent conflicts and to protect people living on either side of the wall from each other from 1969 onwards (see Chapter 5). Initially, only a barbed wire fence was installed, but this was replaced by a high wall (see Fig. 8.4). Roads, which originally served as means for connecting different areas, turned into parts of the border. Gates built into the wall enabled passage, yet they could be closed any time if troubles arose. The wall enclosed entire areas, but was designed as a linear demarcation. It measures up to 8 m high and was intended to prevent people from throwing objects over it. Consequently, the wall was visible from afar, making its separating purpose obvious.

Such walls also serve as means for communication and the proclamation of political statements. Their large vertical surfaces are very suitable for mounting large banners with slogans and images. In Belfast, texts, pictures and memorial stones have been mounted on the wall in order to commemorate the riots, fires and victims (see Fig. 8.4, also Fig 5.3). The surface itself is already present; messages can be written or painted using relatively minimal resources.

ALONG THE BERLIN WALL

One of the most recent archaeological monuments of the Cold War is the former Berlin Wall, which divided Berlin from 1961 to 9th November 1989. A first barricade made from barbed wire was erected on 13th August 1961, intended to stop the numerous refugees who wanted to leave the Soviet-occupied territories for the West, something that was only possible easily in Berlin at that time.

Only a few days later, however, construction of the first concrete wall started, encircling West Berlin with a total length of 160 km. Four expansion phases followed until 1989. The border quickly became not only a barrier cutting through the city, but a staggered system of border and barrier structures. The concrete wall, as it is known to many people from photos, only

Fig. 8.4. Belfast, Peace Wall (© Keith Ruffles, CC BY 3.0, commons.wikimedia.org).

covered the western part of the border system. Indeed, the wall was not positioned directly on the actual border but was some metres off on the East-Berlin side, and thus in GDR territory. As early as 1962, the so-called Hinterland Wall, an expanded metal fence, was erected parallel to the first wall as an additional barrier. The width of the border system ranged between 30 to 500 m at different sections. The strip between the two barriers was fitted with various types of watchtowers, signalling installations, floodlights, dog runs, anti-vehicle trenches, guard paths and some of it was even mined (see Fig. 8.1). Trespassing was almost impossible.

An estimated 1,050 people died attempting to cross the border to the West and escape the GDR. The fall of the Berlin Wall, the succeeding changes in GDR politics ('Wende') and eventually the reunification of Germany led to a rapid dismantling of border installations of the Iron Curtain across Europe. Today, the walls, fences and barriers that divided Europe for decades are barely visible any more. In rural areas, nature has retaken the former border strips. One day after the opening of the Wall on 10th November 1989, Willy Brandt, the mayor of West Berlin during the construction of the Wall, noted, 'Now what belongs together will grow together'. His words reflected the prevailing atmosphere at that time. The Berlin Wall and associated border installations were dismantled to a large extent in the early 1990s. As Berlin and Germany took the first steps on the long path to rebuilding one country that had been divided for so long, the extensive demolition of the Wall was an absolute necessity. A constant presence and visibility of the Wall would not have encouraged the unification process.

In present-day Berlin, only small parts of the Wall have been preserved (see Fig. 8.5), *e.g.* in Bernauer Straße, Niederkirchstraße near the 'Topography of Terror' ('Topographie des Terrors') memorial (see Fig. 1.4; Chapters 6 and 13), as well as the so-called East Side Gallery near Ostbahnhof. This part of the wall is of particular significance, as graffiti and paintings could be applied on the east side of the wall after the fall of the wall for the first time. Until then such paintings were only possible on the western side. In order to preserve this monument the paintings were recently restored. Several segments of the Wall have been transferred to other places in the city, for example to Potsdamer Platz, which was an original site of the border installations, but these segments are not in the original place. The square is a central hub for tourists today, well situated to provide some tourist attractions, including parts of the wall. At the Brandenburg Gate, which is of great symbolic importance

Fig. 8.5. Remains of the Berlin Wall today at the Bornholmer Straße (© Claudia Theune).

Fig. 8.6. In Berlin's inner city the route of the wall is marked by a double line of cobblestones (© Claudia Theune).

has to visit specific locations in Berlin. The border is no longer visible in the ordinary cityscape: the former border strip has been consumed by new building projects and the building styles; once typical of East and West Berlin, the space has been adapted and thus obliterated. Nevertheless, it is this part of history in particular that brings many visitors to Berlin. They want to learn about the two long-separated parts of the city. Quite often tourists ask locals where the wall actually was. Also young Berliners who were born after the 'Wende', or were too young to consciously experience the Cold War, want to know which districts belonged to West or East Berlin.

The Berlin Heritage Office has paid increasing attention to the remains of the Berlin Wall. When remaining parts of the Wall started to deteriorate, renovations were needed in order to preserve them as material witnesses of the Cold War. To date, several of the intact sections as well as three watchtowers have been declared historical monuments. In certain places memorials have been set up and that at Bernauer Straße plays a pivotal role. The aim is to provide information about the inhuman system of border installations that separated families, friends, a city and an entire country for 28 years and enclosed West Berlin.

Since 2007 several surveys and excavations have been conducted (*e.g.* by the Technische Universität Berlin and the Berlin Heritage Office), most of them in the area of the Bernauer Straße Memorial, which demarcates the border between the *Wedding* and *Mitte* districts. The surroundings of the Bernauer Straße site have not been built over yet, and this facilitates documentation of the entire extent of the barrier structures because they are preserved underground. During the GDR period, the western facades of the buildings on Bernauer Straße formed the border between East and West in this area, and their remains are of special importance for the history of the city. The buildings were part of the Soviet zone, while the adjacent pavement belonged to West Berlin. Many people tried to escape to the West through the windows. Later the houses were demolished. The erection of memorial sites as well as construction measures along the former border led to excavations of these remains of the second half of the 20th century, which can be regarded as one of the youngest archaeological features in Germany. With a length of approximately 1,400 m, the memorial site on Bernauer Straße is intended as a window into the recent past by

for both Berlin and Germany, almost nothing remains to remind the visitor of the Wall. As in many other parts of the city, only a barely noticeable cobblestone paving demarcates the course of the former border (see Fig. 8.6). When walking the so-called Mauerweg – a trail along the borders of former West Berlin – one can experience the few still existing remains and explore the vanished border. Numerous panels at relevant sites present information about significant historical events and a commemoration stele has been erected for every victim of the Berlin Wall. Numerous art projects along the route enable different perceptions of the old border.

Comprehensive information panels and memorials have been erected where the Wall is preserved in its original state. Everyone who wishes to see the remains of the Wall and to learn about the division of the city

Fig. 8.7. Excavations at the Berlin Wall show the surviving structures of the border that divided Berlin and Europe between 1961 and 1989 (© Claudia Theune).

making the remains of border installations and cellars visible and the atmosphere comprehensible. Additional texts as well as photographs and audio documents from contemporary witnesses provide information on various topics. Geophysical surveys and excavations were necessary in advance to reveal the foundation walls of the dismantled houses of Bernauer Straße (see Fig. 8.7). Now the borderline is recognizable again. During the GDR period, numerous doors and windows had been sealed to prevent escape attempts. In other areas, the Hinterland Wall and other barrier structures have been excavated. The remains of the 'Versöhnungskirche' (Reconciliation Church), which had been blown up in 1985, were also archaeologically recorded. Headstones and grave markers originating in the former Sophien cemetery, which was demolished for the construction of the Wall, as well as former street levels, were revealed. The archaeological activities were primarily intended to facilitate visibility of the remains for the memorial. In addition to the investigations at the Bernauer Straße, remains of the Wall and its barrier structures have been excavated at various other sites across the city.

Partially excavated escape tunnels bear witness to attempted, successful and prevented escapes. In the Bernauer Straße area, Tunnel 29 extended over a length of 1,300 metres. Geophysical survey has been able to trace the tunnel through which 29 people escaped to

freedom in September 1962. A further tunnel, or more precisely its exit, was discovered in the north of Berlin between the district of Hermsdorf and Glienicke village just outside Berlin (see Fig. 8.8). Starting under the terrace of an apartment building, the tunnel was used by 13 people who escaped below the border constructions to the West. A watchtower, a demolished house and electric cables for the border systems light strips were discovered in the course of these excavations (by the Archäologiebüro ABD-Dressler).

The excavations along the Berlin Wall are a good example of structures from our recent past that may still be present through living memory, but which can also be the focus of archaeological investigations. If destruction is followed by a need for explanations of border-security measures, careful archaeological excavation and documentation is an adequate protocol to better understand such remains and make them accessible and comprehensible.

THE IRON CURTAIN AND OTHER BORDERS

International sites of the Cold War are also being explored archaeologically. The Iron Curtain, which cut through Europe over several thousand kilometres, retains the same meaning as the Berlin Wall.

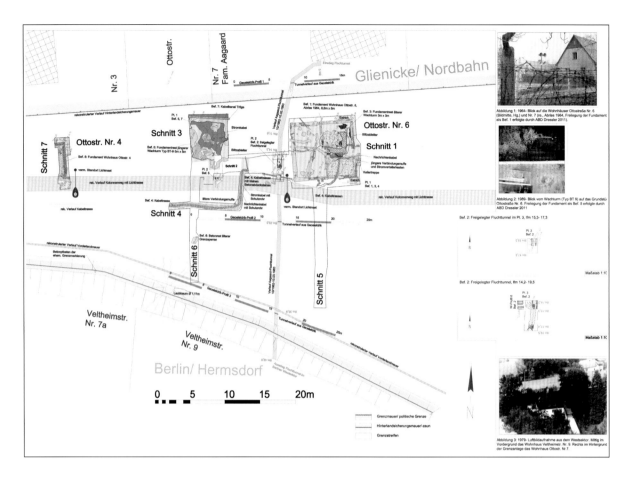

Fig. 8.8. An escape tunnel was excavated on the border between Berlin-Hermsdorf and Glienicke in the suburban area; additional features include a watchtower foundation and remains of the Berlin Wall barrier (© Torsten Dressler).

In several places, including border areas between Italy and Slovenia, Austria and the Czech Republic, and on the internal border within Germany, material remains of the installations and associated buildings have been identified and studied archaeologically. Sites were located mostly by field walking, while the context was informed by contemporary witness statements, archival material and photographs. The number of security systems and bunkers on the eastern side of the former Iron Curtain is considerably greater than on the western side, and the projects document the deterioration of bunkers and respective changes in the landscape.

In Albania, small bunkers scattered throughout the country represent material evidence of the Cold War. Analyses of such remains focus on the development of the border and protective measures between the 1950s and 1980s, but also on what has happened to these features in the years after the fall of the Iron Curtain. Consideration is given to those remains that have been completely restored in the last 25 years, and why; which buildings still exist, and why; which areas have been recaptured by nature and what still remains of the Cold War. Even if no excavations are conducted, the materiality is in the forefront and the clear archaeological interest is present.

FENCES ALONG BORDERS – NEW BOUNDARIES

Within the context of the present-day population crises, archaeologists have recently begun to address questions relating to borders, refugees and global migrations. A project that deserves special attention in this context is the 'Undocumented Migrations Project' (UMP) at the University of Michigan. This long-term study targets places along the border between Mexico and Arizona (USA), where illegal migrants are crossing into U.S. territory. It is the objective of that long-term study to investigate unauthorised border crossings, deportations and human trafficking through archaeological and cultural-anthropological methods. The research starts by surveying all of the regularly used routes, with special regard being given to the desert routes and resting spots. Those places are particularly rich in finds, such as the remains of clothing or of food rations and food containers. The presence of meal wrappers, especially of durable foods, and large numbers of bottled or canned drinks is not unusual in an arid climate, but the clothing that is found indicates that these items were intentionally left behind because they had already outlasted their usefulness. Other explanations appear less likely because why else would the migrants bring so many items of clothing with them and then leave them behind? Among the items that occur in larger numbers are shoes with strong signs of wear and abrasion or even holes, indicating that the migrants have travelled long distances in them. Some of the shoes also appear to be significantly unsuited for a trek across the desert, so it is not surprising that they have fallen apart and were left behind.

Some of the objects show modifications, such as adjustments to make it easier to carry larger loads, or inscriptions and labels that marked individual ownership or held personal messages. These messages are included in the research.

That survey extends to consider the merchants who are selling specific supplies to migrants, such as backpacks, shoes or dark clothes to hide them better in the shadows while they are crossing into U.S. territory. Some of the migrants have also been visited and interviewed about their experience.

CONCLUSION: BORDERS AND SOCIAL BOUNDARIES

Communities involved in and affected by the creation of such borders belong to very different social groups. This applies to opposing factions in war, where people are fighting for different nations and coalitions. In Belfast, different political, as well as religious and social groups were separated by the Peace Wall. The distinctions between the United States and Mexico are perhaps more economic. One side of the border offers a 'land of unlimited possibilities', while the other side wishes to participate in this seemingly economically carefree life by crossing the border.

Similar walls have also been built in recent years in other cities such as Jerusalem (Israel), Nicosia (Cyprus), but also Homs (Syria) or in some cities in Slovakia. The separation in Mostar (Bosnia and Herzegovina) should also be mentioned. The most recent plans for the wall between Mexico and the USA have already been mentioned; several walls in the territories occupied by Israel in the West Bank or the Gaza Strip can also be added. Security aspects are often mentioned as a goal for the new tall dividing lines. In fact, the separation of different groups of people who live there is the result. The walls may indeed have led to a decrease of violent attacks, but it should also be noted that openness and tolerance to the neighbour can barely be promoted this way. The closure of open borders and the construction of walls are more a sign of fear towards others. The dismantling of stationary border controls in large parts of Europe with the Schengen Agreement (1985) promoted an openness and tolerance. The same can be said for Berlin, although it took some time for the city to grow together.

The most extreme social separation is evident in internment camps, former concentration camps and also in prisons. The status of guards and prisoners is entirely different and is emphasised by supporting features that visually distinguish one group from the other, the most obvious being clothing, where guards wear particular formal uniforms and prisoners wear particular informal required clothing.

Future research could take a closer look at the borders described above under the aspect of interaction. The transit areas, the liminality areas between inside and outside would be of particular interest. This is the point where persons from both sides meet and interact.

Chapter 9

PAYING TRIBUTE TO THE DEAD

INTRODUCTION

In the shadow of wars, totalitarianism, internment camps or insuperable borders, deaths always have to be considered as violent deaths. In the preceding chapters, numbers have been given for victims on battlefields, in internment camps and prisons, in mass graves and on borders. The figures are all unimaginably high. Hidden behind these numbers are killed and murdered individuals, each of them with their own name and their own personal biography.

Soldiers who die during war are often said to have 'fallen' in German, while in English the term 'killed in action' is also common. Predominantly it has been young men conscripted for war service who face each other on the world's battlefields. Throughout history, soldiers have fought directly against each other – in a world without tanks, military aircraft, and far-reaching bombs. Industrialization, however, changed warfare fundamentally. Asymmetrical warfare, as described in chapters 4 and 5, has led to the discontinuation of 'classic' battles where large armies encounter each other, eyeball to eyeball. Enemies are now most often killed from a distance. The numbers of soldiers who are killed in battle as well as civilians who are killed intentionally or by accident remain high.

In prisons and internment camps built by the dictatorships and totalitarian states of the 20th century and in the National Socialist extermination camps, people who were considered opponents of the regime were humiliated, degraded, tortured and murdered. In general, the systematic murder of a regime's opponents is not intended to become public knowledge and is conducted 'behind closed doors'. Unauthorised crossings of borders, be they prison walls, fences of an internment camp or state borders, are regarded as attempts to escape or as unauthorised intrusions and are usually punished, sometimes by death (see Chapters 6 and 8). In such cases, a public execution may also be intended as a deterrent.

Deaths occurring in the framework of military actions can be regarded as honourable and a kind of sacrifice for one's homeland. To recover the bodies of soldiers who were killed in action in order to bring them home and provide a proper and honourable burial is often a difficult but very much desired endeavour in which the families of the deceased are also involved. As well as returning the remains of those killed to their families, so too may their personal belongings be returned. In contrast, people murdered by totalitarian regimes are denied such a decent burial and are 'disappeared'. As opponents

The Grave of Karl Peter Welcker (28th September 1925 – 29th July 1944)

Peter Welcker is one of the countless soldiers of World War II to be killed on the front line after brief basic training. During the advance of the Red Army in the summer of 1944, his unit was ordered to hold a bridgehead over the Vistula; the small unit moved forward once more in order to estimate how much time remained for the retreat. At Trzydnik (present-day Poland), on 29th July 1944, the unit was caught in a sudden Soviet attack. Karl Peter Welcker was hit immediately and was killed by a wound to the head; shrapnel had pierced his helmet. A Soviet soldier died nearby. Both men were covered with earth in a makeshift fashion. The next day, local farmers buried the men next to each other on the edge of a wood. The Soviet soldier was later exhumed and returned to his homeland. The local population have cared for Karl Peter Welcker's grave since the end of the war. At first the grave was framed with a simple wooden cross and a lattice of simple twigs.

With the help of the local people, the German Red Cross and documents in the family archive, it became clear that my uncle Karl Peter Welcker was buried in that grave. Members of the family have visited the grave several times and have had contact with the local inhabitants. The school and community maintain the grave and it is always decorated with flowers and eternal candles. The fence and the cross have already been replaced and enlarged twice. Now a plaque with some information also marks the grave. However, there are mistakes in the data given. By 1945, the year in which the death is now stated to have taken place, the Red Army had already advanced much further westwards. But this is of little importance. The grave is a clear sign of the commemoration of Karl Peter Welcker, who died far too young.

Grave of Karl Peter Welcker (not Wecker) at the edge of a forest near Trzydnik, present-day Poland (© Claudia Theune).

of the authorities, they are often regarded as inferior human beings without dignity. Their corpses are secretly disposed of in mass graves and their families are not informed. The concealment or even denial of such deaths stems from attempts to deliberately disguise the crimes committed, since public awareness may lead to a loss of control that threatens the authorities' power.

When excavating crime scenes, archaeologists, forensic archaeologists and anthropologists are often confronted with human remains (see also Figs. 2.1–2.2).

Such discoveries attract a great deal of public attention and are emotionally demanding for everyone involved. Special ethical principles should guide such investigations (see Chapter 2). Archaeologists must act responsibly, giving special regard to the victims and to the needs of living relatives.

The treatment of victims of war actions and those of state terror require case-specific approaches since they can have different objectives. Jewish religious laws, for instance, demand the non-disturbance of the dead's resting places. In this respect, appropriate arrangements need to be made with Jewish communities when investigating Holocaust sites. The active involvement of Jewish communities can permit the uncovering of the National Socialist crimes through excavations and a dignified reburial of the Jewish victims.

To locate the remains of victims of violence and identify the deceased is at the centre of such endeavours. For many years, there have been attempts in eastern Austria to locate a mass grave of approximately 180 Hungarian Jews who were executed in a barn near Rechnitz (Burgenland, Austria) in March 1945, just a few weeks before the end of World War II in Europe. Numerous documents and testimonies have been examined, aerial images evaluated and geophysical surveys and excavations carried out, but so far the mass grave has not been found. In spite of the intensive search, the question of what protocol should be activated should the grave be discovered has not yet been clarified. Is the solution to leave the burials in place or to transfer them to a Jewish cemetery? This case with its indecision shows how the treatment of human remains recovered from crime scenes is handled very individually. The same applies to the handling of personal objects that can be found with the bodies. Artefacts may be returned to the victims' families or handed over to museums and memorials or are buried with the dead.

Forensic anthropologists and archaeologists work together closely when searching for and investigating mass graves. Excavations have to be conducted carefully and include comprehensive documentation with particular attention given to exhuming the corpses in order to ensure that bodies are recovered individually along with any objects that may be associated with them. All relevant geological, botanical, zoological, entomological and, of course, anthropological and pathological traces have to be recorded and evaluated thoroughly in order to elucidate the circumstances and causes of death (see Chapter 3). For the identification process, DNA analyses are essential. Living relatives are usually very supportive and provide necessary samples for comparison. Sometimes personal objects – mostly made from metal – such as crosses, clothing accessories, etc. are associated with the bodies. In the case of soldiers killed in action, identification tags or parts of the uniform or helmets are found. Such items can provide valuable information by identifying the unit to which the soldiers

belonged. The use of metal detectors is central to such work. In many cases, the general locations of mass graves are known prior to investigations beginning. However, it is also possible that valuable knowledge on a site's precise location is kept secret among local populations; perhaps because of a fear that accusations of complicity may be raised by victims' families.

It is important to emphasize that any search and recovery of victims requires the permission of the responsible authorities. Governments that continue to deny mass murders or genocides within their own countries will not give such permission, even if the crimes were committed several decades ago. Such is the case with the Armenian genocide (1915) by the Ottoman Empire that is still denied by the Turkish government (see Chapter 5). Here, excavations could only take place in neighbouring countries. A mass grave of this genocide was exhumed in 2007 in Syria, close to the Turkish border. Where archaeologists operate under governmental supervision, it is important to note that such work may forcefully or willingly interpret the findings of such investigation in accordance with an officially predetermined historical characterisation or narrative.

Briefly, I would also like to mention the treatment of the dead beyond the wars, for example in cemeteries of the 20th century. There are studies of Afro-American communities in Dallas (Texas, USA) from the early 20th century, who apparently died through violence, which was not known to the public but had been covered up. Here too, archaeology was able to contribute to the return of identity to the dead and to document their suffering.

DEATH ON THE BATTLEFIELD

Soldiers killed in action during various wars are quite often discovered subsequently. After the end of the First World War, many of the slaughtered soldiers were buried directly on the battlefields of the Western Front or in war cemeteries erected close to the places of battle. While many graves on the Western Front remain unknown or undetected, there have been several archaeological discoveries in recent years of single bodies as well as larger groups who were mortally wounded in the trenches. The unnaturally crouched position these bodies were found in suggests that the

Fig. 9.1. Mass grave from World War I, with soldiers buried in their uniforms; the shoes were preserved - Monchy-le-Preux (Pas-de-Calais, France) (© Gilles Prilaux, INRAP).

soldier(s) were not properly buried but were simply left at the places where they had been killed. The relentless fighting that defines this theatre of operations presumably prohibited comrades from conducting a proper burial, and supports the photographic records that show corpses lying as fallen scattered across the battle lines. In such cases when they are recovered today, it is often possible to recover the apparel and equipment that the soldiers wore when killed, which can include their helmets, shoes, weapons and all other items. Not all such victims were left as they were killed, and there are examples of where soldiers are buried in simple individual graves or mass graves. Carefully placed bodies have been retrieved from trenches or holes no longer required in the trench warfare. In these cases, the human remains are usually only accompanied by the residues of their uniform, boots and helmet (see Fig. 9.1). Weapons were not put into the graves.

Once the remains are recovered and identified, the deceased will receive a funeral at one of the war cemeteries. If possible, the descendants are informed and – if desired – will receive the personal belongings and information about the circumstances of their relative's death.

Some 5,500 soldiers were killed during the Battle of Fromelles (Dep. Pas-de-Calais, France) in July 1916. In a mass grave were about 2,000 Australian soldiers, 1,400 British and a few German soldiers. Geophysical surveys initiated by the Australian goverment had been carried out, between 2007 and 2009, prior to the excavation. The surveys identified about 300 dead, of whom 250 were eventually exhumed together with a considerable number of related objects, followed by forensic analysis. The analysis of personal items and DNA enabled the identification of approximately 150 Australian soldiers. The soldiers were then reburied in

Fig. 9.2. Pheasant Wood Military Cemetery at Fromelles (Pas-de-Calais, France) (© Wernervc, CC BY-SA 4.0, commons. wikimedia.org).

a newly created war cemetery, the Fromelles Pheasant Wood Military Cemetery (see Fig. 9.2). The German soldiers were identified as members of the 16th Bavarian reserve infantry unit – the unit that Adolf Hitler served in as 'Obergefreiter'.

The United States Defense POW/MIA Accounting Agency (DPAA) dedicates its work to bringing home American soldiers who are listed as prisoners of war and to searching for and recovering the remains of personnel 'missing in action' from all past wars across the world. Predominantly, the agency's recovery teams search for crew members of crashed aircraft, but also for members of infantry units or missing Marines whose bodies are suspected of being contained within sunken ships and submarines. Targeted searches are conducted world-wide on battlefields and sites of the two world wars, in Korea, Vietnam and Laos, as well as in Iraq and Syria and many other countries. The sites of aircraft crashes can often be located quite exactly through archival research and the reports of contemporary witnesses. On-site surveys are conducted to locate parts of the crashed aircraft and to search for missing crew. Identification tags or other personal items, as well as DNA samples where human remains are uncovered, provide evidence for the identity of the dead. The agency's objective is to repatriate the bodies to the United States, return the dead to their families for burial and hand over any personal belongings. Non-governmental organisations (NGOs) like the Red Cross or the military graves registration service states maintain similar institutions that search for soldiers missing in action and rebury retrieved bodies in war cemeteries.

THE KATYN MASS GRAVES

Katyn is a small village in present-day Russia that has become synonymous with the serial mass murder of over 20,000 members of the Polish intelligentsia, officer corps and police in April and May 1940. Further scenes of these massacres include Mednoje near Tver (Russia); Charkiw (Ukraine); and the Bykiwnja forest near Kiev (Ukraine). Between 1991 and 1996, mass graves of these crimes were uncovered in Katyn, Mednoje and Charkiw, and since 2006 excavations have been carried out in Bykiwnja, with 210 mass graves in this location alone. In a wave of arrests in 1939 – prior to the systematic mass executions – about 8,000 Polish officers were sent into Soviet captivity and initially imprisoned in detention camps. In the spring of 1940, Stalin ordered the prisoners' execution as well as the killing of thousands of Polish policemen and intelligentsia, which was carried out by the Soviet Union's secret police – the People's Commissariat for Internal Affairs. The mass graves were discovered by the German Wehrmacht in 1943 (see Fig. 9.3) and an expert commission of forensic doctors from different European countries, Polish exiles and members of the Red Cross was established by the National Socialists to investigate the mass graves. The commission was able to link the massacres to the Soviet secret police on the basis of ammunition found with the corpses. After the Soviet government's decades-long denial of the massacres, it was only in 1990 that Mikhail Gorbachev officially acknowledged the Soviet Union's responsibility. Although the places of the executions and mass graves are not located in Polish territory, it has been of great concern to Polish governments to excavate the mass graves, and they have therefore consistently sponsored the State Council (until 2016) for the Protection of Struggle and Martyrdom Sites (Rada Ochrony Pamięci Walk i Męczeństwa) to support Polish archaeologists and anthropologists during excavations (see Chapter 2).

Aerial photographs taken in the 1940s allowed the precise identification of the sites of mass graves, while the number and size of graves was determined through systematic augering to 5 m depth, and this work has served as a basis for the definition of excavation areas. Osteological analyses of the human remains recovered from the mass graves have provided evidence for the causes of death. The victims were shot in the backs of their heads at close range. In some cases, hand, rib and skull bones show fractures resulting from physical torture and ill-treatment. In addition, there were numerous personal items and military equipment of Polish origin, including identification tags, buttons and other fittings belonging to uniforms, shoes,

Fig. 9.3. Katyn, opening a mass grave in 1943 (Source: Andrzej Leszek Szcześniak, Wikimedia Commons).

personal documents, diaries, combs, toothbrushes, glasses, dishes, cross pendants, cigarette containers and gaming pieces. The combined evidence has helped forensic archaeologists and anthropologists to identify several thousand people killed during these massacres. The objects recovered from the mass graves were taken to Poland, restored and put on display in the Katyn Museum in Warsaw. The murdered, however, have been left in the places of their assassination and memorials have been established on-site.

The investigations have also produced evidence of exhumations carried out by the National Socialists and the Katyn Commission in 1943, as well as evidence for the reopening of the graves by the Soviet secret service. In an attempt to obliterate any traces that might connect them with the crime, the Soviets tried to frame the German Wehrmacht instead by planting false evidence with the bodies in the mass graves' top layers, such as German ammunition and newspapers.

The investigations in Katyn, Mednoje, Charkiw and the Bykiwnja forest are of great importance to the Polish nation. Since archives of war crimes kept by the Russian government are only accessible under restricted conditions and a lot of information on the Katyn massacre is still missing or inaccessible today, the archaeological and anthropological results provide an invaluable resource to explain and understand the detail of this massacre and its cover-up.

THE HEBERTSHAUSEN SHOOTING FACILITY NEAR DACHAU CONCENTRATION CAMP

A shooting facility erected by the National Socialists for mass executions has been partially preserved at Hebertshausen, just a few kilometres from the former Dachau concentration camp. Excavations of the facility revealed evidence for the executions of Soviet prisoners of war in the autumn and winter of 1941/42. In addition, a recent digital terrain model derived from up-to-date laser-scan data clearly shows the remaining features of

the facility: two parallel ramparts with a wooden wall at one end including a bullet trap (see Fig. 9.4). In front of the wall is an iron cuff and the remains of a wooden post were excavated, to which prisoners were tied before being shot. Large amounts of human skull fragments were scattered around the post, a chilling testimony to what occurred here.

MASS GRAVES AND GENOCIDE

The Holocaust, the mass murder and terror of the National Socialists, pervades this volume, as do the extermination camps that are associated with it. How archaeologists approach these sensitive matters is implicit. Undoubtedly, there are many other mass graves across Europe, where people murdered by the National Socialist regime were disposed of. Sometimes the victims are deliberately granted cult status. With regard to the murder and cremation in the extermination and concentration camps of the National Socialists, even human remains such as hair or the ash can be exhibited.

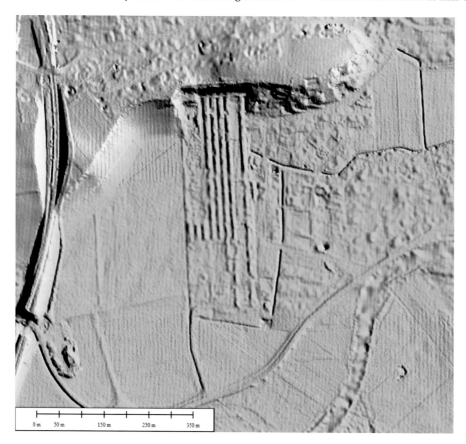

0 m   50 m   150 m   250 m   350 m

Fig. 9.4. Hebertshausen, (Dachau, Germany) LiDAR scan of the shooting facilities (© Landesamt für Vermessung und Geoinformation; editing H. Kerscher, BLfD).

Only recently has Austria decided to bury the ash that was displayed at the Austrian exhibition in the Memorial and Museum Auschwitz. However, it is still sometimes the case that the ash of the corpses is walled into a foundation stone in a ceremonial act.

Additionally we have to consider such camps are also always cemeteries. It is not unusual that archaeologists find cremation ash during excavations (Fig. 2.1). In Mauthausen or Sachsenhausen this ash is reburied in the cemetery areas on-site (Fig. 2.2).

Targeted archaeological surveys and excavations continually aim to identify the sites of mass graves and to recover the bodies of the victims. The dead bodies in these graves are at this point anonymous. Sometimes artefacts or the results of DNA can give information to identify the murder victim (see Fig. 9.5). The investigation seeks to end this anonymity and give back the dead their identity.

There are also those sites and events where other beliefs and totalitarian regimes are responsible, whether because of civil wars, violent conflicts, repressive systems, dictatorships or revolutions and the fight for freedom. One of the essential concerns in dealing with terrorism and mass murder is to find the graves of the murdered and to document them in detail.

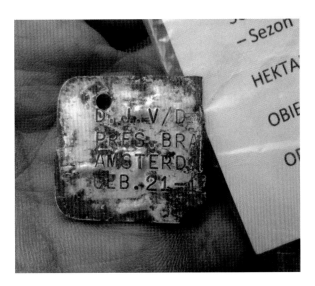

Fig. 9.5. Sobibór, (present-day Poland) tag of David Juda van der Velde, who lived at President Brandstraat 5 II in Amsterdam, born on 21th of November 1932 and murdered aged 10 years on 2nd April 1943 (© Ivar Schute).

Conflicts, regardless of their cause, can quickly lead to inhuman cruelty, including abduction, torture and murder. The victims of such violent excesses are often discarded in mass graves, as the guilty party aims to conceal and deny their crime. The graves are quickly closed to avoid their visibility.

During an ongoing conflict, especially under repressive regimes, it is almost always impossible for relatives and friends to launch an investigation into the disappearance or whereabouts of missing persons or to receive information on whether they are alive or dead. Only after a repressive regime has been disempowered and the violence that threatens personal life has ceased, will families, civil society or non-governmental organisations (NGOs) have the opportunity to demand clarification including judicial punishment. Such attempts depend hugely on the current political situation to be permitted, and often require a temporal distance from the moments of such crimes.

It is important to emphasize that not only are the crimes themselves investigated – the deprivation of liberty, torture and murder – but also the criminal offence of denying and disguising them.

Forensic anthropologists and archaeologists are key to these approaches where they have unequivocal roles in the exhumation of bodies from mass graves, the determination of the causes of death and the investigation of material traces that can be used as evidence for or against the defendants. Matters of international law, war crimes, genocide and crimes against humanity are tried before the International Court of Justice of the United Nations and the International Criminal Court in The Hague. In addition, there are the so-called *ad hoc* International Criminal Courts for the prosecution of mass killings in Rwanda or the former Yugoslavia. Similar courts operate on national levels in Europe and Africa as well as the Americas and the Caribbean.

Every new discovery of a mass grave attracts great media attention and stirs emotions. But it also provides hope for families that their missing relatives are found, that they might get certainty about their whereabouts or at least confirmation of their death. If investigations start soon after the committed crimes, there is a good chance that traces of mass graves are still visible on the ground surface, which facilitates the search for victims.

Air and satellite imagery is also used for the identification of sites. As early as 1984, a year after the end of the military regime in Argentina, the search for missing persons and the discovery of mass graves from the time of the dictatorship (1976–1983) began and was carried out according to the state of the art at the time. Similar investigations were conducted in Guatemala, Chile, Brazil, Colombia, Uruguay, Peru, Ethiopia, Iraq, Afghanistan, Cambodia and not least in Rwanda, Bosnia and Herzegovina, Croatia, Romania, Greece, Cyprus, Libya, South Africa and Zimbabwe, and also next to Nanking (China). Public pressure plays an enormously important role in initiating archaeological investigations into the fate of persons who disappeared or were abducted under dictatorships.

In Europe, the search for victims of the National Socialists has been without doubt one of the most extensive endeavours. Noteworthy are also the more recent archaeological investigations in Spain and Srebrenica (former Yugoslavia). In the course of the Spanish Civil War (1936–1939) and during the Franco dictatorship (until 1975), between 150,000 and 200,000 people were executed and disposed of in mass graves on the Spanish mainland and islands. Many of these victims were simply dumped into flat trenches that demarcated agricultural fields. When the first mass graves of the Franco dictatorship were discovered, some Spanish citizens recognised the opportunity to demand investigations into the fate of their disappeared relatives, although this is a painful process for the whole country.

In Spain, however, the so-called Amnesty Law of 1977 guarantees impunity for all political crimes dating before 1977, thus undermining attempts to clarify the crimes committed by the regime and in general to come to terms with the nation's difficult past. Following a judicial order, the excavation of 19 mass graves was scheduled in 2009 but then stopped by another ruling of the Central Court for Severe Crimes, which prohibited the investigations.

During the Balkan Wars, the so-called Army of the Republic of Srpska and Serbian paramilitaries massacred approximately 8,000 Muslims – almost exclusively boys and men – in and around the town of Srebrenica in July 1995. The murders and atrocities committed in the presence of UN soldiers were hardly conceivable on the threshold of the 21st century in a Europe where, since the end of the Second World War, no war of such an extent had taken place. Several dozen mass graves with several thousand victims were found and excavated, initiated by and under the auspices of the United Nations International Criminal Tribunal for the former Yugoslavia. The main perpetrators were tried in The Hague and sentenced to long prison terms.

In 1994, Rwanda saw the mass murder of 800,000 to 1,000,000 members of the Tutsi ethnic minority in only about 100 days. Following a long-lasting ethnic conflict within the country and eventually triggered by the assassination of President Habyarimana, who belonged to the Hutu ethnic group, the Hutu government launched the mass slaughter of Tutsi. The genocide took place literally under the eyes of the world public, with UN peace corps stationed in Rwanda not intervening at all. The mass graves were opened soon after the genocide, when the traces of the mass graves were still visible. The United Nations International Criminal Tribunal for Rwanda initiated the excavations. The preliminary goal was to identify the victims and provide a dignified burial, but also to enable a criminal investigation. Six national genocide memorials were erected in several places, displaying original buildings, victims' items and perpetrators' weapons. Other memorials exist as well, where residents point to the sites of mass murder. The narratives presented at the national memorial sites and other sites of crime are sometimes controversial and are discussed among the Rwandan population. Rwanda can also serve as an example of further engagement with genocide. Often not only all the inhabitants of a village were murdered but the houses of those murdered were also destroyed and whole villages were wiped out. The archaeological investigation of such abandoned settlements of the late 20th century is an important research field for archaeologists (see Fig. 9.6). This destruction can also be documented as part of the genocide.

Other genocides are silenced and remain largely under-investigated, such as the genocide against the Armenians by the Ottoman Empire 100 years ago; the mass killing of an estimated 2 million Cambodian people by the Khmer Rouge between 1975 and 1978; or the genocide of the Herero and Nama people in Namibia carried out by the German colonial forces between 1904 and 1908.

Fig. 9.6. In the course of the genocide, farms and villages were destroyed in Rwanda, too; only foundation walls are left (© John Daniel Gilbin).

CONCLUSION

As a rule, the archaeological and forensic-archaeological discovery of the dead in the shadow of war can be related to the investigation of one's own history. The search for murdered persons is the focus of the investigations. This is often a central goal. It is a matter of finding and identifying missing persons, and also of clarifying the causes of the killings. Due to these goals, other research questions become less relevant.

The archaeological contribution to the resolution of the dead is to assist in recovering them, investigate carefully how they died, bury them with dignity, involve the relatives, create memorials and exhibitions that discuss the crimes; in such ways, these dead can be given back their names and their personal biographies.

Historical events are often dealt with from a moral point of view. Dead people, the dead from one's own ranks, have a special role to play and are honoured in a special way. Identity and historical-political interests are often in the foreground. This is often implemented in memorials when political symbols are clearly shown. The dead of the others are explicitly excluded from this honour. This can be observed again and again. For example, earth from concentration camps was explicitly buried under the eternal flame in the Hall of Remembrance at the foundation stone laying ceremony of the United States Holocaust Museum in Washington DC. The victims of the September 2011 terrorist attack at the World Trade Center were treated similarly. The victims' families wanted the remains of their relatives to be separated from those of the perpetrators. The perpetrators should not be buried at the same sites and with the same dignity as the victims.

It seems that it is difficult or even impossible to treat all the dead with the same dignity. To ensure that every human life is treated with respect, even after death, is also a task of archaeologists.

Chapter 10

THE WORLD OF SMALL FINDS

INTRODUCTION

Excavations on 20th-century sites tend to recover vast numbers of finds. Large assemblages are mentioned in many excavation reports. Sometimes all finds are presented to a specialist audience and analysed comprehensively, but usually only selected finds that are considered of special interest are presented in detail. In this chapter I would like to discuss the expressiveness of the finds under the special aspects to do with living and surviving conditions in times of war and oppression; in addition, there is the question of whether or not the finds can be attributed to different social groups. Furthermore, aspects of reuse are discussed, as well as how we deal with the sites and finds today.

On war sites, militaria represent the predominant finds category. The spectrum can be very broad, ranging from cartridge cases and firearms to vehicles of all kinds, including tanks, submarines and airplanes, as well as the equipment and personal items of the soldiers themselves.

Despite the different character of detention camps and protest camps – where people were held against their will, and where people voluntarily resided for a while – both types yield finds that testify to daily life, survival, accommodation, clothing and provisioning. It is important to remember that the detention camps in turn hosted two very different groups: prisoners and guards. These camps are often associated with forced-labour places, which may include entire plants with all conceivable industrial facilities. Protest camps generally seem to yield smaller find assemblages.

A large source of finds in the detention camps are garbage dumps or waste pits (see Figs. 10.1 and 10.2). Contemporary witnesses have reported that during the first few years of the detention camps of the National Socialists, the camp administration observed cleanliness and order. However, these aspects got less priority as the war progressed. Particularly towards the end of the war, waste management was a major problem in the concentration camps. The liberators frequently reported large rubbish dumps. Further waste pits were added as various barracks and buildings were demolished after the war. As sites became memorials and buildings were whitewashed to remove National Socialist colours, these places of remembrance were transformed into very clean and cultivated places.

The waste pits are where considerable numbers of finds lie. They can reach dimensions of about 30 m long, 5 m wide and 3 m deep, which corresponds to a volume of around 450–500 cubic metres, as documented in Sachsenhausen (Brandenburg, Germany; see Fig. 10.2).

Trench art ring

In January 2018 we found a metal finger ring among the family's things in a hidden drawer of an old desk. It was obviously a ring for men (UK ring size: Y – 2.2 cm). The ring clearly belongs to the group of objects made in the trenches during the war, and is an example of trench art.

It is a band-shaped ring that broadens towards the ring plate and is thicker at that point. A light trench mortar battery, apparently positioned on a mount, is depicted on the central decorative plate. The barrel is positioned at an angle of something more than 20 degrees; on top is a spring cylinder to bring the trench mortar back in position. At the base of the barrel the artist has added further details, perhaps the aiming device. Towards the edge of the plate a projectile (mine) is shown with the tip pointing downwards. There are some engraved points next to the projectile.

A scanning electron microscope analysis has shown that the ring is made of a Cu-Sn-Zn-Pb alloy; so-called red brass or 'gunmetal', which is a common alloy for cartridge cases.

Overall, it is a simply worked ring with numerous slightly unsmoothed edges and surfaces. No initials, inscriptions or similar marks are recognizable. The ring is probably not one of the very detailed and elaborately-crafted trench art objects that were traded as souvenirs even after the war, as its material and market values are likely to be rather low. However, the individual value for both the owner – who kept and preserved the ring – and its value for their descendants is significant.

The find raises the question of whether the ring could have belonged to a family member who served in artillery units during the First World War. Hans Georg Welcker (1897–1984) served in the 4th Royal Reserve Jäger Battalion of the 195th Division between 1915 and his demobilisation in 1918. This battalion fought at first on the Eastern Front and from 1917 at the River Yser. Trench mortars were used there. It is therefore quite possible that the ring was his property, but we do not have any actual evidence.

Trench art ring with a trench mortar and two projectiles (© Peter Hinterndorfer).

Because of later use and additions, such pits and their contents are multi-period although the objects cannot always be separated stratigraphically.

Other sources of finds are those that were either handed over by former prisoners or were found in the camps after the liberation and put in memorial collections. The opportunities for archaeologists to find objects *in situ* (*i.e.* at the place where they were deposited after their last use) in the memorial sites are limited. The best prerequisites for finding objects *in situ* are presented in peripheral areas that have not been included in the memorial site or been otherwise developed, or at sites where demolition was not followed by massive changes in the terrain.

This applies to Sobibór (present-day Poland). During the extensive excavation there it was observed that the finds recovered near the ramp in the entrance area of the camp were clearly different from those found at the gas chambers at Camp 3. Finds from the entrance area, where prisoners arrived after the train journey, could often be identified as personal belongings brought by the prisoners, such as spectacles, combs, cutlery and other tableware, watches, coins, shaving and sewing kits and toothpaste. These objects were rarely made of valuable materials. The finds illustrate that the prisoners were deprived of their belongings by the SS on arrival. In Camp 3, the site of killing, only a few things were found. These include personal jewellery such as tags, earrings or

Fig. 10.1. Content of an
intact recovered pit with
several hundred single
finds at Hartheim
(© ARCHEONOVA, photo:
Wolfgang Klimesch).

rings, which the victims still carried on their bodies on their final way to the gas chamber (see Chapter 6).

The analyses of these assemblages is very dependent on databases. Traditional archaeological classifications, for example by materials, have proved to be of little use. Classification based on functional aspects is more suitable for the characterisation of camp assemblages. The following criteria have proved useful:

• *Objects of camp facilities and management, including infrastructure.* These may include construction materials and construction elements such as barbed wire, wall and floor tiles, stove tiles, bricks, glass panes, nails and screws, door locks, pipelines, electrical accessories, plumbing appliances and all kinds of tools.

• *Medicinal objects.* The functional category of medicinal products and requisites includes medicines and their containers such as ampoules and vials (some of which still have their original contents), medical accessories and devices such as syringes, cupping glasses, hot water bottles, bedpans, urine bottles, enemas, mortars and pestles.

• *Hygiene and addictive articles* include combs, toothbrushes, shaving equipment, prostheses and glasses. This group also includes cleaning agents. The use of addictive substances is reflected for example in pipes and cigarette tips.

• *Household objects.* Objects associated with the household in its widest sense certainly present the largest group. This group includes elements from the barrack's interior such as furniture and furniture fittings or signs, as well as decorations of all kinds, kitchen accessories such as cooking pots, storage containers (including numerous water, beer and wine bottles), dishes and cutlery as well as other kitchen utensils. In this context, animal bones must also be mentioned. The latter primarily provide an insight into the nutrition of the SS.

• *Toys* and other objects for entertainment can be considered a separate group.

• *Accessories* include watches, hair accessories, pocket knives, amulets and jewellery.

• *Office supplies* include stationery objects.

• *Clothing* comprises prisoners' uniforms or uniforms of the SS, which may have been preserved in the memorials, and various belts or locks, shoes and countless buttons.

• *Militaria* is the final category that includes specific cookware and uniform components, as well as ammunition and weapons.

Other classifications are structured according to the following criteria: camp facilities and administration, local environment, ways to the camp, persecuted, conditions of existence, prisoners' medicine ward, work, leisure and self-assertion. Finds can also be classified into groups referring to the prisoners' society, such as men, women, children, prisoner functionaries, victims and perpetrators.

OBJECTS OF VICTIMS AND PERPETRATORS

Many objects from detention camps can be readily assigned to either the perpetrators or the victims. This especially applies to objects that were obviously produced by the prisoners themselves from the simplest materials and with the simplest techniques, which always occur in larger numbers. Handmade combs and toothbrushes, vessels, spoons and even shoes are typical.

The combs are rarely complete, no matter whether they are industrially manufactured or handmade specimens. It is likely that the combs were deliberately split into parts to create several smaller combs. The self-made combs were usually made by cutting notches into a piece of plastic. The irregularities clearly show that they are hand-made. The toothbrushes have mostly lost their bristles, possibly due to poor preservation conditions. Both object types permit some insight to prisoners' attempts to maintain a minimum standard of body hygiene.

A very impressive example of the plight of the inmates is a self-made shoe from Mauthausen (Austria) (see Fig. 10.4). The sole of the shoe consists of several layers of rubber, which have been cut to the shape of a foot with a shoe size of 5 (38). At the ball of the foot, towards the toes and at the heel, six layers of rubber were placed on top of each other and joined with nails. The heel itself consists of a stronger piece. The profiling indicates that the sole was made from old tires. The sole seems to have been covered by a poorly preserved textile sock lining for protection and comfort. Another piece of rubber tubing served as a back strap. It was inserted and attached between the soles. Wire loops were attached on the sides, which would probably take another strap to provide the necessary support in the toe area. The makeshift shoe shows that the provision of clothes and shoes for the prisoners was completely inadequate. Obviously, one prisoner found him- or herself constrained to make simple shoes in order to protect his feet.

Spoons are always numerous finds in these assemblages, but not the wooden spoons frequently mentioned in written sources and by contemporary witnesses, as they have hardly been preserved. Spoons

were often made from a piece of aluminium (see Fig. 10.5), sometimes joined with a handle from other cutlery. In contrast, forks and knives are relatively rare, but were mostly made of better material. Knives made of stainless steel or even precious metal with artfully engraved initials can be assigned to the guards.

High-quality crockery, in particular porcelain with stamps of the manufacturers Hutschenreuther, Rosenthal, Bauscher, Schönwald, Eschenbach, Kaestner, Villeroy & Boch, Thomas, Kahla or the Royal Porcelain Manufactory Berlin, as has been found in Sachsenhausen, reveals the provenance of the tableware used by the SS. In particular, the SS's own so-called Bohemia factory in Neurohlau, now in the Czech town of Nová Role, produced porcelain for the SS staff in the concentration camps. In Mauthausen, crockery was also obtained from retailers based in the nearby town of Linz. Besides the trademarks, the crockery often contains stamps such as 'SS Reich', 'Waffen-SS' or the swastika and, from the early 1940s, a year stamp (see Fig. 10.6).

Objects that can be assigned to the victims often show handmade engravings or monograms, such as prisoner numbers, initials, names or other markings (see Fig. 10.7). They provide clues to their owners and offer a chance to assign pieces to certain prisoners, illuminating their stories.

Overall, the objects from the detention camps are very worn and have numerous repair patches. Such condition suggests the general scarcity and under-supply at these camps.

Fig. 10.3. Brass fingerring with skull and crossed legs of the SS-guards from Buchenwald (© Sammlung Gedenkstätte Buchenwald).

Fig. 10.4. Self-made shoe from Mauthausen (© Claudia Theune).

Fig. 10.5. Self-made spoon from Sachsenhausen (© Anne Kathrin Müller).

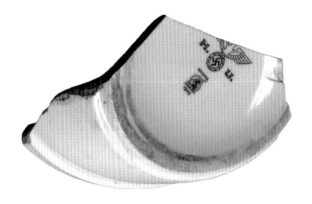

Fig. 10.6. Porcelain with National Socialist symbols from Sachsenhausen (© Anne Kathrin Müller).

Fig. 10.7. Self-made mug, spoon that belonged Guy Pinardon (mug) and a bowl from Nikolaj Maksimowitsch Resnikow (bowl) imprisoned in Flossenbürg (© KZ-Gedenkstätte Flossenbürg).

SELF-ASSERTION AS SURVIVAL STRATEGY

The finds allow deep insights to the prisoners' societies, their lives and survival strategies. In the following section I would like to discuss this in further detail, taking the concentration camps as a starting point.

Today, more than 70 years later, the diversity of the internment and detention camps as well as the different prison conditions and the different prisoners' communities tend to be overlooked. However, we are very well informed about the complex social structure of the prisoners' community, for instance by the descriptions by Eugen Kogon and Paul Martin Neurath. Kogon was imprisoned in Buchenwald (Thuringia, Germany) from 1939 until his liberation in April 1945. After the war he wrote a book based on a report to the Psychological Warfare Division, in which he gives a detailed description of the internal structures of the camp. Neurath was detained from 1938 to 1939, first in Dachau (Bavaria, Germany), then also in Buchenwald. He was released, emigrated to

the United States and wrote his PhD thesis on social life in the camps. Both authors emphasise that the prisoners' community was a multi-layered society based on internal solidarity, but also on competition. In particular, both mention clear hierarchies between different nationalities, as well as a competition for leadership positions within the prisoners' community between prisoners who were detained for alleged political offences and those accused of criminal activities. Probably due to better internal organisation and thus also stronger social structuring, the political prisoners eventually proved stronger and managed to occupy key positions in the camps.

The hierarchy imposed on the prisoners by the SS is better known. Since the SS was not able to fully control all events and processes in the camps, it rapidly designated prisoner functionaries or 'kapos'. This so-called second camp hierarchy was responsible for order in the barracks, certain tasks in the administration, the sick bays or the kitchens, and was also extended to have oversight of certain work processes at the forced-labour sites. The structure gave these functionaries access to power, albeit in a fragile context.

The procedures and torments, to which the prisoners were exposed in the concentration camps, reveal the efforts of the SS to deprive prisoners of their identity in respect of their origin, social status and social position in the outside world. They show absolute humiliation and both open and subtle (symbolic) violence. The forced surrender of the last personal belongings and clothing, the shearing of hair, the nakedness, the compulsion to wear the blue-and-white striped prisoner suit and uncomfortable wooden shoes, and the replacement of names by numbers are but some elements of this degradation. The main objective was undoubtedly to humiliate, physically and mentally expose, subject and dehumanise the prisoners and break their will. The detainees should be deliberately excluded from human society. Former norms and laws, social positions and stratifications should be extinguished, sociality and socialisation should be destroyed. The inhuman treatment aimed at robbing the prisoner's personality, individuality, identity and their humanity.

Kogon and Neurath describe how newly arrived prisoners, after their initial shock at these torments, were quickly taken up by certain groups who helped them as far as possible. This was especially the case for prisoners who shared a certain ideological, political or religious disposition, such as political prisoners or Jehovah's Witnesses. It applied less to Jewish prisoners, who were deported to the camps because of their racial affiliation – as defined by the National Socialists – and less because of their religious confession. Certain behavioural rules, social practices and actions, shared and understood by fellow inmates through their socialisation could be fostered. Even in the extreme situations of a concentration camp, the *habitus*, which accompanies the sociality of human beings in every life situation and is incorporated in every person, is not lost. Basic concepts and social constants of human society and different levels of social behaviour and social action that serve to create and maintain identity, communality and dignity were also maintained in the detention camps. In this context so-called cultural capital, *i.e.* the personal, deep-rooted cultural abilities and skills, plays an important role. This includes, for example, reading books and newspapers in the limited spare time, having food in a civilized manner, praying, secretly reciting poems even during the lengthy musters, decorating objects such as prisoner tags (see Fig. 10.8), writing down your own name, writing poems and diaries (see Fig. 10.9), crafting of items necessary for survival, creating drawings that show the life in the camp or writing poems, as was done, for example, by numerous women in Ravensbrück (Brandenburg, Germany). Many such poems and drawings have survived to this day. We also have to take into account graffiti with names, political statements, drawings on walls or even engraved in tree bark, as was done by forced labourers at the so-called Eastern Wall next to the Rivers Oder and Wartha (present-day Poland) or in Luxembourg at the Western Front. In addition, education should be included as the prisoners taught all kind of subjects in various camps. Other forms of self-assertion refer to regular body care.

Objects as an expression of self-assertion in detention camps

In the archaeological record these actions are represented by objects inscribed with prisoners' initials and names, or decorated with lovely motifs such as flowers, a heart, boat, city view etc.; or we find little things that may have been used as toys like homemade dolls or gaming pieces

Fig. 10.8. Prisoner tag of Carlo Ceggion who died on April 29th, 1945 in Mauthausen. Inscription: KL Mauthausen – 97827 – C C Venezia - A M Napoli – 1945 (Concentration camp Mauthausen, prisoner number – cc initials Venezia his birthplace; AM initials Napoli (unknown person) (© Marlene Schütze).

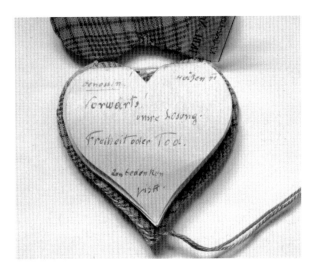

Fig. 10.9. Textile heart with some fixed heart-shaped papers and the motto: 'Comrades, forward our slogan, freedom or death. In memory Lisa' (Genossen, vorwärts unsere Losung – Freiheit oder Tod. Zum Gedenken Lisa). (© Marlene Schütze).

Fig. 10.10. Plectrum fom Sachsenhausen, made from a piece of plastic (© Anne Kathrin Müller).

(see Figs. 10.12–10.23. The crafting of spoons, vessels, combs and the secret production of knives (see Figs. 10.5, 10.7, 10.15) or shoes (see Fig 10.4) similarly reflect the will to preserve one's personal dignity and identity. Combs and toothbrushes show the will to maintain a minimum standard of hygiene. Other objects express religious faith (see Fig. 10.14). These objects symbolise self-assertion and the will to survive. Such actions allowed prisoners to build on familiar ways of living and familiar or learned habits within the camp walls. Such acts were mostly carried out secretly, without knowledge of the SS, which in turn is a sign of the powerlessness of the prisoners. Other activities, such as the exercise of sport or music (see Fig. 10.10), were tolerated by the SS, sometimes even arranged, as demonstrated by sports competitions and music events. The SS also instructed some artistically talented painters to produce certain paintings. This does not change the fact that life in the camp was completely dominated and overshadowed by the strict rules and the absolute power of the SS.

Conversely, prisoners who abandoned their self-assertion strategies often gave up their will to live, which almost inevitably meant death. As many contemporary witnesses reported, survival was only possible as long as prisoners had the will to live and felt a communal solidarity, despite permanent malnutrition, physical

Fig. 10.11. Self-made wooden heart from Sachsenhausen (© Anne Kathrin Müller).

exploitation, catastrophic hygienic conditions or serious disease.

Similar activities that reflect personal cultural identity can also be observed in other internment camps. In almost all of these camps a general lack of basic things can be stated, too. The lack of tableware in the Soviet Special Camp Buchenwald led to the production of ceramics such as cups and bowls by the prisoners themselves (see Fig. 10.16).

Many prisoners from the Soviet Special Camps have recounted the gruelling idleness and forced inaction. They also reported that the detainees sought diversion

Fig. 10.12. Doll from Mauthausen (© Marlene Schütze).

Fig. 10.14. A Star of David pendant as a sign of Jewish faith from Sobibór (© Ivar Schute).

Fig. 10.15. Self-made knife and a fragment of a comb from Jugendschutzlager Uckermark (© Brandenburgisches Landesamt für Denkmalpflege und Archäologisches Landesmuseum).

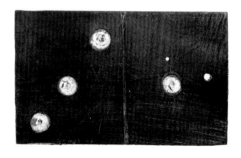

Fig. 10.13. Gaming piece (dominoes) from Buchenwald (© Sammlung Gedenkstätte Buchenwald).

to escape the daily monotony. It was not until 1948 that board games and similar activities were tolerated. As with objects from the concentration camps, finds from the Soviet Special Camp Sachsenhausen are also often marked with names and are decorated (see Chapter 6). The so-called sugar tins need to be mentioned in particular. Sugar tins are small cylindrical cans made of aluminium, measuring 2 cm high and 5 cm in diameter.

Their very uniform design, shape and size indicate that they were manufactured industrially and centrally procured. According to contemporary accounts, the camp administration started distributing these tins to the prisoners at the beginning of 1947. The prisoners received small rations of sugar, jam and similar food products in the tins, which for the first time allowed them to store their rations. Prisoners soon started to mark their sugar tins with their initials or complete names. Other inscriptions such as 'sugar', 'jam' or 'butter' refer to the specific use for the storage of food rations. The cans had matching lids to better protect the contents. No doubt other things were collected in them as well. Some sugar

Fig. 10.16. Ceramic mug from the Soviet Special Camp Buchenwald, made of clay occurring nearby (© Sammlung Gedenkstätte Buchenwald).

Fig. 10.17. So-called sugar tin from the Soviet Special Camp Sachsenhausen with prison bars and year dates (© Anne Kathrin Müller).

tins were also modified. By drilling holes in the bottom they could be turned into a sieve, or by bending the rim they could become a small bowl. One specimen with a handle may have served as a small pan. According to contemporary witness accounts, sugar was heated and caramelised in the tins to make sweets, which seems to be confirmed by one of the finds. Due to the softness of aluminium, it was easy to apply engravings. There is a good percentage of cans that are simply and sometimes complexly decorated (see Fig. 10.17 and 10.18). Some of the decorations were even filled with colour, giving a two-colour or multi-colour pattern. Many tins also bear a year marking. Since the engraved years all fall into the second half of the 1940s, they confirm that the sugar tins were only in use in the special camp.

One of the decorated sugar tins shows a face behind a cross-hatched pattern symbolising a prison and the inscription '1946–194?' (see Fig. 10.17). Other specimens show punched or engraved hearts, geometric patterns, animals, ornamental bouquets, houses or city views, detailed drawings of sailing ships or inscriptions (*e.g.* 'Eat your norm and you will stay in form'). Such motifs and inscriptions can again be regarded as statements, as expressions of wishes and hopes, as self-assertion. The unusually high percentage of decorated tins may be due to the low occupation opportunities. Some sugar tins

Fig. 10.18. So-called sugar tin from the Soviet Special Camp Sachsenhausen with a bunch of flowers (© Anne Kathrin Müller).

wandered through several hands, as can be deduced from superimposed engravings. In two special find contexts, sugar tins as well as other small aluminium containers were discovered inside a larger rectangular metal box. An analogy with pre- and protohistoric finds suggests that these are hoards. One of the boxes is made of aluminium and about 30 cm long (see Fig. 10.19). It contained one complete spoon and fragments of two other spoons,

Fig. 10.19. Aluminium container with spoons, 'sugar tins' and other items (© Claudia Theune).

Fig. 10.20. Tara Brooch made from a spoon and a coin by John 'Blimey' O'Connor in Tintown (© Joanna Brück).

four sugar tins, a small bowl, glass and porcelain sherds, and the lid of an aluminium cooking pot. In the second case a sugar tin was deposited in an iron box along with a small bowl, a small green glass bottle, and various pieces of porcelain and glass. In both cases the prisoners had probably stowed their important belongings in small boxes. Unfortunately, the objects do not carry any engravings, and so the owners cannot be identified.

Other internment camps have yielded finds with a similar character. National symbols are known from internment camps where the British imprisoned Irish Republicans and nationalists who had been captured in Dublin during the Easter Rising in 1916 (see Chapter 5). The internment camp at Frongoch (Wales) was first used as a prison for German soldiers during the First World War, before hosting around 2,500 Irish detainees. The camp was a former whiskey distillery that had been extended with wooden barracks. A number of objects from the camp have been handed down by the prisoners. The objects in these camps were produced by the prisoners themselves and express their national, political and personal identity. The objects include harps carved from bones, as well as miniature round towers and the famous Tara Brooch (see Fig. 10.20). Some objects are decorated with braided ornaments, which copy those on prehistoric and medieval objects from Ireland. They obviously express a strong connection with nationalist Ireland, with reference to the Gaelic world that was celebrated as Gaelic Revivalism and which was used by the revolutionaries to claim their honourable link with

an Irish past. Some objects show Roman Catholic motifs, such as crosses, small cups and monstrances, decorated with the Sacred Heart. A large number of the objects have been specially made by the men for women, including handbags of macramé, brooches and other personal things. Some objects show personal inscriptions. Through these objects and motifs, prisoners were able to express their social and national identity. The prisoners were allowed to send their self-made objects home and received useful things for life in the camp in return. This way, families expressed and confirmed their strong mutual bonds. The nationalist symbols strengthened the politically motivated prisoners' community. It is not for nothing that the camp Frongoch is also known as the 'University of Revolution'. The Easter Rising was prosecuted by a relatively small group of rebels. However, a large number of detainees were politicised in Frongoch, and further plans for the struggle for Irish independence were made there. The designation Irish Republican Army was used for the first time at Frongoch. While the rebellion had originally concentrated on the Dublin area, revolutionary ideas were carried throughout Ireland after the prisoners' release.

The internment camp Manzanar in California (U.S.) belongs to a very different time and region. Here, and in nine other main internment camps, some 120,000 Japanese and Japanese-born Americans who were regarded as enemy aliens were imprisoned after the attack on Pearl Harbour. Excavations have confirmed that detainees in Manzanar pursued an

Fig. 10.21. Feature of a Japanese garden in Manzanar, California (© Jeff Burton).

Fig. 10.22. Embroided view from the inside of a barrack with three windows with flowers and garden; unkown internee from the Gulag camp Inta (Workuta region) (Source: Collection 'Memorial' Moscow; © Peter Hansen / Gedenkstätte Buchenwald).

activity that is specific to Japanese culture: planting and maintaining gardens (see Fig. 10.21). The strange environment, in terms of both the landscape itself and of being imprisoned in a camp, was redesigned in such a way as to create a place reminiscent of home. Personal preferences were also taken into account. Gardening and the cultivation of Japanese cultural traditions contributed to stabilizing prisoners' personal identity and strengthening their community.

The production and use of things that are familiar and that form a link to earlier socialization are a basic concept and social constants of human society that can be observed all over the world in prison camps or prisons. The examples given could easily be supplemented. The preservation of one's own identity and dignity is preserved and strengthened through these objects and actions. This seems essential to survive or maintain a will to live in extreme situations like life-threatening danger of imprisonment.

TRENCH ART

Trench art is the term used to describe objects that soldiers have produced, either during breaks in combat or in prisoner-of-war camps. Trench art is primarily associated with theatres of war. Particularly well known are the artefacts produced in the trenches of the Western Front of the First World War, but trench art is not limited to this. It should be noted that even after the wars, especially in the period between the two world wars, trench art was produced. In such cases, the objects may also have been manufactured by persons who were no (longer) soldiers.

These objects were made by soldiers from war materials. The most frequently used material were shell casings of different calibre, which were available in large quantities but which were to be collected and surrendered for recycling. However, they were also used to produce artistic objects (see Fig. 10.23). Large-calibre artillery shells, rifle bullets, shrapnel, parts of crashed aircraft or other military equipment were also used; indeed, anything that was not vital to maintaining life and was capable of being adorned or worked became a chosen medium for such art. Vessels of all kinds are among the most frequently produced objects, the shape of the shell casings being predestined for this purpose. Artistic design, elaboration and decoration of the upper end and the body were applied to create vases, pots, goblets or tankards, but also other objects such as elaborate table bells, ashtrays, lighters, letter openers, jewellery, miniature aircraft or ships, small containers (for matches, for example) or Christian symbols such as crosses. Inscriptions and engravings with dates and

Fig. 10.23. Windmill built from cartridge cases (© Claudia Theune).

names provide additional information on when, where or by whom the object was made. Bone, wood and textile were also used, but these materials are rarely preserved in archaeological contexts. After the war, civilians also produced similar objects. They were traded as souvenirs of war and became widespread throughout Europe. The memory of the war is kept alive by such art in domestic living rooms. In some cases, production debris or other evidence found in dugouts and trenches shows that this art was made there.

Trench art gives an insight into the soldiers' situation. Producing the works offered soldiers a diversion during breaks in fighting. More than a pastime, however, it helped them maintain their own cultural traditions. It reflects self-assertion strategies. As with prisoners in the camps, the depiction of beautiful ornaments, coats of arms, landscapes, floral patterns, animals, people or other scenes may have stirred pleasant memories and offered some distraction to the soldiers. Crosses and other symbolic objects may have served as amulets or lucky charms. After the war they became souvenirs. Matchboxes, tobacco cans or ashtrays also served a practical function. Such objects may have been bartered or traded for other valuables or money. This is reported by contemporary witnesses. Allied British and French soldiers taught each other songs. In return, they received trench art rings made of – enemy – artillery grenades. It might be of interest for future research to ask whether soldiers opposed to each other also exchanged such objects.

The overarching conclusion is that even in extreme situations that are overshadowed by war and captivity, basic constants of social coexistence remain valid in every form of detention. Such constants are expressed in activities and objects, in drawings and poems, and all build on personal cultural capital that serve the preservation of dignity and identity.

OBJECTS AS EXPRESSION OF HUMILIATION IN DETENTION CAMPS

There is plenty of evidence in written and oral records that the so-called 'functionary prisoners' were esta-blished to police the concentration camp inmates and provide day-to-day organisation. They represented a second hierarchy that made it easier for the National Socialists to control the camps.

The systematic humiliation of prisoners by the SS is also revealed in some helmets. During excavations in former workshops of the Mauthausen concentration camp in 2002, four helmets were discovered. They are essentially M16 helmets, a standard model introduced during the First World War, which was gradually replaced by the successor model M35 from 1935 onwards. An iron spike has been welded to the old helmets, so that at first glance they look like the 'Pickelhauben' of the German Empire. The helmets from Mauthausen also show remains of a white paint (see Fig. 10.25). A photograph taken in 1941 or 1942 shows two functionaries of the so-called camp police wearing such whitened helmets with an attached spike (see Fig. 10.24). The two functionaries, prisoners themselves, wear a uniform that is obviously too large for them, with a belted tunic, trousers and boots. A sabre is attached to the belt. The uniform may be original but it includes outdated uniform elements; they are a caricature – such a treatment is a deliberate form of humiliation exerted by the SS. The two camp policemen in the photograph are inspecting Soviet prisoners of war who have just arrived in the camp. The pseudo-uniforms, including the modified helmet and sabre, which clearly

Fig. 10.24. Prisoner functionaries with white-painted helmets with a welded-on spike and an old-fashioned uniform (© Fotoarchiv der KZ-Gedenkstätte Mauthausen).

refer to the imperial period, give them a military appearance. Behind these pseudo-uniforms, and thereby the military appearance of the so-called camp police,

lies a deliberate strategy of the SS humiliating both the concentration camp prisoners, even if they have special tasks, and the Soviet prisoners of war as well.

The clear difference from the usual striped prisoner clothing demonstrates the special position of the camp police. At the same time, the pseudo-uniforms of the camp police do not resemble those worn by SS guards in any way. The latter were perfectly tailored to size and were in an excellent or at least good condition. Ranks and the affiliation with the 'SS-Totenkopfverbände' were clearly displayed on the collars. In line with the military organisation, which was regulated by the camp management, the clothing established a clear hierarchy that highlighted positions of power. Within the hierarchy of the detainees, the functionaries of the camp police held a high position. They might wear pseudo-uniforms; they might also be distinguished by certain markings on their triangular emblems and prisoners' numbers.

Fig. 10.25. Helmet (type M16) with a welded-on spike and remains of the white paint (© Claudia Theune).

OBJECTS AS EVIDENCE FOR ORIGIN, TRANSPORTS, TRANSFERS AND EXCHANGE

Some archaeological finds from detention camps illustrate the many transports and transfers that the prisoners had to endure. Anne Frank, for example, was transported from Westerbork (The Netherlands) to

Fig. 10.26. Memorial stone for Anne Frank and her sister Margot (© Claudia Theune).

Fig. 10.27. Mauthausen, embroidery with the initials G J on a pocket of a prisoners' jacket (© Marlene Schütze).

Fig. 10.28. Cooking pot with Hungarian inscription from Gunskirchen (Upper Austria), a sub-camp of Mauthausen (© Claudia Theune).

Auschwitz (present-day Poland) before she was taken to Bergen-Belsen (Lower Saxony, Germany) in the spring of 1945, where she died of mental and spiritual exhaustion a few days before liberation (see Fig. 10.26). Many of the names inscribed on objects found in Mauthausen can be assigned to prisoners who were first imprisoned in Flossenbürg (Bavaria, Germany) and then transported to Mauthausen, where they perished.

An alteration made to a black prisoner's jacket with a blue-white striped patch on the back from Mauthausen can illustrate transfers of clothing. At breast height is affixed the badge with the prisoner's number 65347 and a red triangle, showing that the owner was categorised as a political prisoner. In the right inside of the jacket is a rectangular-shaped pocket sewn in by hand. On the pocket is handmade embroidery, where one of the owners or wearers marked the jacket with his initials G in yellow and J in red (see Fig. 10.27). The prisoner number 65347 belongs to the Hungarian prisoner Rudolf Andorka, who was an envoy and who came to Mauthausen in May 1944. As the number and the initials do not fit together, it seems likely that a former owner or wearer with the initials G J marked the jacket, while Rudolf Andorka was another person who wore the jacket in Mauthausen. These objects also illustrate the victims' path of suffering.

Inscriptions written in foreign languages provide clear indications of the origins of the detainees. Many objects from Mauthausen and Gunskirchen (Austria), for example, show Hungarian markings (Fig. 10.28). They can be attributed to the numerous Hungarian Jews who

were deported to Mauthausen and then to Gunskirchen towards the end of the war. Obviously, they carried their pots, eating ware and toothbrushes with them.

In prisoner-of-war camps archaeological finds can reveal the origin of the imprisoned soldiers. This applies, for example, to Quedlinburg (Saxony-Anhalt, Germany), which had a prisoner-of-war camp during and after the First World War (see Chapter 6). The remains of several barracks, the camp fence and the canteen were uncovered during excavation work. Among the finds are numerous fragments of glasses, bottles, tableware and cutlery. Although contemporary accounts state that the prisoners cooked for themselves, they could also buy food and drinks in the canteen. Numerous beer bottles and glasses with trademarks of local breweries indicate a regular supply of beer from the region to the camp. The assemblage also includes water and lemonade bottles. While beer bottles were found throughout the investigated area, glasses were only found in the surroundings of the canteen. This implies that the canteen also served draft beer, and that beer bottles could be taken to the accommodations. One beer bottle clearly stands out from the rest as it does not come from a local brewery but is from Reims in northern France (see Fig. 10.29). There are other fragments of beer bottles from northern France as well as porcelain and shoelaces produced by French companies. These things were sent to the soldiers in the camp by relatives from home. Such connection to the homeland is only apparent for the French prisoners. Uniform buttons and military equipment from Russia and Great Britain, for example,

Fig. 10.29. Beer bottle from a brewery in Reims, France (© Landesamt für Denkmalpflege Sachsen-Anhalt).

Fig. 10.30. Beer bottle from a local brewery in Oranienburg found in Sachsenhausen (© Anne Kathrin Müller).

show that the camp hosted numerous soldiers from other countries as well.

Many objects, especially those that were industrially manufactured, show trademarks. The trademarks help to show which companies supplied the camps. In the case of Mauthausen, an activity report of the administrative manager has been preserved that records deliveries to the camp between 1st October 1941 and 28th December 1944. The report provides an interesting insight into the nature and size of the deliveries, and so into the organisation of the camp. The camp management received goods from both regional companies and from large companies from across the Reich. In several cases, the origin and nature of the archaeological finds agree with the suppliers and manufacturers mentioned in the report, but the archaeological evidence adds a number of other suppliers to the list. This is illustrated by a map showing the location of companies listed in the activity report and represented by trademarks on the objects (see Fig. 10.31). The report

does not cover the full operating time of the camp (August 1938 – May 1945). It is therefore theoretically possible that at least some of the objects were delivered before 1941 or in 1945 and were therefore not mentioned.

Similar observations have been made at other camps. In Sachsenhausen and in the Uckermark camp (both in Brandenburg, Germany), firebricks bearing the label 'Schamottewerke Colditz' were found. This is a company from the Leipzig-Dresden area (Sachsen, Germany). Numerous beer bottles bear the inscription 'August Wiegand Oranienburg unverkäuflich (not for sale)' (see Fig. 10.30) or 'Hansabrauerei Stendal unverkäuflich' (not for sale). The SS could buy beer in the canteens, but it was forbidden for the prisoners to drink or buy alcohol.

Sometimes archaeological finds tell a different story from the narrative gleaned from oral traditions. This is illustrated by finds from the excavation of a position from the Spanish Civil War on El Castillo Hill, in Abánades (Guadalajara) in central Spain. The excavation (by the

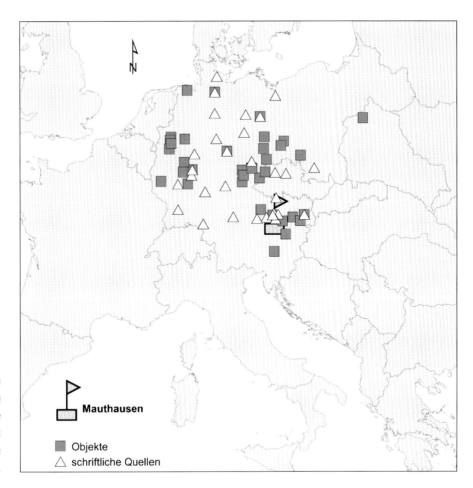

Fig. 10.31. Map with both the companies listed in the report and those represented by trademarks from Mauthausen (© Barbara Hausmair).

Spanish National Research Council) revealed various concrete elements, a protective trench, shelters and bunkers of the Nationalists. In addition to the structural remains, several artefacts such as remains of dishes and food cans were discovered. Interestingly, the tin cans found in the trenches and shelters prove that the fighters ate a great deal of tuna, while the accounts of the veterans mention sardines. Memory and fact in this instance reflect different aspects. One possible interpretation could be that the sardines, which are easier to eat, are more easily remembered than the pieces of tuna, which are difficult to share. The food tins can be assigned to factories in regions that were controlled by the Nationalists and that also hosted armament factories. The food supplies were therefore part of a wide provisioning network for the Nationalist soldiers.

Various militaria and other objects from the Spanish Civil War also reveal links with German-National Socialist and Italian-Fascist units, and with the International Brigades. It illustrates the close relationship between the dictatorships on the one hand, and the international commitment to the Republican side on the other. The sense of a proxy war comes into full focus when archaeological work reveals these connections. Of particular interest are the militaria found in the trenches of the various Civil War parties. While cartridge casings from numerous countries are found in Republican positions reflecting the International Brigades, Nationalist trenches have only yielded Spanish and German munitions. The Italian-Fascist units are also represented, but in lesser amounts. An Italian helmet was found, for example, that was used predominantly during the First World War (see Fig 11.1).

Elemental for the history of Great Britain and Ireland are the remains of the long-standing conflict that defines the history of Ulster (Northern Ireland). The museums dealing with 'The Troubles' on the Irish island use objects in a variety of ways to show the backgrounds, people involved, fighting and violence (see Chapters 5 and 13).

Bullet holes and blood traces on the textiles show the extent of the fighting. Certainly, different points of view and perceptions are presented in this way. In the spirit of reconciliation, for example, the Bloody Sunday Trust's project 'in their footsteps' in Derry tries to give a voice to as many relatives of the victims as possible. The call of 2014 says: '...we are asking families/individuals to each bring or contribute a pair of shoes to represent their absent loved one...' Those who were injured are also invited to contribute a pair of shoes for display. Each pair should have a note inside, explaining who they represent, how they died or were injured, and any demands or hopes that the particular family may have. We believe this collection of shoes will prove a powerful visual tool symbolizing lost and ruined lives'. Again, objects play an important role in the memorizing of victims.

SECONDARY USE

Archaeological investigations of 20th century sites often focus on very short periods, be it the two world wars which lasted four and six years respectively, the reigns of totalitarian regimes, or phases of use at detainment and protest camps. However, many of the structures and objects were also used later. Items that were still useful continued to be used. There are clear examples from the National Socialist period, which include the entire infrastructure and barracks of their camps. Smaller objects such as dishes and cutlery or medical devices and medicines were also often in continuous use. On a cup from the Sachsenhausen garbage dump, the name of the Bohemia porcelain manufactory, which had specially produced crockery for the concentration camps, has been scratched. Somebody using

a mug at the camp Loibl-Nord – a secondary camp of the Mauthausen concentration camp in Carinthia (Austria) – went one step further. The 'Reichsadler' (imperial eagle) with the SS signet has been scratched away completely,

Fig. 10.33. Mug from the sub-camp Loibl-Nord with the scraped-off Reichsadler with the swastika (© Claudia Theune).

Fig. 10.34. Donation box (8 cm high) for the so-called Winter Relief (inscription: Winterhilfswerk des Deutschen Volkes 1933/34 - Winter Relief of the German People 1933/34); here, too, the swastika was scraped away and the tin was used as a container for old nails in a village in the Lausitz for a long time (© Claudia Theune).

Fig. 10.32. Red Army soldiers engraved a five-pointed (red) star on the reworked padlock, formerly equipped with a swastika (© Thomas Kersting).

leaving only the wing tips visible (see Fig. 10.33). It is not clear who used the cup with the scratched-out swastika but the cup with the intact swastika was not thrown away. The cup was reused and it was important to the user that the National Socialist symbol was no longer there. Similarly the owner of the collecting box for the so-called Winter Relief acted (see Fig. 10.34).

The same applies to the objects redesigned by Red Army soldiers. Here, they went even one step further. The swastika was not only removed, but the symbol of the victors, the five-pointed star, was engraved on it (see Fig. 10.32).

VALUATION OF THE OBJECTS TODAY

Historical sites are always subject to constant change. This also applies to the appreciation of places as places of remembrance. It has already been pointed out that major changes have been made to the memorial sites, historical structures have been removed, many things have been dumped in rubbish pits, original paintings have been covered with fresh paint. This approach also reflects the valuation and the change of value for objects. The changed value of movable and immovable objects is expressed, for example, by their disposal. Things that were left on-site may or may not have been useful to the former owners. As subsequent users of the site removed and disposed of some of these objects, the latter were declassified as worthless. Today, these objects are cherished again as archaeological evidence and sources of historical information. Finds from former detention camps, protest camps, burial sites and battlefields serve as witnesses of the past. In exhibitions they bear an additional public value. Last but not least, emotional value may be attached to them by survivors, bereaved relatives and their descendants.

This leads to the question of how we deal with the vast amount of objects that are being kept in storage in museums and heritage institutions, and how we should value the sites themselves. While archaeologists and heritage managers for a long time maintained the view that all archaeological finds must be kept and preserved, the masses of finds from medieval and post-medieval (including 20th century) complexes have triggered a debate on this matter.

There is, however, no single definition of the term value. It can refer to the pure material value, it can concern a region, a nation or a landscape. Things can be of historical, scientific or artistic value. They can be valuable to former owners, survivors, museum visitors, or they can have a social value for a larger community, for example as a reference to a common identity. In cultural heritage management, value may refer to a class of monuments or objects.

No one will object to the permanent preservation of the personal objects of soldiers, prisoners and protesters, as discussed in this chapter. But what about the tens of thousands of industrial nails from prisoners' barracks, door and window fittings, barbed wire fences, countless fragments of glass panes, water, beer or wine bottles, porcelain dishes and many other small finds? What about the innumerable field sites, such as bunkers and gun batteries that crowd the landscape of the Siegfried Line, the Atlantic Wall and other linear alignments? What should be preserved? Do we resolve the matter by simply allowing these assemblages to decay as it is often discussed at the moment? Certainly, neither everything nor every place can be protected and preserved; there is simply too vast an assemblage. Decisions have to be made on their selection. But whatever is decided, none of these places and items should be forgotten as they remain witnesses to a great deal of human suffering and serve to remind all generations of the error of their architects.

CONCLUSION

In this chapter I discussed a number of possible interpretations of different objects. Large and small finds have a great potential for insights into living conditions in times of war and under oppression. However, only a small spectrum of finds from the large number of different categories could be presented. Much could only be touched upon, many things remained unmentioned, such as the multitude finds from the medical field. In addition, it is also clear that a number of research questions will undoubtedly remain open for future investigations. This refers, for example, to networks of different social groups, to regional or global exchange of objects between friend and enemy; to a comparison of available objects in different internment camps or different theatres of war and many other things. The world of small finds is endless.

Chapter 11

A GLOBAL PERSPECTIVE

INTRODUCTION

Globalisation refers to the growing and close economic, political, cultural, environmental, institutional, as well as ideological and communications networks that interlace and connect individuals and societies across the globe. The driving forces behind this process include rapid technological development, known as the Digital Revolution, and the meteoric increase in the mobility of people and goods over long distances. Developments in one region often yield great impacts across the world and reveal the complex interconnections that exist. This is an historic dynamic of human society that can be traced into antiquity. Post-Columbian settlement of the New World established networks that crossed both major oceans, paving the way for large-scale transport and trade between Africa, the Americas and Europe, and creating the so-called Atlantic trade triangle. A shadow of this expansion was the enslavement and overseas sale of Africans.

With the successful laying of the first trans-Atlantic telegraph cable in the 1860s, the time needed for spreading news and exchanging information between the North American and European continents was greatly reduced. At the same time, steam engines made travel by land and water considerably faster. Since around 1900, combustion engines have accelerated this development,

while automobiles and aviation have revolutionised transportation and travel. In the 1920s, radio receivers became accessible to many people and shortly afterwards the moving pictures of the early film industry allowed people, for the first time in human history, to watch what was happening at the other end of the world in motion. Globalisation has deep roots. For an archaeology of the 20th century, it is the technical developments in particular that play an important role for the study of global interdependencies.

Forty nations from all continents participated in the First World War. In the Second World War sixty nations took part. To this can be added the respective colonial territories of the combatants – most of them located in Africa. The industrialization of war; the rapid development in military technology; the employment of tanks, submarines and aircraft; and the consistent use of railways for the transportation of troops helped to create a massive engine of war; equally it facilitated countless deaths, casualties and prisoners of war, all of which rose to a scale previously unknown in history. Incarceration became a global phenomenon, whether of soldiers or of people interned for contrary political views, ethnic identity or religion. Deportation was possible over great distances.

A Mosque in a First World War prisoner-of-war camp south of Berlin

The global presence of objects and ideas from other regions, transported and distributed through personal transfer or trade is not a feature of the modern period alone. International networks, individual contacts and small and large groups in the political, cultural and economic fields are very extensive. Objects that bear witness to the globalised world of the 20th century are discussed in many places in this book. Soldiers from all over the world fought in many theatres of war and prisoners were held at very different sites.

The mosque built in the First World War prisoner-of-war camp at Wünsdorf south of Berlin is nevertheless one of the most remarkable sites. The building in the so-called 'Crescent Camp' is the earliest mosque in Germany, apart from a few prayer rooms.

The Muslims there had mostly gone to war for the colonial powers of Britain and France. Germany was allied with the Ottoman Empire and, by allowing the prisoners to fulfil their religious duties and to pray together, sought to strengthen the coalition by exploiting the situation for propaganda purposes. At the same time, the Ottoman Sultan/Caliph called for Jihad against the colonial powers.

A century after its construction in 1915, the foundations and plan of the building were excavated by a team from the Free University of Berlin led by R. Bernbeck and T. Dressler. The walls and the dome of the building were built lightly in wood. The building included a polygonal prayer room and a minaret, and a room for the preachers, a room for washing the dead, a bathhouse and a forecourt with a well. The prayer room had a diameter of 12 m. The excavation revealed not only the ground plan, but also details on the floor surfaces, sherds from the windows of the dome and ceramic tiles from the washroom. By 1930 the mosque was in need of renovation and was demolished.

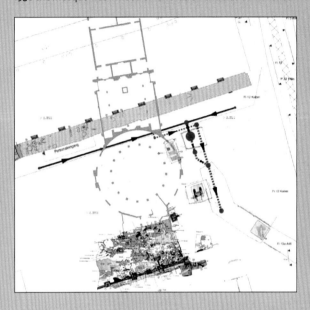

Plan of the excavation of the Mosque at the so-called Halbmondlager (Crescent Camp) (© Torsten Dressler).

The supplying of the soldiers as well as of the prisoners with clothes, food and other necessities created an immense trade network for all kinds of goods. A lot of trade was on a local or regional level, but there were also many companies and especially institutions of nation states that operated on a supra-regional and/or international level.

A new wave of protest movement arose in the second half of the 20th century during the Cold War, when the United States and the Soviet Union invested in massive military rearmament and the arsenal of weapons, including nuclear weapons, grew. This threat led to an engagement of people from all over the world. They were engaged in various resistance movements protesting against nuclear tests, the stationing of atomic bombs or against other human-induced environmental threats (see Chapter 7). Later, other causes, such as the demand for compliance with basic human rights prompted protest. The protestors coordinate and organise themselves worldwide, especially through social media.

The numerous finds in protest camps of the second half of the 20th century may reflect the ideological attitude of the protesters as well as their origin, and so the solidarity among these groups.

In recent years, cultural-historical disciplines have engaged in a lively discussion on global networks and in interaction from a historical point of view. Historical processes in different regions of the world have been examined on an equal basis and their global networks and interdependencies have been taken into consideration. The long-prevailing Eurocentric or Western perspective has given way to more regionally focused perspectives. Alternatives to looking at the world within the limitations of Western-dominated narratives have become increasingly relevant in archaeology, especially for research in non-Western areas like Africa. Here, Western concepts of linear time, spatial order or moral values do not necessarily apply to local traditions and thinkings and have to be taken into account for historical-archaeological projects of the 20th century.

With regard to such interactions, regional and global events and structures as well as persons and groups can be considered from different perspectives and complex connections observed. Questions may focus on networks and interactions of different groups; the kinds of communication with the country of origin or with and within the new environment; the (dis)continuation of cultural practices; forms of acculturation, integration and assimilation; but also persistence, the adaptation to a different climate and environmental conditions; to other mentalities; the supply of food or clothing; or the treatment of foreigners by the local population. Another interesting aspect would be further investigation into the fate of internees or migrants from a long-term perspective: did displaced people return to their homelands or did they eventually integrate without

considering a return to their countries of origin? In the context of dictatorships and repressive regimes, research touches on the essential question of access to objects of all kinds as opposed to victims' absolute lack of even the most basic of necessities for survival.

By including pictorial and written sources, an archaeology of the 20th century can reveal such profound interdependencies (see Chapter 3). Small and large (archaeological) objects provide a detailed impression of the nature and the extent of the multi-layered international networks of the two world wars, the Cold War, the many other wars and numerous protest movements.

A REGIONAL PERSPECTIVE

In this chapter, I will return to some aspects that I have addressed in previous chapters, but will discuss them from a global perspective. However, it must be stressed that the potential for comprehensive global analyses of archaeological remains would certainly be greater if archaeological materials recovered during excavations and stored in museum or memorial collections were published with greater accessibility.

Even today, the two world wars and also the Cold War are mostly viewed from a predominantly European or Western perspective. Narratives deriving from such approaches neglect the fact that soldiers from

Fig. 11.1. Italian helmet found on a battlefield of the Spanish Civil War (© Alfredo González Ruibal).

all continents, including the European and American colonies, took part in the wars in Europe, the Pacific and Africa and died on battlefields across the world. Through material culture, it is relatively easy to determine the origin of dead soldiers and of people imprisoned in internment camps. Identification tags or inscriptions and trademarks on objects associated with victims of war can provide such information about identification (see Chapters 9 and 10). Excavations on battlefields as well as in camps from various wars repeatedly reveal the worldwide origin of fallen soldiers or captured people (see Fig. 11.1). Weapons recovered from battlefields provide further insights. Archaeological investigations of remnants of the Spanish Civil War, for instance, have shown that members of the opposing parties involved in the conflict can be identified by militaria as well as other objects, revealing the international character of the various factions. Italian-made weapons attest to a similar access to arms for opponents in Libya.

Close study of prisoner camps can also reveal the identity of the prisoners. In Edelbach (Austria) a National Socialist prisoner-of-war camp for high-ranking French officers, the so-called OFLAG XVII A, was partially excavated recently. Similar investigations have been conducted in the STALAG III A, a prisoner-of-war camp in Luckenwalde (Brandenburg, Germany), where the National Socialists detained mainly Soviet soldiers. In the United States, investigations have taken place in several prisoner-of-war camps for German captives of the Second

World War (see Fig. 11.2). Many objects of German origin were found. The same is true for the objects found at the Inari Peltojoki (Finland) military base and prisoner-of-war camp. The finds there also show a slightly broader pattern of distribution. They originate not only from Germany, but also from the territories occupied during the war, *e.g.* those regions which belonged to the so-called Axis Powers (see Fig 11.3).

The battle in the Pacific and its far-reaching interconnections have been highlighted by investigations in the so-called 'Jappenkampen' in Indonesia, where members of the former Dutch colonial power were interned between 1943 and 1945.

Objects recovered from these sites suggest that prisoners continued practices from their homelands. Through writing letters, detainees kept in touch with their relatives and friends and so their country of origin, while at the same time maintaining their socialization. The gardens erected by Japanese-born prisoners in

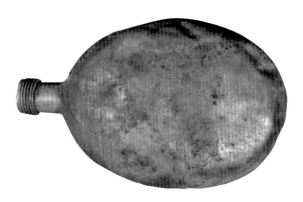

Fig. 11.2. German military water bottle, from the prisoner-of-war-camp in Whitewater, Prov. Manitoba, Canada (© Adrian Myers).

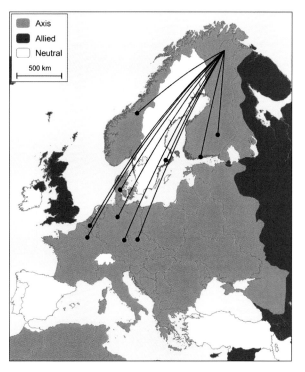

Fig. 11.3. Provenances of objects found at the Inari Peltojoki military base and prisoner-of-war camp (Finland); the borders correspond to the current national boundaries (© Oula Seitonen et al. 2017 with modification).

Second World War internment camps in the United States represent a particularly impressive example of material practices that maintained connections to one's homeland (see Chapter 10).

Other activities of prisoners of war can be characterised in a similar way. At the Whitewater camp some dugout canoes were found. This is a very uncommon way to make a canoe in the region, where the indigenous people would make their canoes out of birch bark or animal hides. Diaries of German prisoners of war note that the prisoners saw a birch bark canoe in a magazine and developed the idea to make canoes, and they did so in a manner that the prisoners were more familiar with – dugout canoes.

Another important means of keeping in touch with the world outside the camps was the radio. Contemporary witnesses repeatedly emphasize the importance of radios as a medium to receive news from home or keep informed about the progress of the war and crucial political events. Letters or newspapers reached the prisoners only irregularly or not at all. Both radios and letters belong to the material culture preserved from sites of internment. Another form of contact is materialised in the remains of telephone sets and most recently mobile phones.

Further contacts with the homeland become evident in commodities that were sent by relatives to their imprisoned loved ones, such as beer bottles produced in Reims (France) that were found in a German World War I prisoner-of-war camp in Quedlinburg (Fig. 10.29). The absence of such objects, on the other hand, indicates that other groups of prisoners had difficulties or were not able to maintain such contacts.

At former places of National Socialist terror, the immense efforts to identify the regime's victims have led to the creation of long, yet countable lists of the names of detainees. The recovery of some victims' identities may represent at least a small consolation for the anonymity of the uncountable people murdered in the concentration and extermination camps (see Fig. 11.5; see also Figs. 9.5, 10.7, 10.8). An increasing number of books containing the names of people who perished in the terror facilities of Hitler's regime have been published by memorials in recent years and inscriptions of the names on the walls of the former camps remember the dead. Although the full names of many Jews killed at the Bełżec death camp (present-day Poland) could not be recovered, at least the first names of identified victims were carved into a memorial wall on-site, as were the dates and places

Fig. 11.4. Dugout canoe from the prisoner-of-war camp Whitewater, Prov. Manitoba, Canada (© Adrian Myers).

from where people were deported to the extermination centre. In addition to the profound meaning of returning names and thus personal biographies to the victims of the National Socialists, these efforts also provide insights into the geographical extent of National Socialist terror. The deportation routes began in towns and villages across Europe and reveal the enormous scale of the terror network that encompassed large parts of the continent (see Chapter 6).

On the other hand, material culture also has the potential to bring local and regional relationships to the fore, be it through objects produced and used by indigenous populations or items that travelled together with their creators and users as part of forced migrations, for example when people from Africa were enslaved and forcefully brought to the Americas. Such approaches enable an historical engagement that is not dominated by a Eurocentric point of view. Migrations from Asian regions are increasingly studied by archaeologists, for example in the United States, where the living quarters of Chinese-born migrants, their ways of life and traditions have been studied through material culture. Excavations of 18th- and 19th-century sites connected with the African-American community have focused on the intra- and interrelations of different groups with a particular sensibility for the African-American perspective.

The migratory movements of the present, be it war refugees or people forced to leave their countries for economic reasons in order to find a place to live, necessitate a global approach. This is true for the migrations from Africa and Asia across the Mediterranean Sea and into Europe and also for other places in the world. Mobile telephones play an immensely important role in communication, as can be seen in the study of the economic migrants who cross the Mexican-American border into the United States (see Chapter 8). This is also very well-known for those migrants coming to Europe.

The high importance of things and objects for migrants can also be seen when they ask themselves: 'What should I bring to Europe?' It is obvious that before embarking on the arduous and dangerous journey migrants deliberately think about what objects they take with them. These will probably be only a few objects that serve to remind them of their homeland, family and friends; objects designed to preserve this memory in a new world.

Material culture, letters, photographs and testimonies of contemporary witnesses are equally valuable for investigations from a global historical perspective. Targeted investigations as well as studies of supra-regional networks emerging from more locally rooted analyses provide insights into wars, totalitarian regimes, internments and protest movements. Analysing such phenomena over a longer period of time allows for a better understanding of their causes, developments and effects. However, it needs to be re-emphasised, the proper disclosure and publication of archaeological documentation and finds is a precondition of successful analyses.

Fig. 11.5. Commemorative stone in memory of Wolf Polak, who was murdered in the extermination camp Sobibór on May 21st, 1943 with the Dutch inscription: Papa je hebt nu, in 2010, 10 Joodse achterkleinkinderen, waarvan 1 naar jou is vernoemd. Dank tot in de eeuwigheid. Levie Wolf Polak (Dad, in 2010 you have now 10 Jewish grandchildren, one of them was named after you. Thanks forever and ever. Levie Wolf Polak) (© Claudia Theune).

Chapter 12

ARCHAEOLOGY BEYOND WAR

INTRODUCTION

The major focus of this book is on contemporary archaeology as the archaeology of conflict and oppression. We now consider widening the subject to include other aspects of the diverse matrix that constitutes human existence in the modern period. The choice and the range is vast. Archaeological sites of the 20th and 21st centuries provide valuable insights into historical processes, social conditions of the last 100–150 years and current socio-political challenges. With regard to a long-term contextualisation, it might be useful to include remnants from the 18th and 19th centuries.

The thematic fields encompass places, object assemblages and items of daily life, infrastructure, public life, work and trade, leisure time, religion and cult, deposits and death as well as human remains (see Chapter 1 and 10). Many of these topics can be subsumed under the aspect of everyday life, primarily living, consumption and work. It is an archaeology that is very closely related to our own life. Some of the sites have been abandoned over time. Economic reasons can lead to the abandonment of shopping malls or airports. Film sets of completed films are sometimes preserved. Fewer communications monitoring stations, which were built everywhere during the Cold War, even in the Arctic on Greenland, are needed in peacetime. Other places have been abandoned due to disasters, of which Chernobyl or Fukushima are examples. All these sites can be of interest for archaeological studies.

Indeed the everyday life of archaeologists can also make for interesting study. The so-called Van-Project of the University of Bristol (England) considered a Ford Transit van that was used for archaeological projects from 1991–1999 and then by works and maintenance teams of the Ironbridge Museum (1999–2005). The project has provided deep insights into everyday work, in particular archaeological work, and included an analysis report of contemporary witness reports, photographs and other written sources. The main interest lay in the condition of the vehicle and the artefacts left over after almost 15 years of use by different persons, the traces of the archaeologists. The van was dismantled systematically and all findings were documented. Many parts of the van itself, in particular the engine and its components were still original, and/or in good condition, from which we can assume the van was maintained and regularly serviced. Some finds like sherds, slag and coins can be allocated to the archaeologists and their projects. Screws, wire, pencils or even a sherd from a champagne glass, as well as confetti seem to be leftovers from the users, from their work and also from celebrations.

Modern deserted settlements

Desertions, abandoned settlements or parts of them are a common field of research for archaeologists. Normally these are settlements from long-gone eras. However, there are numerous places from the last 100 years or so that have been abandoned and whose remains have not been removed afterwards. They remain instead as desolate ruins that are often quite overgrown, and include, for example, unprofitable shopping malls, unused religious buildings, disused factories or even whole villages.

On the outskirts of today's cities in particular there are such empty buildings, which are then used by many other people, be it by young people as a meeting place or by homeless people as free accommodation. The new uses can remove objects that are still useful, introduce new objects or perpetuate themselves through graffiti. Whatever the case, subsequent uses that have nothing to do with the original use become inscribed in those places.

One example is Fordlândia on the Rio Tapajós in the Amazon region, where Henry Ford built a small town in 1920 for about 8,000 people to extract high-quality rubber for windscreen wipers, doormats and tyres as part of his automobile production. However, the North American way of life and work could not be communicated to the local workers, who rebelled against the working conditions. Following the invention of synthetic rubber, production was abandoned with high losses.

Such modern abandoned settlements can be enormous in size and the often still-standing walls with extensive infrastructure and remaining interior furnishings, as well as the endless number of finds, mean that no excavations are actually carried out in the strict sense of the word, but that the condition of the site is recorded by survey. These places are undoubtedly important witnesses to our recent history and certainly a worthwhile destination for archaeological and historical projects, assuming there is an interesting research question to investigate.

The old warehouse in Fordlândia (© Rodrigo Cruzatti, CC BY 4.0, commons.wikimedia.org).

RUINS OF NATIONAL SOCIALIST BUILDING ACTIVITIES

Before presenting further topics and examples I would like to draw attention to National Socialist buildings that are still preserved throughout Europe, especially in Berlin, Munich, Nuremberg (all Germany) Linz and Vienna (both Austria), and are used for various purposes. Well-known examples in Berlin include the Tempelhof Airport, the Olympic Stadium, the Ministry of Finance (formerly the Reich Aviation Ministry), the building of the Ministry of Foreign Affairs (formerly the Reichsbank), and also the Olympic village to the west of the city. The heavyweight cylinder (Schwerbelastungskörper) served for the preparation and testing of the underground solidity for the gigantic buildings of so-called Germania, planned for Berlin by Albert Speer, Hitler's architect. It still stands in the middle of Berlin (see Fig. 12.1). The Prora seaside resort on the island of Rügen (Germany), which was never completed, was to accommodate up to 20,000 holidaymakers ('Kraft durch Freude' - 'Strength through Joy'). In Oranienburg (Brandenburg, Germany), the tax office uses the so-called T-building of Sachsenhausen, in which the so-called 'Inspektion der Konzentrationslager' (administration of the concentration camps) was housed after 1938. The

Munich University for Music and Theatre is located in the former NSDAP-Führerbau. In Nuremberg is the large area of the Reichsparteitagsgelände with the Zeppelin platform. The list could go on. Usually small memorials, museums or documentation centres are found in these buildings, where visitors get information about the place and its history. Other buildings were bombed during the war and then partially demolished. In Bavaria this includes one of the major centres of National Socialist power, the Obersalzberg with Hitler's Berghof (see Fig. 12.2) and other estates of high-ranking National Socialist politicians. Hitler spent a third of his entire dictatorship here. He used the impressive rural alpine mountain landscape specifically for his political goals. Many guests of state were welcomed. Another example is the Brown House in Munich. The same applies to lesser-known building ruins, such as the old, never completed motorway in the Spessart area (Germany) or a number of so-called Thingstätten, in which seasonal celebrations or festivities with an apparently Germanic background were held. These include the Waldbühne in Berlin, the Loreley open-air theatre near St. Goarshausen (Rhineland-Palatine, Germany), the Kalkberg Stadium in Bad Segeberg (North Rhine-Westphalia, Germany), used for the Karl May Festival, the Heiligenberg in Heidelberg (see Fig. 12.3) or more unknown or disused arenas in Passau or Eichstätt (both Bavaria, Germany), which have become visible again through the use of digital terrain models. The relics of the National Socialist era are still preserved in many places in Germany and Europe, even if we do not necessarily always recognize them as such.

Buildings that were specifically destroyed by the National Socialists because of their ideology should also be mentioned, such as synagogues. The location of the synagogue in Marburg (Germany) has changed

Fig. 12.1. Berlin, heavyweight cylinder (Schwerbelastungskörper) to test the stability of the subsoil (© Claudia Theune).

several times over the years. At the end of the 19th century a large new building was built at a central place in the city. On three sides the prayer room was surrounded by women's temples, and on the fourth side the shrine with the Torah rolls was elaborately presented. In addition, a school hall and other rooms were added; a mikvah was installed in the basement, which was filled with rainwater. After its destruction during the pogroms on November 8–9th, 1938, the remaining walls were completely demolished and the Jewish community was forced to sell the property below its value. The site stood idle for a long time,

Fig. 12.4. Marburg, excavation of the synagogue with the mikvah (© Ulrich Klein, IBD Marburg).

and the property was transferred back to the Jewish community in 2002. Excavations documented differences between planning and execution, and uncovered the still well-preserved mikvah with its water-supply system (see Fig. 12.4). A memorial was built here, a garden of remembrance.

RUINS OF THE 2ND HALF OF THE 20TH CENTURY

We have created a large number of ruins on earth in the very recent past. Ruins from the Cold War are not only the border installations mentioned above (see Chapter 8) but also numerous interception stations, radar installations, bunkers, military facilities and much more all over the world. Often the places were simply left behind without taking along the written documents or uninstalling devices. Other sites, like military training grounds or sites of manoeuvres, were archaeologically investigated. The innumerable finds give information about the origin of the units; furthermore it is possible to date the manoeuvres.

Numerous other ruins everywhere, be they airports, train stations, roads and railway sections, shopping malls, industrial estates, adventure parks and other places that are no longer in use are scattered around the world. Some

of these places are also referred to as 'lost places' or also as 'non-places'. This draws attention to the fact that at these locations were only mono-functionally used areas located in urban and suburban areas. Usually, economic inefficiency is the reason for the abandonment of the places. They seem to have little or no history and identity, or there is no interest in maintaining, preserving or reusing the sites.

Sometimes it is quite easy to get access to such places. Random persons may take useful things with them or leave new messages like graffiti or other objects. In any case, these places are subject to further change. They do not always reflect the state when the structures lost their functions, but they are ruins of our generation.

ABANDONED SETTLEMENTS

In the Kölner Bucht between Eschweiler in the West, Brühl in the South and Erkelenz in the North, in the Lausitz south of the Spreewald, in Boxberg in the north-east of Saxony or in the surroundings of Leipzig (all Germany), brown coal is exploited in large open-cast mines. The mining tears deep wounds in the landscape and does not stop for settlements. Occasionally in the first half of the 20th century and in the 1950s, but particularly since the 1960s, people have had to abandon their villages and

Fig. 12.5. Breunsdorf, devastated village during the excavation (© Landesamt für Archäologie, Sachsen).

towns and give way to new mining districts. Houses, homesteads, churches, schools, shops, streets and roads, sports grounds and many other buildings have been vacated and demolished. Planning for new extensions of brown-coal mining regions is a time-consuming process and very often it is accompanied by intense and protracted protests and delays. When the eviction of settlements is finally put into practice, extensive archaeological investigations are conducted. Not only the medieval or early modern features and basements under existing houses or the soon-to-be demolished buildings themselves are of interest, but also the entire building stock, including changes of the 20th century.

One example of such an extensive investigation of a village took place in Breunsdorf (Saxony, Germany). The village was cleared in the mid-1990s. Comprehensive historical building analyses (Landesamt für Archäologie and the Universität Tübingen) of the empty but not yet demolished houses and barns produced a precise chronological sequence. The village was founded in the course of medieval settlement and cultivation processes ('Landesausbau'), east of the River Elbe in the 1130s. The first written reference to the village dates to 1267. Initially it was assumed that the medieval layout of the village would resemble the linear scheme of the 20th century village (see Fig. 12.5). The houses of the early phases, dating to the 12th century, however, took up far less space and were loosely scattered. The discovery of a farm building beneath the later village's main road in turn suggested that the linear arrangement was only implemented at a later point in time. The medieval and early modern homesteads were partially devastated by various fires at the end of the 18th and in the first half of the 19th century. Apart from the medieval church, no buildings of the village's early days survived into the 20th century. Most residential or commercial buildings date back to the 19th and 20th centuries. Structural changes seem to have occurred constantly. With the emergence of new types of crops in the 19th century, farms were restructured to accommodate new buildings for crop storage.

A similar project was conducted at Allentsteig (Lower Austria, Austria) (Universität Salzburg), an area evacuated for military exercises. Questions regarding socio-economic processes and the dynamic development of settlement structures from the Middle Ages to the modern period were the focus. Among other results, the construction of stables and barns shows the growing role of livestock housing during winter. New small houses in the outskirts make social differentiation in the village clear.

Such examples show how crucial it is for detailed archaeological analyses of village structures and farmstead layouts to be completed, to avoid misconceived assumptions about medieval origins and the development of modern settlement. As the cases of Breunsdorf and Allentsteig have clearly revealed, settlement patterns can originate from far more recent periods than older research might have considered.

The comprehensive study of villages that must be abandoned to accommodate new development provide invaluable insight to researchers and to those inhabitants who are forced to build new lives elsewhere. The work can support them in maintaining their memories and so their former identities.

Other examples worth mentioning are studies that concern the interiors of abandoned houses. In December 2003 the village Bam (Iran) was destroyed by a heavy earthquake that killed many of its inhabitants. Nothing could be rescued from the devastated houses, but large efforts were made to recover the bodies of the victims from the ruins and bury them properly. Five years later, archaeologists (Buali Sina University) visited Bam and documented the features and finds in six houses. There was a clear contrast between structures that were publicly visible and accessible and those dedicated to private usage. Especially in private areas, objects were found that are not in accordance with national traditions and norms. While in the exterior (public) part of the houses socio-economic status and evidence of a life according to religious rules was evident, objects were found that show a lifestyle less regulated by religion in the inner parts of the house.

Abandoned settlements of the 20th century can also be found in a part of today's Czech Republic, the former Sudetenland. Until 1945 the majority of the population was of German origin, and they had to leave the country after the Second World War. Some of the villages and the cemeteries were no longer used. Detailed archaeological studies (University of Pilsen) are being undertaken to investigate the villages. The questions of interest consider which parts of settlements and which cemeteries were abandoned by which parts of the population. The research is also looking at those parts that were reused and those that were abandoned but still maintained.

In this case, the documented material culture covers all aspects of life, because the event happened without

Fig. 12.6. Remains of 'tramping sites' in the Czech Republic (© Pavel Vařeka).

warning and caught everyone by surprise, something that is also called the 'Pompeii Premise'. Other projects deal with a planned leaving; they show social or spatial shifts. The legacy of a single mother and her children were documented in a council house in England, where the family seemed to have left abruptly without taking many belongings with them. In Spain, farmhouses that were abandoned by their owners were studied. In the English and Spanish examples, the abandonment was planned and so it is reasonable to expect that only objects of little value would be left behind, objects that would be of no use in the new life situation. However, this was not the case. A multitude of unbroken objects were discovered in England and in Spain that were still intact and possible to use. Remarkably, there were also many items of a very personal nature, such as private letters and photographs that the inhabitants had abandoned. It suggests in these instances that the owners deliberately broke with their past lives, and that the choice to do so was their own.

Studies in the Czech Republic conducted by the University of Pilsen in cooperation with the University of York have focused on the archaeology of leisure time, in particular informal camping grounds or 'tramping sites'. One of the goals of the project was to get an insight to the marking of the landscape through these leisure activities. The sites show new types of temporary settlements, residential sites and built-up areas with wooden cabins, camping grounds and tramping settlements, which incorporated woodcraft, hiking, camping and scouting, and were also used by hippies. The camps were related to the Czech 'tramping movement' mainly in the second half of the 20th century. Tramping groups roamed the forests on weekends, spending time away from the state authorities among like-minded people. The camps can be easily found, while contemporary witness reports give insights into the experiences within the movement. Benches, fireplaces, and other remains can still be found near the city of Pilsen (see Fig. 12.6). Investigations on

Fig. 12.7. Foundations of a house at Viðey, Iceland (© Gavin Lucas).

sites of adventure parks, as in Derbyshire (England), and festival sites like Woodstock (August 1969) can be added in this context.

To capture the deep history of places was also the motivation behind other projects. Researchers have examined the ruins of abandoned residential buildings, industrial facilities, shopping centres, military bases and abandoned settlements of the last century such as the Soviet mining town Piramida on the Norwegian territory of Spitsbergen (1921–2000) or Viðey in the bay of Reykjavík (Iceland). Where contemporary witnesses were still alive, their testimonies were included in the analyses. One detailed case study focused on Viðey, where former agricultural land had been restructured around 1907 in order to build a large fish factory. A harbour and a village for the workers were built adjacent to the factory. The venture soon ran into trouble because of expensive loans, high salaries of the company management and some bad business decisions, eventually leading to bankruptcy in 1914. A second company was founded in 1924 and although the island's community initially benefited economically, it took only a few years until the company collapsed in 1931. In the following years, until 1943, the last inhabitants left Viðey and all buildings were demolished. The ruins of the fishing village attest to the failure of a local employer and the resulting abandonment of an entire village (see Fig. 12.7). Archaeological research (University of Iceland) at Viðey has primarily focused on commodities. Since the factory and all related facilities were built from scratch in 1907, the import of all goods was a precondition for a successful implementation. The study traced the origins of goods as found by the archaeologists. The majority of items came from Germany, but also from Sweden and England, as well as Japan and the United States. Hardly any object originated from Iceland itself.

INDUSTRIAL PLANTS OF THE 19TH AND 20TH CENTURY

The sites of abandoned factories and remnants of industry might become monuments that are worthy of archaeological study in their own right. Those remains, particularly in England where the Industrial Revolution was so great, attract special attention, and English archaeologists have led the field in close documentation and research. The oldest iron bridge spanning the River Severn at Coalbrookdale (Shropshire, England) is a known study. Such work includes the study of canal systems. Many of these facilities are now listed historical monuments.

The Ruhr area between Duisburg and Dortmund (North Rhine-Westphalia, Germany) has long epitomised heavily industrialised landscapes with dense population. Iron ore deposits and rich resources of coal were the basis of its development. The 19th-century industrialization brought rapid growth in many ways. After ironworks were installed in the middle of the 18th century, the exploitation of coal increased manifold in the 19th century, while coke that was required for iron- and steelworks was produced in coking plants. The unprecedented boom attracted more and more workers. Small villages grew rapidly from the end of the 18th century onwards. By the late 1800s, more than five million people lived in the Ruhr area. While the economy continued to flourish into the first half of the 20th century, the coal and steel industry began to decline in the late 1950s. More and more mines and collieries had to close. Today, only a small number of coal mining pits remain in operation. The end to these now low-profit mines will come in the medium term. The closely related steel industry suffers from strong global competition. Today, the industry has lost the pervasive status it enjoyed until the middle of the 20th century, and the Ruhr area is experiencing massive structural change. Historically, the workers and inhabitants lived close to the mines and the ironworks and steel mills, and this proximity was a large part of the regional identity. The structural changes being experienced today risk the loss of this recent social history. There have been attempts to counter this by preserving several winding towers and industrial facilities as cultural monuments. The industrial facilities of the Zollverein in Essen, for example, have been declared a UNESCO World Heritage Site, highlighting their importance for the region.

To do justice to the detailed documentation of such sites, it is necessary to trace the sites back to their 19th-century origins. Among the best known is Krupp's Gussstahlfabrik in Essen, a cast-steel factory, founded in 1811 by Friedrich Krupp. Starting with only one melting shop and Krupp's parent house, the complex was developed into a large industrial area with mines, coking plants, steelworks, railway facilities and accommodation for the workers. The company expanded, and its armaments sector alone accounted for a large part of Germany's production in the First and Second World Wars. Forced labour was used here, from Humboldtstraße, a sub-camp of the Buchenwald concentration camp. The Kruppwerke was targeted during Allied air raids during World War II, and much of the site was destroyed as part of war reparations.

As new development plans have emerged in recent years, archaeological investigations have also been carried out (by the Stadtarchäologie Essen). Conventional archaeological methods are not suitable in such extensive areas. The very large and oversized objects could not be excavated or even retrieved in a 'classical' way. The aim was to document the remains as much as possible, especially with photographs. Remains of the 19th and 20th centuries, such as the Krupp parent house, the old main administration building, the so-called Hauptcomptoir of 1874, and the Probierhaus H (founded in 1871), in which the Siemens-Martin process for improved steel production was developed, have been revealed. Two cast-iron fluted columns were unearthed in the debris of the old administrative building, measuring almost 5 m long (see Fig. 12.8). Additional columns were found in the basement. The use of pillars to decorate important entrances and interior areas in the 19th century was common. The pillars in Krupp's administration building were probably installed around 1880, but they were subsequently walled up, suggesting a change in architectural style, as is seen also in contemporary buildings. Interestingly, the cast-iron columns themselves were not recycled.

Small workshops can also be considered in this vein. There have been very few close studies of old handicrafts, including workshops with traditional crafting tools as well as techniques. Before the last of those workshops is abandoned and evidence no longer exists, archaeologists should document such small enterprises. Only small potteries have been investigated so far. One future goal for contemporary archaeology should be to broaden this field of research.

GARBAGE AND WASTE

The first archaeological projects to consider contemporary rubbish dumps have been carried out in the United

Fig. 12.8. Cast-iron columns from the old administrative building of the Krupp cast-steel factory in Essen (© Detlef Hopp).

Fig. 12.9. My bin (© Claudia Theune).

States. Waste is the material for which we have no further use or which we want to get rid of. Every day, garbage accumulates, whether it is the paper of unfinished and revised manuscripts, newspapers from the previous day, food packages made of different materials, food scraps, or defective or no longer usable devices of all kinds. This list could be endlessly extended and a look in our own rubbish bins records the daily quantity of garbage (see Fig. 12.9). An analysis of this disposal behaviour and the garbage itself provides a wide range of information about us and our lifestyles.

Rubbish dumps have been investigated (University of Arizona) in the so-called Tucson Garbage Project since 1973. The study was accompanied by public surveys to compare self-assessment with the results of the waste analysis. Specific questions concerned, for example, alcohol consumption, which was generally heavily underestimated, as expected. Other topics covered the handling of hazardous waste and dangerous substances, and the different local approaches to the disposal of waste in different districts or cities. The results reveal insights into the purchasing and processing of fresh food with less packaging, compared to fast food or ready-made meals, which produce significantly more waste, and larger amounts of leftover food. In the 1970s, paper accounted for up to 50% of domestic waste. Publication of these results and the general attention the project attracted led to a change in behaviour and ultimately to waste separation and recycling. Today, it has become normal for many of us to collect paper separately and reuse it as raw material for new types of paper.

FURTHER RESEARCH QUESTIONS AND CONCLUSION

An imminent topic for contemporary archaeologists in this context could be plastic. It is one of the main materials of today's world. Questions about production methods, the sites of the factories, and the route of the products to the consumers, the use and consumption in industry and in private households are central. Although plastic is recycled and reused, the problem of plastic waste is currently central to the world. It is not only an object that is recovered from our bins. Plastic has a global dimension, as the waste from the Western World is often brought to Africa without caring for the environment there. More and more waste, especially plastic waste, is dumped in the world's oceans. The animal world suffers from it; plastic particles are also found in food. There are many points for contemporary archaeologists to study.

Projects focusing on waste as a category of archaeology have been increasing in recent years. As in the projects in the United States, the study of rubbish dumps and domestic refuse from village and city dwellers can reveal issues associated with social differences and the affordability of different products.

Contemporary archaeology raises relevant and timely social questions. In principle, it is not only about documenting and uncovering abandoned structures; instead specific questions can highlight characteristics of and effects on our present society. For example, the Garbage Project has been able to provide information on consumer behaviour and sustainability. Studies of everyday objects, such as the Van Project or the products from an Icelandic fishing village, focus on production and exchange on a small scale or mass production in the context of globalisation, a field that has been called 'Ikea archaeology' in recent times. The projects in different settlements show the changes in those settlements up to the present time; they reveal local and regional characteristics as well as social differences, distinctions between private and public areas; they show different social groups, including migrants. For some time, the living conditions of different groups have been examined in the United States according to their origin, *e.g.* the African-Americans or the Native Americans. More recently, Chinese immigrants and their lifestyle are coming under the spotlight. Popular culture and leisure are also key topics of research. The questions are manifold and interesting and valuable themes for archaeological study.

Chapter 13

ARCHAEOLOGY AND COMMEMORATION

INTRODUCTION

Commemoration in the first place is an intimate personal sentiment that affects each of us as an individual. We remember the good episodes and times of our lives but also the less pleasant ones. Episodes that we experience with family, friends or colleagues are committed to our memories and remembered for a long time regardless of how trivial they were. Memories can be affected by external influences and they are also likely to fade, or even to sink into oblivion altogether. Memory and forgetfulness lie very close together but conversations, items and pictures have the power to evoke the memories and bring them to the forefront again. Our memories are often tied to specific places and can be triggered by a picture of that place.

Major occurrences, which affect the wider public, be they political or social events, triumphs or defeats, attacks by terrorists or natural disasters, are reported via the worldwide web, radio stations, television, newspapers or other media. Normally we have no first-hand experience of such events, but the detailed information on the place and the incident provided by the media keep us involved. The reports of events inscribe themselves into the memory of countless people and become a part of the collective memory, linking the place to the events, and creating a site to commemorate the incident. The day that the Berlin Wall fell (9th November 1989), for instance, or the attacks on the Twin Towers, NYC of 11th September 2001 (9/11) remain exceptional in this regard and are etched into the memories of many millions of people around the world (see Fig. 13.1). Our awareness of the most significant events of both world wars is being constantly renewed through the same media channels, and this prevents the memory of the wars from fading.

Numerous records and episodes from past eras are meaningful because of a specific focus on tradition and the continuation of traditions. These events and traditions become part of a collective memory. Some of them have become national holidays. It should also be emphasised that a historical memory can be consciously (re-)constructed by us and suitable historical places of remembrance are chosen and charged with a corresponding meaning. They can be public and private, address different groups and often address the phenomenon of identity. The archaeological and cultural heritage plays an important role.

In some parts of Europe prehistoric sites of the Iron Age period can be seen as testimonies of a far older Celtic tradition. In 1971, the Shah of Persia used the fact that the royal capital of Persepolis was founded by Darius I 2,500 years earlier as a substantial enough reason to

Fig. 13.1. Flowers as a sign of individual commemoration at Ground Zero, New York, USA (© Claudia Theune).

Fig. 13.2. An eternal candle as a sign of individual com–memoration at the Loibl-Nord/Loibl-North memorial, Austria (© Claudia Theune).

legitimate his claim to power. Roman and late Roman sites are often treated as the cradles of Western culture regardless of the fact that the trajectories of development from the Classical Age are not always sufficiently clear and were often at best discontinuous. Medieval- and early-modern-period sites often become the places where history and national history come together and still incite fascination. Such sites exist in each nation. The burial mounds of Jellinge in Denmark, the royal site and earthworks on the Hill of Tara in Ireland, Thingvellir in Iceland, or the Nidarosdom in Trondheim (Norway) are examples of such places, although in each case close study will reveal the elements of discontinuity that challenge such attributions. Aachen Cathedral (Germany) will forever be the iconic coronation site of the medieval kings of the Holy Roman Empire. All Saints' Church (Castle Church) in Wittenberg (Germany) is where Martin Luther attached his Ninety-five Theses to the cathedral door and began the Reformation. The German cities of Münster and Osnabrück staged the treaty of the Peace of Westphalia, 1648. This ended the destruction of the Thirty Years' War that had devastated Middle Europe from 1618 to 1648. It marked a decisive turning point away from the religious wars sparked by the Reformation and Counter-Reformation. In the same fashion, Waterloo, the battlefield south of Brussels (Belgium) is forever associated with the events that saw the last and final defeat of Napoleon I in June 1815, in the epic battle against the combined forces commanded by Irish-born British General Wellington and Prussian Generalfeldmarschall (Field Marshal) Blücher.

PLACES OF REMEMBRANCE

It appears to be a constant feature that remembrance and commemoration are tied to a specific place. Such sites are unalterable and physically present, and offer a place for remembrance. In the context of the terrorist attacks of 9/11, the obvious site was immediately apparent, namely the site of the Twin Towers, now known as Ground Zero, at the southern tip of Manhattan, New York City. In the case of the Berlin Wall the locus is more difficult to pinpoint as it reached over 160 km in length. In addition to the Bernauer Straße memorial, there are several smaller sites that have become representative for the commemoration of all the victims of the Greater Berlin area (see Chapter 8). This is not the role of the Brandenburg Gate – that site is used for the ceremonies to do with the reunification of Germany and not for the remembrance of a darker history.

Destruction of heritage

The meaning of important sites of national and transnational history is even more pronounced in situations involving violent conflict or full-scale wars that target cultural heritage. Large-scale destruction of places of major importance has occurred repeatedly in the course of our violent past, and is not a feature peculiar to the modern world. While sites may be destroyed accidentally in the course of a battle, many other sites are directly targeted and their destruction is part of politically-motivated actions aimed at the redefinition of a nation's history by destroying and eliminating the vestiges of previous societies that held or hold contrary views. Such destruction and damage, theft and plunder is banned by the Hague Convention for the Protection of Cultural Property in the Event of Armed Conflict, signed in 1954. However, this convention is often contravened.

Pol Pot and the Khmer Rouge attacked Buddhist monasteries, Christian churches and Islamic mosques and their holy scrolls in Cambodia in the 1970s. The Yugoslav Wars of the 1990s destroyed many churches and mosques. The 16th-century bridge at Mostar (Bosnia-Herzegovina) was an icon and symbol that connected Christian and Muslim areas. A striking symbol of unity and connectedness, it was destroyed by a targeted strike during the Bosnian War in 1993. The large Buddha statues at Bamiyan were destroyed in 2001. Terrorists have also vandalised and ransacked the famous ancient sites at Aleppo and Palmyra in Syria and Nimrud and Hatra in Iraq, not to mention the intentional destruction of ancient statues that were part of the treasures of the Iraqi museums. Recently, there have been the Taliban incidents in Afghanistan where an allegedly Islamic movement has been consciously destroying the cultural histories of the region. Such a list could be endless. The targets are usually World Cultural Heritage sites and places that have a distinctive meaning with regard to the identity and self-image of a certain group, country or nation. Such violent crimes at cultural heritage sites are also acts of psychological warfare, aimed at undermining a national identity. The looting and trafficking of valuable cultural objects is an aspect of these activities and is known to play a major role in financing such wars.

The destroyed Buddha statues in the Bamiyan Valley (Afghanistan) (© UNESCO, Alessandro Balsamo, CC BY-SA 3.0 IGO, whc.unesco.org).

Where even more extensive sites are concerned, such as the 10,000 km long Iron Curtain, the task of focusing the commemoration at a certain place becomes even more difficult. Nevertheless, every country that shared a border with the Iron Curtain has established National Memorials. Without any doubt, all the camps are also historical sites, sites of remembrance (see Fig. 13.2). With cemeteries, the situation is very similar, be they the large war cemeteries on the battlefields of World War I with their endless seas of white crosses in Belgium and across northern France, or the single graves, where local people buried individual soldiers (see Chapters 4 and 9).

It is often presumed that sites of remembrance remain authentic even after several decades have passed and the places have been transformed. Such discussions are commonly associated with former concentration camps. Present-day memorial sites with only a few remaining buildings and large tidy open areas in between have little in common with what the same camp actually looked like some 70 years ago. While the camps were in operation, they held thousands of prisoners, crammed together and struggling to survive in inhumane conditions. The overpopulated barracks stood closely together and vital goods were in permanently short supply. There was no hope of escaping the omnipresent threats of repression, terror and death. It is a challenge to show this narrative today. In many instances, the darkest chapters have been whitewashed or even erased. This is where archaeologists have a role in making them visible again. Present-day visitors are driven by a desire to learn more about concentration camps and fascist terror. The tasks of the memorial sites have changed. While the survivors and the relatives of the victims predominated among visitors to the memorials in the first decades after the war, young people and many tourists from all over the world today want to experience this part of history. Sometimes they behave like tourists, in ways that deviate from the expectations of the first or second generation of victims.

The sites themselves, although only some areas of the former internment camps are part of the memorials, have become museums and centres for civic and historic education where younger people and tourists can learn about National Socialist terror and the importance of maintaining and upholding fundamental democratic principles. They are transnational memorials for the victims of the Holocaust and the National Socialist dictatorship. The remains clearly offer a more direct approach than any other media could ever hope to achieve precisely because the sites are literally saturated with the essence of their cruel past. Nevertheless, the memorials cannot be described as authentic places. Our perception cannot truly relate to the conditions the prisoners experienced. The decisive distinction between former detention camps and a present-day memorial is that the gates are open today and no threats await. Nothing stops us from leaving and nothing restricts our freedom. Nevertheless, every visitor should engage with these former places of suffering and remember the victims; they are undoubtedly places of remembrance. Such a commemoration can also be seen as part of the process of coming to terms with the past.

Many of these commemoration sites are well known and remain so thanks to continued media attention. There are also places where public awareness is reduced, which is often true for the areas outside the fences of the internment camps, like work sites. Such places come to attention because of single and relatively local incidents. Several countries now regularly identify the homes of National Socialist victims by placing inset markers in the adjacent footpaths. The markers, so-called 'Stolpersteine' (stumbling stones), are inscribed with the biographical data of the individual victims. The stones are highly visible and are located in public places, purposefully intended to inspire commemoration.

COMMEMORATION THROUGH OBJECTS

Not every commemorative experience is located at the place of the historical event, as French historian Pierre Nora points out ('Lieux de mémoire'). Relevant events without direct ties to a fixed location are also remembered. Objects of collective commemoration that are put on display in carefully selected places such as museums, for instance, are also likely to gain that status. This is because the viewer feels a connection with the objects and/or the person/s being remembered. The blood-soaked clothes displayed in an exhibition in Derry (Northern Ireland) commemorate the 13 victims who died on Bloody Sunday (30th January 1972, see Fig. 13.3). The incident took place during a peaceful demonstration against internment, and the killings incited the escalation of violence in Ireland that became The Troubles. The display of this material makes the museum itself the focal point of commemoration (see Chapters 5 and 9).

COMMEMORATION, IDENTITY AND CONTESTED MEMORIES

Initiating and promoting cultural memories of certain moments and places in history is a consciously set

Fig. 13.3. Jacket from Jim Wray with marked bullet hole (old exhibition at Museum Free Derry, Northern Ireland, United Kingdom (© Elizabeth Crooke).

and controlled process, which also says a lot about those who direct such processes. Specific narratives are considered valuable by the societies, politicians or goverments to become places of remembrance. Places of remembrance can therefore also be recalled at will. The continued public commemoration when paired with a strategically concentrated narrative is furthering that process. Events not integrated into the narrative, however, are not being conveyed and are likely to fade into oblivion. Sites of shared remembrance can help to forge confidence and identity if their historical meaning within a region or nation is substantial enough. It is rarely achieved through the spread of detailed knowledge, however, as the conveyance usually favours a more simplified citation of events or is actually creating myths. It is also the case that the sensitivity of sites change over time, so that the public association and significance of some sites can grow over time, while others can dissipate. The constructed

past allows individuals or larger groups to claim a historically justified position.

The official narrative that is passed down to the public is centrally important in this, but it does not require or receive the support of all segments of society. Contrasting views and perceptions may not be given much space or even tolerated. The negotiations of meaning of places of remembrance is a subject of disputes. In particular at places of protest, contested perceptions and memories are emphasized by different groups. In many respects, it may be argued that Germany is the single country that has grappled with this issue and has created the most 'honest' statement of the horrors effected by its wartime government and society. Other countries and other contexts where the perpetrators of injustices remain in or close to power have had less success. The negotiations regarding the historical meaning of sites can be very arduous processes. Places of protest in particular are often met with contested perceptions and memories by the stakeholders. Individual perception emphasizes one perspective over another. The annual parades held mostly in Northern Ireland to commemorate the Battle of the Boyne in 1690 when King William of Orange defeated the Catholic King James, for instance, are organised principally by the Protestant Orange Order, and can still ignite riots today. The Battle of Waterloo – 200 years after the actual event – is still an emotive moment for the French, in contrast to the celebratory tone of the victors. At Greenham Common (England), although a memorial was eventually established to honour the protests against nuclear weapons, it was a long struggle to get the English government to recognize this and the women remained in their camps until an agreement was reached to acknowledge the place as a memorial and to create a documentation centre (see Chapter 7).

The difficulties that can occur should the instigators of protests challenge the official narrative on history are further illustrated by the events at the site of nuclear testing in the USA. The Nevada Test Site Guide focuses largely on the achievements of nuclear testing and the invention of nuclear weapons, while mention of the protests, and the reasons for such protests, is marginalised and pushed to the background. Protest and resistance should be addressed by a critical civil society.

Such persistent enquiry into the past has recently exposed the case of the St Mary's Mother and Baby Home,

in Tuam (Co. Galway, Ireland). It is symptomatic of a wider issue that is not particular to Ireland and is a truly dark shadow on post-war Western society in general. At St Mary's, women who found themselves pregnant were rejected and essentially ostracised by 'polite society'. Infant mortality at the time was high, but it is the conditions under which these young women were placed, and the absence of humility and respect for the infants who died that makes the issue so hard to accept or even believe. Hundreds of dead infants were disposed of before the house closed in 1961, many placed in an obsolete septic tank. The discoveries are only now coming to light, but already the names of all 796 victims are published and the first markers are being installed on the site of the atrocities (see Fig. 13.4). It allows a first commemoration, but there are far too many details still looming in the dark that will require further investigations.

The voices of the opposition, of the lost and the disappeared cannot be allowed to become diffused and forgotten by denial, discrimination, injustice and terror. To stand against these atrocities and to use these as lessons to ensure that such things must not be repeated is critically important. The need for commemoration is key in this.

Archaeology has a complex relationship with memorials, and contemporary archaeology particularly so because it focuses on the period of the last 100 years – on this period of living memory that encompasses the 20th and 21st centuries and the wartime horrors

that unfortunately distinguish the period. The darker episodes of our shared past cannot be ignored and should be approached from a profound historical perspective where archaeologists can make significant contributions. The Second World War was not forgotten, but the many concentration camps, Gestapo barracks or the former Berlin 'Reichssicherheitshauptamt' (RSHA/ Reich Security Head Office), which is a part of the present-day documentation centre 'Topographie des Terrors' (see Chapter 6), were removed from the cultural memory for decades. Declared as 'bad places', 'traumatic sites', or involuntary memorials, they remained tabooed and shunned. However, the discussions of the 1980s that demanded a reconciliation of history and a conscious remembrance with particular regard to the victims of the National Socialist terror drew public attention back to them. It cannot be ignored either, that such places of trauma have another, profound moral component.

Excavations are exposing crime scenes of the past. Through a careful analysis of the remains, individuals and their actions are put in context, both in terms of their personal environment, and in terms of the greater historical background. The fate of the victims is the most consuming subject of such investigations, and while the two world wars and the ensuing Cold War attract particular attention, the same applies to places of protest and resistance.

The roll-call at former National Socialist concentration camps is often chosen as a reference point for the remembrance. At the site of the former concentration camp

Fig. 13.5. Sarcophagus at the roll-call in Mauthausen (© Lucignolobrescia).

Mauthausen (Austria), the pre-planning for a memorial began as early as 1947. It became the main objective of the victims' associations, in particular the political detainees, who had a big say in the project. The aim was to focus on the roll-call and the surrounding SS buildings (laundry, kitchen, killing areas, detention cells and sick bay area), with the prisoner barracks opposite. This was to be the central place of mourning and commemoration. The other barracks were explicitly not considered worth retaining. Consequently, they were dismantled to be reused for other purposes. The roll-call was considered to have highly symbolic significance with respect to the victims' suffering. A sarcophagus was installed in the centre of the place (see Fig. 13.5) bearing the Latin inscription 'Mortuorum sorte discant viventes' (From the fate of the dead, the living are to learn). In some memorials the gate is the critical point for commemoration, being places where the infamous inscriptions, such as 'Arbeit macht frei' ('Work liberates') or 'Jedem das Seine ' ('To each his own') were positioned.

There are examples of other concentration camps where the former gas chambers or crematoria are considered a better-suited locale to focus the mourning and commemoration. This is frequently the case in Poland, for instance, a nation that undoubtedly suffered more than others under National Socialist rule. The existence of the extermination camps has an emphasised meaning there and they are mainly perceived of as places of defeat, loss and exodus. At the end of the war, though, those sites above others became iconic for the liberation from National Socialist dictatorship. It was a major change in paradigm that altered the view from one of oppression and defeat to one of resistance and perseverance. This became formative in creating identity and a trigger to re-evaluation. Here, as in other places, excavations created

Fig. 13.6. Wall with first names of the victims at the Bełżec memorial (© Claudia Theune).

and revealed findings that provided reference points for mourning and commemoration (see Chapter 6).

In some former concentration camps, archaeological surveys and excavations were needed to locate the roll-calls, and their extended forecourt areas were often included in both the archaeological prospection and in the design plans for commemoration. So-called 'time windows' become a means to put the excavated remains on display and are often complemented by further visuals.

The exposure of visual evidence of the National Socialist reign has always been one of the key motives for archaeologists in instigating acknowledgement and facilitating remembrance. From the moment that those remains return to light after decades of denial and oblivion they become tangible again. The additional provision of information about each site yields deeper insight. The commemoration of the victims is coming to the fore. In the past, visitors were mainly looking at anonymous numbers; now the individual names of victims are presented, ranging from a few individuals to several thousand. It is a harsh reminder of the victims' fates, of life journeys brutally cut short before their time, of the absolute cruelty and baseless behaviour that the human psyche is capable. Sometimes the records are lacking and the names are incomplete, and this is common where the extermination camps are concerned. In Bełżec (present-day Poland), for instance, only the first names are provided, many of the surnames are unknown; they are displayed on two walls (see Fig. 13.6). It actually seems as if there is even more power inherent in first names since they are confronting the visitor on a much more personal level.

Battlefields are also places of remembrance. The *USS Arizona* was bombed during the Japanese surprise attack on Pearl Harbor and has become iconic for the American disaster that led to the United States' direct involvement in World War II. Despite the fact that the fleet at berth did not represent the active fighting force, which was at sea at the time, the attack was quickly transformed into the *cause célèbre* to justify America's

Fig. 13.7. On stelae on the site of the former Westerbork transit camp, reference is made to the transports to Auschwitz (© Claudia Theune).

engagement in the war effort. The wreck still lies at the bottom of Pearl Harbor. It has been surveyed, mapped and accurately drawn to scale. The resting place of the *Arizona* is a registered national memorial, dedicated on 30th May 1962 to all those who died during the attack, and a museum now straddles the ship's hull (see Fig. 13.8). The site represents the first defeat that the Americans suffered during World War II. At the same time, it is a proud reminder of how that defeat was overcome and eventually turned to the epic achievement of a victory won alongside their wartime allies. As victors, the Americans can tell this story. As archaeologists, we can study and understand the reality of the *Arizona* and appreciate how the experience of a defeat can be transformed into a positive, and forge a sense of national identity and unity.

Between September and December 1944, the Huertgen Forest south of Aachen (North Rhine-Westphalia, Germany) became a battleground when the advancing Allied Forces collided with the German Wehrmacht. In the aftermath of that battle, the whole area was left as a destroyed wasteland with countless covered military installations, corpses and items of war machinery in the woods. During the post-war era, many of the casualties were located and repatriated, while archaeologists surveyed several of the former positions. Although initially promoted by dedicated locals, the authorities eventually realised the importance of commemoration and reconciliation. Their focus stayed mostly on the war cemeteries, where countless war dead are buried. A few individuals are also remembered at the sites where they were killed. This is not atypical; in fact it is a common occurrence, and local people will often maintain a vigil and respect for the deceased they have buried, regardless of their nationality and affiliation.

When it comes to reunification, the Berlin Wall Memorial is iconic. Archaeological observations at the border strip along Bernauer Straße are an integral part of the memorial. In strong contrast, except for a double row of deeply inset cobblestones, no traces are visible today above ground level at Brandenburger Tor – the iconic gate that was blocked by the wall for 40 years. The Berlin Wall itself is clearly not a part of the memorial there. Instead, the Brandenburger Tor has become the symbol of German reunification and is a public stage for many events that have a positive meaning. During the Cold War era, the Brandenburger Tor was a place for repeated demonstrations against the Wall. U.S. president Ronald Reagan, for example, addressed the Russian president with a speech only two years before the Wall fell, on June 12th, 1987 in that same spot on the West side, challenging: 'Mr. Gorbachev, open this gate. Mr. Gorbachev tear down the wall'. The story of the wall is to be found 3 km away, in Berlin Wall Documentation Centre. It includes a stretch of the former border strip that extends 1.4 km in length, and it provides multiple insights into the border fortification system that was the Wall. A reconstruction of both the wall and the Hinterland wall, including the obstacles that lay within, can be visited in a separate area of the wall memorial. This place was designed to commemorate the fugitives who lost their lives along the Berlin Wall (see Chapter 8). The exhibition carefully addresses selected aspects of the history of the

Fig. 13.8. USS Arizona, Pearl Harbor, Hawaii, United States (© PH3(AW/SW) JAYME PASTORIC, USN, wiki commons).

German divide that are presented through a number of commemorative events along its length.

The prison on Robben Island where Nelson Mandela was detained for 27 years following his political opposition against the Apartheid regime in South Africa later became a memorial site. The same is true for several places closely linked to the Hutu genocide in Rwanda or the protest sites such as the camp of Greenham Common, where a commemoration centre was installed in one of the nine former camps. The list of memorial sites overshadowed by wars is endless.

Archaeology contributes to commemoration in a way that is educational; it emphasises tolerance and human rights, by revealing the atrocities of the National Socialists and other totalitarian regimes and dictatorships. Archaeology confronts the perpetrated crimes and demonstrates the importance of democratic values. Contemporary archaeology assumes social responsibility. Some commemoration centres at German and Polish concentration camps, for instance, are organising workshops for young people that last several weeks and offer profound and critical education about the strategies of National Socialist terror. The initiators are hoping for longer-lasting impacts than those that can be achieved by the usual short visits that include only a quick guided tour and a couple of presentations. At the same time, such field schools are supposed to compensate for the increasingly dwindling numbers of contemporary witnesses who could share stories of their dramatic experiences.

The range of other significant 20th-century cultural or historical sites incude former industrial plants that used to be the main employer of the region, for instance; the local sports venue that saw the great achievements and also devastating defeats; and certain buildings that influenced the style of either individual artists or whole groups of them. Archaeologists are tasked to actively help to preserve such sites and monuments, to assess their cultural value, and to document and witness of the structure's role in the past and its roles into the future. Such assessment must go beyond the usual categorization, and include considerations of what future generations might want to be preserved, what they would label a monument or a site of commemoration.

In this context, archaeologists have a special social responsibility to treat all the dead, all victims of terror, violence and dictatorship, all victims of wars with dignity. Only in this way can remembrance and also reconciliation be sought and achieved.

BIBLIOGRAPHY *

Chapter 1. The beginnings of contemporary archaeology during the short and the long 20th century

Andrén, Anders 1998
Between artefacts and texts. Historical archaeology in global perspective. New York, London.

Andrén, Anders 2009
Archaeology of a densley documented time. In: Scholkmann, Barbara *et al.*, Zwischen Tradition und Wandel. Archäologie des 15. und 16. Jahrhunderts. Tübinger Forschungen zur historischen Archäologie 3. Büchenbach, 3–6.

Appadurai, Arjun 2001
The Globalisation of archaeology and heritage: a discussion with Arjun Appadurai. In: Journal of Social Archaeology 1 (1), 35-49.

Arndt, Betty – Müller, Ulrich 2015
Klasse trotz Masse. Zu einer Archäologie des 19. – 21. Jahrhunderts. In: Blickpunkt Archäologie 2015 (3), 177-183.

Baeriswyl, Armand 2000
Wo ist die Höhe Null? Über die angebliche Grenze zwischen Bauforschung und Bodenarchäologie. In: Schumann, Dirk (ed.), Bauforschung und Archäologie, Stadt und Siedlungsentwicklung im Spiegel der Baustrukturen. Berlin, 21–31.

Bernbeck, Reinhard 2017
Materielle Spuren des Nationalsozialistischen Terrors. Zu einer Archäologie der Zeitgeschichte. Bielefeld.

Bernbeck, Reinhard – Pollock, Susan 2013
'Archäologie der Nazi-Zeit' Diskussionen und Themen. In: Historische Archäologie – Online-Zeitschrift. [www.histarch.uni-kiel.de/2013_Bernbeck_Pollock_high.pdf], accessed December 2017.

Buchli, Victor 2000
An archaeology of socialism. London.

Buchli, Viktor – Lucas, Gavin (eds.) 2001
Archaeologies of the contemporary past. London.

Buchli, Viktor – Lucas, Gavin
The absent present. In: Buchli, Viktor – Lucas, Gavin (eds.), Archaeologies of the contemporary past. London, New York, 3-18.

Burström, Mats 2008.
Looking into the recent past. Extending and exploring the field of archaeology. In: Current Swedish Archaeology 15-16, 21-36.

*Several articles, edited books and monographs were important for several chapters. They will be quoted for each relevant chapter.

Burström, Mats – Gustafsson, Anders – Karlsson, Håkan 2006
The air torpedo of Bäckebo. Local incident and world history. In: Current Swedish Archaeology 14, 7-24.

Council of Europe 1992
European convention on the protection of the archaeological heritage [Europäisches Übereinkommen zum Schutz des archäologischen Erbes]. SEV.Nr. 143. Valetta. [www.coe.int/en/web/conventions/full-list/-/conventions/treaty/143], accessed October 2017.

Dixon, James 2011
Is the present day post-medieval? In: Post-Medieval Archaeology 45 (2), 313–322.

González-Ruibal, Alfredo 2008
Time to destroy. An archaeology of supermodernity. In: Current Archaeology 49 (2), 247-279.

González-Ruibal, Alfredo 2013
Reclaiming archaeology: beyond the tropes of modernity. London.

González-Ruibal, Alfredo 2014
Archaeology of the contemporary past. In: Smith, Claire (ed.), Encyclopaedia of global archaeology. New York, 1683-1694.

González-Ruibal, Alfredo 2016
Archaeology and the time of modernity. In: Historical Archaeology 50 (3), 144-164.

González-Ruibal, Alfredo 2016
Ethnoarchaeology or simply archaeology? In: World Archaeology 48 (5), 687-692.

Gould, Richard A. – Schiffer, Michael B. 1981
Modern material culture: The archaeology of us. New York.

Graves-Brown, Paul (ed.) 2000
Matter, materiality and modern culture. London 2000.

Graves-Brown, Paul – Harrison, Rodney – Piccini, Angela (eds.) 2013
The Oxford handbook of the contemporary world. Oxford.

Hansen, Todd A. 2016
The archaeology of the Cold War. Gainesville.

Harrison, Rodney 2011
Surface assemblages. Towards an archaeology in and of the present. In: Archaeological Dialogues 18 (2), 141-161.

Harrison, Roddney – Schofield, John 2010
After Modernity. Archaeological approaches to the contemporary past. Oxford.

Hobsbawm, Eric 1998
The age of extremes. The short 20th century, 1914-1991. London.

Hodder, Ian 2016
Studies in human-thing entanglement. Online-publication. [www.ian-hodder.com/books/studies-human-thing-entanglement], accessed December 2017.

Holtorf, Cornelius – Piccini, Angela (eds.) 2011
Contemporary archaeologies. Excavating now. Frankfurt/Main.

Jeute, Gerson H. 2015
Was kommt nach der Archäologie des 20. Jahrhunderts? Überlegungen und Beispiele zu einer Archäologie der Gegenwart. In: Mitteilungen der Deutschen Gesellschaft für Archäologie des Mittelalters und der Neuzeit 28, 29-36.

Kerscher, Hermann 2012
Neue Beobachtungen an bayerischen Denkmälern und Kulturlandschaften durch Prospektion und ALS-DGM-Daten. In: Archäologisches Jahr in Bayern, 179–182.

Klein, Ulrich 2015
Archäologische Untersuchungen an der Marburger Synagoge. In: Mitteilungen der Deutschen Gesellschaft für Archäologie des Mittelalters und der Neuzeit 28, 155–164.

Kunow, Jürgen 1996
Zu den Aufgaben und Zielen der Bodendenkmalpflege bei Objekten aus unserer jüngsten Vergangenheit. Fallbeispiele des 20. Jahrhunderts aus dem Land Brandenburg. In: Archäologisches Nachrichtenblatt 1, 315–326.

Lazzari, Marisa 2011
Tangible interventions: the lived landscapes of contemporary archaeology. In: Journal of Material Culture 16 (2), 171-191.

Little, Barbara J. 2007
Historical archaeology. Why the past matters. Walnut Creek.

Leone, Mark P. – Potter, Parker B. – Shakel, Paul A. 1987
Toward a critical archaeology. In: Current Anthropology 28 (3), 283-302.

Leone, Mark P. 2010
Critical historical archaeology. Walnut Creek.

Lyons, Claire L. – Papadopoulos John K. 2002
The Archaeology of colonialism. Los Angeles.

McGuire Randall, 2008
  Archaeology as political action. California series in
  public anthropology 17. Berkeley.

Mehler, Natascha (ed.) 2013
  Historical archaeology in Central Europe. Society
  for Historical Archaeology. Special publication
  number 10. Rockville.

Mehler, Natascha
  Die Archäologie des 19. und 20. Jahrhunderts zwischen
  Akzeptanz und Relevanz. In: Mitteilungen der
  Deutschen Gesellschaft für Archäologie des Mittelalters
  und der Neuzeit 28, 23-28.

Moshenska, Gabriel 2012
  The archaeology of the Second World War.
  Uncovering Britain's wartime heritage. Barnsley.

Moshenska, Gabriel 2013
  Conflict. In: Graves-Brown, Paul – Harrison, Rodney –
  Piccini, Angela (eds.), The archaeology of the
  contemporary world. Oxford, 351-363.

Mrozowski, Stephen A. – Wurst LouAnn 2014
  Preface: the future is now: common problems,
  common threads. In: International Journal of
  Historical Archaeology, special issue: Studying
  history backward: toward an archaeology of the
  future, 1-2.

Müller, Ulrich 2013
  Die Archäologie des Mittelalters und der Neuzeit
  im Gefüge der historischen Archäologie. In: Ridder,
  Klaus – Patzold, Steffen (eds.), Die Aktualität der
  Vormoderne. Berlin, 67–98.

Myers, Adrian
  Contemporary archaeology in transit: The artifacts
  of a 1991 van. International Journal of Historical
  Archaeology 15 (1), 138-161.

Neyland, Robert S. 2011
  Underwater archaeology of the world wars. In: Ford,
  Ben – Hamilton, Donny L. – Catsambis, Alexis (eds.),
  The Oxford handbook of maritime archaeology.
  Oxford, 708–733.

Olivier, Laurent 2013
  Time. In: Graves-Brown, Paul – Harrison, Rodney –
  Piccini, Angela (eds.), The archaeology of the
  contemporary world. Oxford, 167-177.

Orser, Charles E. 2009
  Twenty-first-century historical archaeology. In: Journal
  of archaeological research 18, 111-150.

Petrikovits, Harald von 1962
  Vorwort. In: Rheinisches Landesmuseum Bonn (ed.),
  Kirche und Burg in der Archäologie des Rheinlandes.
  Kunst und Altertum am Rhein. Führer Rheinisches
  Landesmuseum Bonn 8. Düsseldorf.

Rathje, William L. 1979
  Modern material-culture studies. In: Advances in
  archaeological method and theory 2, 1979, 1-37.

Schofield, John 2005
  Matériel culture: the archaeology of twentieth-
  century conflict. London.

Schofield, John 2005
  Combat archaeology. Material culture and modern
  conflict. London.

Schofield, John 2009
  Aftermath. Readings in the archaeology of recent
  conflict. New York.

Scholkmann, Barbara 2003
  Die Tyrannei der Schriftquellen? Überlegungen
  zum Verhältnis materieller und schriftlicher
  Überlieferung in der Mittelalterarchäologie. In: Heinz,
  Marlies – Eggert, Manfred K. H. – Veit, Ulrich (eds.),
  Zwischen Erklären und Verstehen? Beiträge zu den
  erkenntnistheoretischen Grundlagen archäologischer
  Interpretation. Tübinger Archäologische Taschenbücher
  2. Münster, 239-257.

Scholkmann, Barbara – Kenzler, Hauke – Schreg, Rainer
(eds.) 2009
  Archäologie des Mittelalters und der Neuzeit.
  Grundwissen. Darmstadt.

Schreg, Rainer 2007
  Archäologie der frühen Neuzeit. Der Beitrag der
  Archäologie angesichts zunehmender Schriftquellen.
  In: Mitteilungen der deutschen Gesellschaft für
  Archäologie des Mittelalters und der Neuzeit 18,
  9–20.

Schute, Ivar 2012
  Archäologie des 20. Jahrhunderts in den
  Niederlanden. In: Fundberichte aus Österreich 51,
  130–135.

Shanks, Michael – Tilley, Christopher 1992
  Re-constructing archaeology: Theory and practice.
  London.

Theune, Claudia 2010
  Historical archaeology in National Socialist
  concentration camps in Central Europe. In:

Historische Archäologie Online-Zeitschrift [www.histarch.uni-kiel.de/2010_Theune_low.pdf], accessed December 2017.

Theune, Claudia 2012
Zeitgeschichtliche Archäologie. Forschungen und Methoden. In: Fundberichte aus Österreich 51, 121–126.

Theune, Claudia 2013
Archaeological research in former concentration camps. In: Mehler, Natascha (ed.), Historical archaeology in Central Europe. Society for Historical Archaeology. Special Publication Number 10. Rockville, 241–260.

Theune, Claudia 2015
Bedeutung und Perspektiven einer Archäologie der Moderne. In: Mitteilungen der Deutschen Gesellschaft für Archäologie des Mittelalters und der Neuzeit 28, 11–22.

Theune, Claudia 2015
Grundlagen und Perspektiven einer Archäologie des 20. Jahrhunderts. In: Blickpunkt Archäologie 2015 (3), 164–176.

Theune, Claudia 2016
Archäologie an Tatorten des 20. Jahrhunderts. Zweite durchgesehene und erweiterte Auflage. Wissenschaftliche Buchgesellschaft: Darmstadt.

Theune, Claudia 2016
Zeitgeschichtliche Archäologie in ehemaligen Konzentrationslagern – Erinnerungsort, Denkmalpflege, Forschung. In: Kersting, Thomas – Theune, Claudia – Drieschner, Axel – Ley, Astrid – Luth, Thomas (eds.), NS-Lagerstandorte: Erforschen – bewahren – vermitteln. Petersberg, 7-16.

Vařeka, Pavel 2013
Archeologie 19. a 20. století. Přístupy – Metody – Témata. Plzen.

Vařeka, Pavel – Balý, Radek –Funk, Lukáš – Galusová, Lucie 2008
Archeologický výzkum vesnic středověkého původu na Tachovsku zaniklých po roce 1945 – Die archäologische Grabung der nach 1945 verschwundenen Dörfer mittelalterlichen Ursprungs in der Tachauer Gegend. In: Archaeologia Historica 33, 101–117.

Vařeka, Pavel – Vařeková, Zdeňka 2016
Contemporary cemeteries in the district of Tachov/Tachau (Western Bohemia) as an evidence of population and settlement discontinuity in the 2nd half of the 20th century. In: Tod und Gedenken in der Landschaft. Siedlungsforschung: Archäologie – Geschichte – Geographie 33, 225-244.

Voss, Barbara – Casella, Eleanor 2012
The archaeology of colonialism. Cambridge.

Wagner, Karin 2014
Archäologie der Neuzeit. Berlin: Ausflüge im Spree-Havel-Gebiet. In: Führer zu Archäologie, Geschichte und Kultur in Deutschland 58. Stuttgart, 79–85.

Chapter 2. Contemporary archaeology and ethics

González-Ruibal, Alfredo – Moshenska, Gabriel 2016
Ethics and archaeology of violence. New York, Heidelberg, Dordrecht, London.

Gonzáles-Ruibal, Alfredo – Ayán Vila, Xurxo – Caesar, Rachel 2015
Ethics, archaeology, and civil conflict: the case of Spain. In: González-Ruibal, Alfredo – Moshenska Gabriel (eds) Ethics and the archaeology of violence. Ethical archaeologies: the politics of social justice. New York, 113- 136.

Moshenska, Gabriel 2008
Ethics and ethical critique in the archaeology of modern conflict. In: Norwegian Archaeological Review 41(2), 159-175.

Nicholas, George – Hollowell, Julie 2007
Ethical challenges to a postcolonial archaeology: the legacy of scientific colonialism. In: Hamilakis, Yannis – Duke, Phillip (eds.), Archaeology and capitalism: from ethics to politics. Walnut Creek, 59-82.

Steele, Caroline 2008
Archaeology and the forensic investigation of recent mass graves. Ethical issues for a new practice of archaeology. In: Archaeologies 4 (3), 414-428.

Chapter 3. Sources and methodology

Amishai-Maisels, Ziva 1993
Depiction and interpretation: the influence of the Holocaust on the visual arts. Oxford.

Appadurai, Arjun (ed.) 1986
   The social life of things. Commodities in cultural perspective. Cambridge.

Attfield, Judy 2000
   Wild things. The material culture of everyday life. Oxford, New York.

Baberowski, Jörg 2005
   Der Sinn der Geschichte. Geschichtstheorien von Hegel bis Foucault. München.

Bachmann-Medick, Doris 2006
   Cultural turns. Neuorientierungen in der Kulturwissenschaft. Reinbek.

Beyer, Andreas (ed.) 1992
   Die Lesbarkeit der Kunst. Zur Geistes-Gegenwart der Ikonologie. Berlin.

Boehm, Gottfried 2007
   Wie Bilder Sinn erzeugen. Die Macht des Zeigens. Berlin.

Botz, Gerhard (ed.) 2007
   Schweigen und Reden einer Generation. Erinnerungsgespräche mit Opfern, Tätern und Mitläufern des Nationalsozialismus. Wien.

Bräunlein, Peter 2012
   Material turn. In: Georg-August-Universität Göttingen (Hg.): Dinge des Wissens. Die Sammlungen, Museen und Gärten der Universität Göttingen. Göttingen, 30-44.

Brock, Thomas – Homann, Arne 2011
   Schlachtfeldarchäologie. Auf den Spuren des Krieges. Archäologie in Deutschland, Sonderheft 2/2011. Stuttgart.

Burke, Peter 2003
   Augenzeugenschaft. Bilder als historische Quelle. Berlin.

Büttner, Frank – Gottdang, Andrea 2006
   Einführung in die Ikonographie. Wege zur Deutung von Bildinhalten. München.

Cochran, Matthew – Beaudry, Mary 2006
   Material culture studies and historical archaeology. In: Hicks, Dan – Beaudry, Mary (eds.), The Cambridge companion to historical archaeology. Cambridge, 191–204.

Deetz, James 1977
   In small things forgotten. The archaeology of early American life. New York.

Dejnega, Melanie – Theune, Claudia in press
   Das Sanitätslager in Wort, Bild und Objekt. Warum die Zusammenarbeit von HistorikerInnen und ArchäologInnen Sinn macht. In: Prenninger, Alexander et al. (eds.), Leben und Überleben in Mauthausen. Mauthausen überleben und erinnern 2.

Endlich, Stefanie 2005
   Kunst im Konzentrationslager. In: Benz, Wolfgang – Distel, Barbara (eds.), Der Ort des Terrors. Geschichte der nationalsozialistischen Konzentrationslager, Bd. 1: Die Organisation des Terrors. München, 274-295.

Fewster, Kathryn 2013
   The relationship between ethnoarchaeology and archaeologies of the contemporary past: a historical investigation. In: Graves-Brown, Paul – Harrison, Rodney – Piccini, Angela (eds.), The archaeology of the contemporary world. Oxford, 27-39.

Fowles, Severin – Heupel, Kaet 2013
   Absence. In: Graves-Brown, Paul – Harrison, Rodney – Piccini, Angela (eds.), The archaeology of the contemporary world. Oxford, 178-191.

Frankl, Viktor 1977
   …trotzdem Ja zum Leben sagen. München.

Goetz, Hans-Werner 2006
   Proseminar Geschichte. Mittelalter. Stuttgart.

Hahn, Peter 2005
   Materielle Kultur. Eine Einführung. Berlin.

Hamburger Institut für Sozialforschung (ed.) 2002
   Verbrechen der Wehrmacht. Dimensionen des Vernichtungskrieges 1941-1944. Ausstellungskatalog Hamburg.

Hamling, Tara – Richardson, Catherine (eds.) 2010
   Everyday objects: Medieval and early modern material culture and its meanings. Farnham.

Hausmair, Barbara 2016
   Jenseits des 'Sichtbarmachens'. Überlegungen zur Relevanz materieller Kultur für die Erforschung nationalsozialistischer Lager am Beispiel Mauthausen. In: Kersting, Thomas – Theune, Claudia – Drieschner, Axel – Ley, Astrid – Luth, Thomas (eds.), NS-Lagerstandorte: Erforschen – bewahren – vermitteln. Petersberg, 31-46.

Heese, Thorsten
   Vergangenheit 'begreifen'. Die gegenständliche Quelle im Geschichtsunterricht. Schwalbach/Taunus.

Heinz, Marlies – Eggert ,Manfred K. H. – Veit, Ulrich (eds.)
2003
    Zwischen Erklären und Verstehen? Beiträge zu den
    erkenntnistheoretischen Grundlagen archäologischer
    Interpretation. Tübinger Archäologische
    Taschenbücher 2. Münster.

Heitzmann, Birte 2010
    Archäologische Ausgrabungen in der KZ Gedenkstätte
    Neuengamme. In: Hammaburg 15, 191–205.

Hicks, Dan – Beaudry, Mary (eds.) 2010
    The Oxford handbook of material culture studies. Oxford.

Hoffmann, Detlef 1998
    Das Gedächtnis der Dinge. KZ-Relikte und KZ-
    Denkmäler 1945–1995. Frankfurt a. M.

Jäger, Jens 2009
    Fotografie und Geschichte. Historische Einführungen
    7. Frankfurt a. M., New York.

Juwigm, Carsten – Kost, Catrin (eds.) 2010
    Bilder in der Archäologie – eine Archäologie der
    Bilder? Tübinger Archäologische Taschenbücher 8.
    Münster.

König, Gudrun (ed.) 2005
    Alltagsdinge. Erkundungen einer materiellen Kultur.
    Tübinger kulturwissenschaftliche Gespräche 1.
    Tübingen.

Kranebitter, Andreas 2012
    Zahlen als Zeugen. Quantitative Analysen zur
    'Häftlingsgesellschaft' des KZ Mauthausen-Gusen.
    Diplomarbeit Universität Wien [http://othes.univie.
    ac.at/19397/1/2012-03-28_0009519.pdf], accessed
    December 2017.

Latour, Bruno 2005
    Reassembling the Social. Oxford.

Marotzki, Winfried – Niesyto, Horst (eds.) 2006
    Bildinterpretation und Bildverstehen. Methodische
    Ansätze aus sozialwissenschaftlicher, kunst- und
    medienpädagogischer Perspektive. Wiesbaden.

Maurer, Michael (ed.) 2002
    Aufriß der Historischen Wissenschaften. Band 4:
    Quellen. Ditzingen.

Mauthausen Memorial 2007
    Kunst und Kultur im Konzentrationslager
    Mauthausen 1938-1945. Wien.

Mehler, Natascha 2012
    Written sources in post-medieval archaeology and the
    art of asking the right questions. In: Post-Medieval
Studies 4: Written and iconographic sources in post-
medieval archaeology. Prague, 11-24.

Moreh-Rosenberg, Eliad – Smerling, Walter (eds.) 2016
    Kunst aus dem Holocaust. 100 Werke aus der
    Gedenkstätte Yad Vashem. Köln.

Myers, Fred R. (ed.) 2009
    The empire of things. Santa Fee.

Panofski, Erwin 1994
    Ikonographie und Ikonologie. In: Kaemmerling,
    Ekkehard (ed.), Bildende Kunst als Zeichensystem.
    Ikonographie und Ikonologie, Band 1 Theorien –
    Entwicklung – Probleme. Köln, 207–225.

Pollak, Michael 2016
    Die Grenzen des Sagbaren. Lebensgeschichte von
    KZ-Überlebenden als Augenzeugenberichte und als
    Identitätsarbeit. Wien.

Samida, Stefanie – Eggert, Manfred K.H. –Hahn, Hans
Peter 2015
    Handbuch Materielle Kultur. Stuttgart, Weimar.

Sieradzka, Agnieszka 2016
    Das Skizzenbuch von Auschwitz. Oświęcim.

Theune, Claudia 2011
    Das Gedächtnis der Dinge. In: Berger, Heinrich et
    al. (eds.), Politische Gewalt und Machtausübung im
    20. Jahrhundert. Zeitgeschichte, Zeitgeschehen und
    Kontroversen. Festschrift für Gerhard Botz. Wien,
    Köln, Weimar, 543–560.

Theune, Claudia 2015
    Archäologische Fundmassen und Massenfunden aus
    ehemaligen Konzentrationslagern. In: Hofer, Nikolaus (ed.),
    Massenfunde – Fundmassen. Strategien und Perspektiven
    im Umgang mit Massenfundkomplexen. Fundberichte aus
    Österreich, Tagungsband 2. Wien, 37–42.

Veit, Ulrich et al. (eds.) 2003
    Spuren und Botschaften. Interpretationen materieller
    Kultur. Tübinger Archäologische Taschenbücher 4.
    Münster.

Wendland, Jörn 2008
    Bildgeschichten von Häftlingen der Konzentrations-
    und Vernichtungslager. Kontinuitäten und Wandel
    in Funktion, Ikonografie und Narration vor und nach
    1945. In: Heß, Christiane et al., Kontinuitäten und
    Brüche: neue Perspektiven auf die Geschichte der NS-
    Konzentrationslager. 15. Workshop zur Geschichte
    der Nationalsozialistischen Konzentrationslager 2008
    in Oranienburg und Fürstenberg. Berlin, 142–164.

Woodward, Ian 2007
Understanding material culture. New York.

Yaneva, Albena 2013
Actor-network-theory approaches to the archaeology of contemporary architecture. In: Graves-Brown, Paul – Harrison, Rodney – Piccini, Angela (eds.), The archaeology of the contemporary world. Oxford, 121-134.

Chapter 4. Sites and monuments of the two world wars

Banks, Iain 2014
Digging in the dark: the underground war on the Western Front in World War I. In: Journal of Conflict Archaeology 9 (3), 156-176.

Banks, Iain – Pollard, Tony 2014
Beyond recall: searching for the remains of a British Secret Weapon of World War I. In: Journal of Conflict Archaeology 9 (3), 119-155.

Bauer, Ute (ed.) 2010
Erinnerungsort Flakturm. Der ehemalige Leitturm im Wiener Arenbergpark. Wien.

Bulgrin, Lon E. 2005
The Tudela site: fire and steel over Saipan, 15 June 1944. In: Journal of Conflict Archaeology 1 (1), 1-18.

Burt, Richard et al. 2007
Pointe-du-Hoc Battlefield, Normandy, France. In: Scott, Douglas – Babits, Lawrence – Haecker, Charles (eds.), Fields of conflict– Battlefield archaeology from the Roman Empire to the Korean War. London, 383–397.

Church, Robert A. – Warren Daniel J. 2008
The 2004 deepwrecks project: analysis of World War II ear shipwrecks in the Gulf of Mexico. In: International Journal of Historical Archaeology 12, 82-102.

Daly, Lisa M. 2011
Survey of World War II aircraft crash sites in and around Gander, Newfoundland. In: Archaeological Review 9, 27–33.

Deal Michael – Daly, Lisa M. – Mathias, Cathy 2015
Actor-Network Theory and the practice of aviation archaeology. In: Journal of Conflict Archaeology 10/1, 3-28.

Desfossés, Yves – Jacques, Alain – Prilaux, Gilles 2008
L'Archéologie de la Grande Guerre. Rennes.

Dillon, Brian (ed.) 2011
Ruins. Cambridge.

Doyle, Peter – Barton Peter – Vandewalle, Johan 2005
Archaeology of a Great War dugout: Beecham Farm, Passchendaele, Belgium. In: Journal of Conflict Archaeology 1 (1), 45-66.

English Heritage 2013
The First World War, Conservation Bulletin 71/Winter 2013. [www.historicengland.org.uk/images-books/publications/conservation-bulletin-71], accessed May 2017.

Falch, Wolfgang 2013
Aviation archaeology in the Alps. In: Mehler, Natascha (ed.), Historical archaeology in Central Europe. Society for Historical Archaeology. Special publication number 10. Rockville, 325–335.

Faulkner, Neil – Saunders, Nicholas J. 2010
Fire on the desert: conflict archaeology and the Great Arab Revolt in Jordan, 1916–18. In: Antiquity 324, 514–527.

Fings, Karola – Möller Frank (eds.) 2008
Zukunftsprojekt Westwall. Wege zu einem verantwortungsbewussten Umgang mit den Überresten der NS-Anlage. Köln.

Freeman, Philip (ed.) 2001
Fields of conflict: progress and prospect in battlefield archaeology; proceedings of a conference held in the Department of Archaeology, University of Glasgow, April 2000. Oxford.

Hettlage, Bernd 2015
Denkort Bunker Valentin Bremen. Bremen.

Hollebeeke, Yannick van – Stichelbaut, Birger – Bourgeois, Jean 2014
From landscape of war to archaeological report: Ten years of professional World War I archaeology in Flanders (Belgium). In: European Journal of Archaeology Vol. 17 (4), 702-719.

Hoppe, Wiebke – Wegener, Wolfgang 2014
Stätten der Katastrophe. In: Archäologie in Deutschland 2014/1, 8–13.

Hoppe, Wiebke – Wegener, Wolfgang 2014
Archäologische Kriegsrelikte im Rheinland. Führer zu archäologischen Denkmälern im Rheinland Bd. 5. Essen.

Huber, Florian 2015
>   Innerhalb einer Stunde sank Boot ganz weg'- der Untergang des deutschen U-Bootes S.M. UC 71 vor Helgoland 1919. ('Within the hour boat sank completely' - the sinking of the German U-boat S.M. UC 71 near Helgoland 1919). In: Historische Archäologie, Online-Zeitschrift. [www.histarch. uni-kiel.de/2015_Huber_high.pdf], accessed December 2017.

Irlinger, Walter 2015
>   Dokumentation, Erfassung und öffentlichen Darstellung der KZ und KZ-Aussenlager in Bayern. In: Schädler-Saub, Ursula – Weyer, Angela, Geteilt vereint! Denkmalpflege in Mitteleuropa zur Zeit des Eisernen Vorhangs und heute. ICOMOS Journals oft he German National Committee LIX. Petersberg, 207-216.

Jaquemot, Stéphanie – Legendre, Jean-Pierre 2011
>   Vestiges de guerres en Lorraine. Le Patrimoine de conflits Mondiaux. Marly.

Kersting, Thomas 2015
>   Orte der Zeitgeschichte im Fokus der Landesarchäologie Brandenburg In: Blickpunkt Archäologie 2015 (3), 193-199.

Kirby, Magnus – Ross, Alasdair – Anderson, Sue 2013
>   The excavation of a World War II Army camp at Mortonhall, Edingburgh. In: Journal of Conflict Archaeology 8:2, 106-135.

Knecht, Rick, – Price, Neil – Lindsay, Gavin 2012.
>   WWII battlefield survey of Peleliu Island, Peleliu State, Republic of Palau. Archive report lodged with the bureau of arts and culture, Koror, Palau, and the US National Park Service, Guam.

Kok, Ruurd – Vos, Wouter K. (eds.) 2013
>   Archeologie van de tweede Wereldoorlog. Rapportage Archeologische Monumentenzorg 211. Amersfoort.

Konrad, Helmut – Hämmerle, Christa – Rauchensteiner, Manfried 2013
>   Der Erste Weltkrieg. Die großen Erschütterungen und der Keim des Neuen. Graz.

Korsgaard, Annika – Gibbs, Martin 2015
>   Shipwrecks as archaeological signatures of a maritime industrial frontier in the Solomon Islands, 1788–1942. In: International Journal Historical Archaeology 20, 105-126.

Landa, Carlos – Lara, Odlanyer Hernández de (eds.) 2014
>   Sobre campos de Batallas: Arqueología de conflictos Bélicos en América Latina. Buenos Aires.

Landolt, Michaël 2015
>   Der Kilianstollen. Eine deutsche Stollenanlage aus dem Ersten Weltkrieg bei Carspach (Elsass, F). In: Mitteilungen der Deutschen Gesellschaft für Archäologie des Mittelalters und der Neuzeit 28, 135–146.

Lanoy-Ratel, Philippe 2004
>   La bunker archéologie: principes et études de cas sur le littoral du Nord-pas-de-Calais (Bunker archaeology: principles and studies of samples on the Nord-Pas-de-Calais coast). In: Bulletin de l'Association de géographes français 81 (3), 405-417.

Legendre, Jean-Pierre 2006
>   Archaeology of World War 2: the Lancaster bomber of Fléville (Meurthe et Moselle, France). In: Buchli, Victor – Lucas, Gavin, Archaeologies of the contemporary past. London, 126–137.

Lowry, Bernard (ed.) 1999
>   20th century defence in Britain. An introductory guide. Practical Handbooks in Archaeology 12. Council for British archaeology. York.

Masters, Peter – Stichelbaut, Birger 2009
>   From the air to beneath the soil– revealing and mapping Great War trenches at Ploegsteert (Comines-Warneton), Belgium. In: Archaeological Prospection 19 (4), 279–285.

McCartney, Innes 2012
>   The armoured cruiser HMS Defence: a case-study in assessing the Royal Navy shipwrecks of the battle of Jutland (1916) as an archaeological resource. In: The International Journal of Nautical Archaeology 41 (1), 56–66.

McKinnon, Jennifer F. – Carrell, Toni L. (eds.) 2015
>   Underwater archaeology of a Pacific Battlefield. New York.

Meyer, Mathieu de – Pype, Pedro 2007
>   Scars of the Great War (Western Flanders, Belgium). In: Scott, Douglas – Babits, Lawrence – Haecker, Charles (eds.), Fields of conflict– battlefield archaeology from the Roman Empire to the Korean War. London, 359–382.

Moshenska, Gabriel 2012
>   The archaeology of the Second World War. Uncovering Britain's wartime heritage. Barnsley.

Myles, Franc
   The research and production pant, Parkgate, Dublin: archaeological investigations of a Word War II munition facility. In: Journal of Conflict Archaeology 6 (2), 73-96.

Natho, Heinrich 2012
   Bröckelnder Beton und rostender Stahl – Überreste des Zweiten Weltkrieges. In: Archäologie in Deutschland 2012/6, 60–61.

Neumayer, Heino 2005
   Archäologie des Grauens. Funde und Befunde des 2. Weltkrieges in Berlin. In: Der Bär von Berlin 54, 119–130.

Osborn, Mike 2008
   Pillboxes of Britain and Ireland. Stroud.

Page, Robin – Forbes, Neil – Perez, Guillermo 2009
   Europe´s Deadly Century. Perspectives on 20th-century conflict heritage. London.

Passmore, David G. – Harrison, Stephan 2008
   Landscapes of the battle of the Bulge: WW2 field fortifications in the Ardennes Forests of Belgium. In: Journal of Conflict Archaeology, 4 (1-2), 87-107.

Passmore, David G. – Harrison, Stephan – Capps Tunwell, David 2014
   Second World War conflict archaeology in the forests of north-west Europe. In: Antiquity 88, 1275-1290.

Petchey, Peter 2015
   Second World War Japanese defences on Watom Island, Papua New Guinea. In: Journal of Conflict Archaeology 10 (1), 29-51.

Pollard 2014
   Taking the hill: archaeological survey and excavation of German communication trenches on the summit of Mont St Quentin. In: Journal of Conflict Archaeology 9 (3), 177-197.

Pollard, Tony – Banks, Iain 2006
   Past Tense. Studies in the archaeology of conflict. Leiden.

Pollard, Tony – Banks, Iain 2007
   War and sacrifice. Studies in the archaeology of conflict. Leiden.

Pollard, Tony – Banks, Iain 2008
   Scorched earth. Studies in the archaeology of conflict. Leiden.

Price, Jillian – Howey, Meghan 2016
   Nation, college, wartime: archaeology at a WWI Student Army Training Corps Camp at New Hampshire. In: International Journal of Historical Archaeology 20, 289-317.

Price, Neil – Knecht, Rick 2012
   Peleliu 1944: the archaeology of a South Pacific D-Day. In: Journal of Conflict Archaeology 7, 5-48.

Price, Neil et al. 2013
   After the Typhoon: multicultural archaeologies of World War II on Peleliu, Palau, Micronesia. In: Journal of Conflict Archaeology 8:3, 193-248.

Rass, Christoph – Lohmeier, Jens 2011
   Transformations: Post-battle processes of the Hürtgenwald battlefield. In: Journal of Conflict Archaeology 6 (3), 179-199.

Robertshaw, Andrew – Kenyon, David 2008
   Digging the trenches: the archaeology of the Western Front. Barnsley.

Sagona , Antonio et.al. 2011
   The ANZAC [Arıburnu] Battlefield: New perspectives and methodologies in history and archaeology. In: Australian Historical Studies 42:3, 313-336.

Saunders, Nicholas 2002
   Excavating memories. Archaeology and the Great War 1914–2001. In: Antiquity 76, 101–108.

Saunders, Nicholas (ed.) 2004
   Matters of conflict. Material culture, memory and the First World War. Oxford.

Saunders, Nicholas 2007
   Killing time. Archaeology and the First World War. Stroud.

Schofield, John 2005
   Combat archaeology. Material culture and modern conflict. London.

Schofield, John – Beck, Colleen M. – Johnson, William Gray (eds.) 2002
   Matériel culture. The archaeology of 20th century conflict. London.

Schofield, John – Klausmeier, Axel – Purbrick, Louise (eds.) 2006
   Re-mapping the field: New approaches in conflict Archaeology. Westkreuz: Berlin.

Scott, Graham – Gane, Toby 2015
   Aviation archaeology offshore: the recovery of a rare

Ju88 Aircraft Wreck during work for the New London Gateway Port. In: Journal of Conflict Archaeology 10 (2), 75-95.

Spennemann, Dirk 2013
Hindcasting the Japanese Military Base on Midway Atoll (Central Pacific). In: Journal of Conflict Archaeology 8 (2), 136-159.

Stadler, Harald 2007
Zeithistorische Archäologie. Osttirol und seine Nachbarn seit 1918. In: Kofler, Martin (ed.), Spurensuche 3. Teil III. Randlage im Wandel; Osttirol 1850 bis zur Gegenwart. Innsbruck, 30–37.

Stadler, Harald 2008
Die Kosaken im Ersten und Zweiten Weltkrieg. Innsbruck.

Stadler, Harald 2011
Der Beitrag der Archäologie zur Geschichte des Ersten Weltkrieges in Westösterreich. In: Nicolis, Franco (ed.), Archeologia della Grande Guerra – Archaeology of the Great War. Atti del Convegno Internazionale – Proceedings of the International Conference 23/24.06.2006 Luserna, Trento. Trento, 67–78.

Stichelbaut, Birger 2005
The application of Great War aerial photography in battlefield archaeology: The example of Flanders. In: Journal of Conflict Archaeology, 1, 235–243.

Stichelbaut, Birger 2011
The first thirty kilometres of the Western Front 1914-1918: an aerial archaeological approach with historical remote sensing data. In: Archaeological Prospection 18 (1), 57–66.

Threuter, Christina 2009
Westwall. Bild und Mythos. Petersberg.

Tzalmona, Rose 2011
Traces of the Atlantikwall or the ruins that were built to last, Third Text 25 (6), 775– 786.

Virilio, Paul 2009
Bunker archaeology. New York.

Wegener, Wolfgang 2016
Kulturlandschaft – Erinnerungskultur – Erinnerungslandschaft. Projekt Hürtgenwald: Eine kritische Betrachtung von Erinnerungskultur und Kulturlandschaft des Zweiten Weltkriegs. In: Siedlungsforschung. Archäologie – Geschichte – Geographie: Tod und Gedenken in der Landschaft 33, 163-176.

Willems, Willem – Koschik, Harald 1997
Der Westwall. Vom Denkmalwert des Unerfreulichen. Führer zu archäologischen Denkmälern des Rheinlandes Bd. 2. Köln.

Wilson, Ross 2011
Landscapes of the Western Front. Materiality during the Great War. London.

Zeiler, Manuel – Buthmann, Norbert – Pfnorr, Sebastian 2015
Untersuchung von Anlagen des Flughafens Lippe bei Burbach aus dem Zweiten Weltkrieg. In: Archäologie in Westfalen-Lippe 2014, 195-198.

Chapter 5. Local wars, totalitarianism and resistance against state authorities

Auwera von der, Sigrid 2012
Contemporary conflict, nationalism, and the destruction of cultural property during armed conflict: a theoretical framework. In: Journal of Conflict Archaeology 7 (1), 49-65.

Godsen, Lisa 2015
Making 1916: Material and visual culture of the Easter Rising. Liverpool.

González-Ruibal, Alfredo 2006
The dream of reason. An archaeology of the failures of modernity in Ethiopia. In: Journal of Social Archaeology 6 (2), 175-201.

González-Ruibal, Alfredo 2007.
Making things public. Archaeologies of the Spanish Civil War. In: Public Archaeology 6 (4), 203–226.

González-Ruibal, Alfredo 2010.
Fascist Colonialism: The Archaeology of Italian Outposts in Western Ethiopia (1936–41). In: International Journal of Historical Archaeology 14 (4), 547-574.

González-Ruibal, Alfredo – Sahle, Yonatan – Vila, Xurxo Ayán 2011
A social archaeology of colonial war in Ethiopia. In: World Archaeology, 43 (1), 40-65.

González-Ruibal, Alfredo 2012
From the battlefield to the labour camp: Archaeology of civil war and dictatorship in Spain, Antiquity 86/332, 456-473.

González-Ruibal, Alfredo 2014
Digging Franco's trenches: an archaeological investigation of a nationalist position from the Spanish Civil War. In: Bjørnar Olsen – Þóra Pétursdóttir (eds.), Ruin memories materialities, aesthetics and the archaeology of the recent past. London, 97-123.

González-Ruibal, Alfredo 2014
An archaeology of resistance. Materiality and time in an African borderland. Lanham u. a. MD.

McAtackney, Laura 2014
An archaeology of the Troubles. The dark heritage of Long Kesh/Maze prison. Oxford.

Müller, Ulrich 2017
Contested identities. Die Nevada Test Site, Nevada, und das Welterbe Le Morne, Mauritius. In: Scholz, Anke – Bartelheim, Martin – Hardeberg, Roland – Staecker, Jörn (eds.), Resource cultures. Sociocultural dynamics and the use of resources – theories, methods and perspectives. Tübingen, 271-298.

O'Farrell, Mick 1999
A walk through rebel Dublin 1916. Cork.

Pollard, Tony – Banks, Iain – Arthur, John – Clark, Jane – Oliver, Neil 2005
Survey and excavation of the Anglo-Zulu War Fort at Eshowe, KwaZulu-Natal, South Africa. In: Journal of Conflict Archaeology 1 (1), 133-180.

Rubio-Campillo, Xavier – Hernàndez – Francesc, Xavier 2015
Combined arms warfare in the Spanish Civil War: The assault on the republican defence line at Fatarella Ridge. In: Journal of Conflict Archaeology 10 (1), 52-69.

Saunders, Nicholas J. (ed.) 2012
Beyond the dead horizon: Studies in modern conflict archaeology. Oxford.

Scott, Douglas – Babits, Lawrence – Haecker, Charles (eds.) 2007
Fields of conflict– battlefield archaeology from the Roman Empire to the Korean War. London.

Scott, Douglas – McFeaters, Andrew P. 2011
The archaeology of historic battlefields: a history and theoretical development in conflict archaeology. In: Journal of Archaeological Research 19, 103-132.

Seitsonen, Oula – Kunnas, Lisa 2009
Ahvola 1918: Archaeological reconnaissance of a Finnish Civil War battlefield. In: Journal of Conflict Archaeology 5 (1), 57-80.

Wilson, Ross 2011
Remembering and forgetting sites of terrorism in New York, 1900-2001. In: Journal of Conflict Archaeology 6 (3), 200-221.

Chapter 6. Concentration camps and internment camps

Accessing Campscapes 2017
Inclusive strategies for using European conflict heritage. [http://www.campscapes.org/wp-content/uploads/2017/04/bulletin_ACCESSING-CAMPSCAPES_no1_Winter-2017.pdf], accessed December 2017.

Agamben, Giorgio 2002
Remnants of Auschwitz. The witness and the archive. New York

Aiko, Utsumi 2013
Soldaten und Zivilisten in japanischer Gefangenschaft während des Pazifikkrieges, 1941-1945. In: Greiner, Bettina – Kramer, Alan (eds.), Die Welt der Lager. Zur 'Erfolgsgeschichte' einer Institution. Hamburg, 245-275.

Amesberger, Helga – Auer, Katrin – Halbmayr, Brigitte 2007
Sexualisierte Gewalt. Weibliche Erfahrungen in NS-Konzentrationslagern. Wien.

Antkowiak, Matthias 2000
Erinnerungsarbeit und Erkenntnisgewinn. Die Konzentrationslager Ravensbrück und Sachsenhausen im Spiegel der Bodenfunde. In: Archäologie in Berlin und Brandenburg, 149–151.

Antkowiak, Matthias 2000
Dokumentiert und konserviert – Ein Außenlager des Konzentrationslagers Sachsenhausen in Rathenow, Landkreis Havelland. In: Archäologie in Berlin und Brandenburg, 147–148.

Antkowiak, Matthias, 2002
Struktur eines Rüstungsbetriebes – Barackenlager in Kleinmachnow, Landkreis Potsdam-Mittelmark. In: Archäologie in Berlin und Brandenburg, 165– 171.

Antkowiak, Matthias – Meyer, Angelika 2007
Grundlagen und Arbeitsweisen neuzeitlicher Archäologie am Beispiel des Jugendschutzlagers Uckermark. In: Veröffentlichungen zur Brandenburgischen Landesarchäologie 39/40, 299–336.

Antkowiak, Matthias – Meyer, Angelika 2000
Der wiederentdeckte Ort – archäologische Ausgrabungen in Uckermark. In: Limbächer, Katja – Merten, Maike – Pfefferle, Bettina (eds.), Das Mädchenkonzentrationslager Uckermark. Münster, 219–231.

Artner, Gottfried – Farka, Christa – Hofer, Nikolaus – Krenn, Martin 2004
Archäologische Untersuchungen im ehemaligen Konzentrationslager von Mauthausen. In: Bundesministerium für Inneres (ed.), Das Gedächtnis von Mauthausen. Wien, 26–29.

Banks, Iain 2011
Control or repression: contrasting a prisoner-of-war camp and a work camp form world war II. In: Myers, Adrian – Moshenska, Gabriel (eds.), Archaeologies of internment. New York, 111-128.

Baumann, Zygmunt 1989
Modernity and the Holocaust. Ithaca, N.Y.

Benčic, Andriana 2017
Jasenovac and the Persistence of the Past. In: In: Accessing Campscapes. Inclusive strategies for using European conflicted heritage 2, 4-11 [www.campscapes.org/wp-content/uploads/2017/12/e-journal-ACCESSING-CAMPSCAPES_no2-1.pdf], accessed December 2017.

Benz, Wolfgang – Distel, Barbara (eds.) 2005-2009
Der Ort des Terrors. Geschichte der nationalsozialistischen Konzentrationslager, Band 1 bis 9. München.

Bernbeck, Reinhard – Pollock, Susan 2007
'Grabe, wo Du stehst!' An archaeology of perpetrators. In: Hamilakis, Yannis – Duke, Phillip (eds.), Archaeology and capitalism: From ethics to politics. Walnut Creek, 217–231.

Bernbeck, Reinhard – Dressler, Torsten – Gussone, Martin – Kersting, Thomas – Pollock, Susan – Wiegmann, Ulrich 2016
Archäologie der Moderne. Ausgrabungen im Gelände der Moschee und des 'Halbmondlagers' von 1915. In: Brandenburgische Denkmalpflege, 1, 99-113.

Burton, Jeffrey F. 1996
Three farewells to Manzanar: The archaeology of Manzanar National Historic Site, California. Publications in Anthropology 67. Tucson.

Burton, Jeffrey F. – Bergstresser, Laura S. – Tamura, Anna H. 2003
Minidoka Internment National Monument: Archaeology at the gate. Tucson.

Camp, Stacey Lynn 2010
Preliminary archaeological investigations at Idaho's Kooskia Interment Camp (May 1943–May 1945) Phase I October 2009 to May 2011. University of Idaho [www.uidaho.edu/class/kicap/pubs], accessed February 2016.

Carr, Gilly 2013
'My home was the area around my bed": Experiencing and negotiating space in civilian internment camps in Germany, 1942–1945. In: Mytum, Harold – Carr, Gilly (eds.), Prisoners-of-war: archaeology, memory, and heritage of 19th and 20th century mass internment. New York, 189-204.

David, Wolfgang 2001
Archäologische Ausgrabungen im ehemaligen Konzentrationslager Dachau (18.9.–6.10.2000). Vorbericht. München.

David, Wolfgang 2003
Archäologische Ausgrabungen in der ehemaligen SS-Schießanlage bei Hebertshausen 2001 Vorbericht. München.

Demuth, Volker 2009
'Die das Schlachtfeld überlebten …' Archäologische Untersuchungen in einem Kriegsgefangenenlager des Ersten Weltkrieges bei Quedlinburg. In: Meller, Harald. (ed.), Schlachtfeldarchäologie – Battlefield Archaeology. 1. Mitteldeutscher Archäologentag 2008 in Halle (Saale). Halle/Saale, 259–267.

Diver, Luke 2017
German internees at the Curragh Camp. In: History Ireland 25 (2), 48-50.

Dressler, Torsten et al. 2017
Halbmond über Wünsdorf: Moschee im Kriegsgefangenlager 1915. In: Globalisierung. Mitteilungen der Deutschen Gesellschaft für Archäologie des Mittelalters und der Neuzeit 30, 125-136.

Fröhlich, Roman – Jovanović-Ratković, Mira – Siebeck, Cornelia – Wiedemann, Frank 2013
  Zentrum und Peripherie. Die Wahrnehmung der nationalsozialistischen Konzentrationslager. Berlin.

Gilead, Isaac – Haimi, Yoram – Mazurek, Wojciech 2009
  Excavating Nazi extermination centres. In: Present Pasts 1, 10-39.

Golden, Juliet 2003
  Remembering Chelmno. Heart-wrenching finds from a Nazi death camp. In: Archaeology 56 (1), 50–54.

González-Ruibal, Alfredo 2011
  The archaeology of internment in Francoist Spain (1936-1952). In: Myers, Adrian – Moshenska, Gabriel (eds.), Archaeologies of internment. New York, 53-74.

Götze, Bettina – Keil, Juliane 2004
  Archäologie der Zwangsarbeit: das KZ-Nebenlager Rathenow. In: Morsch, Günter (ed.), Die Außenlager der Konzentrationslager Sachsenhausen und Ravensbrück: Vorträge und Manuskripte des Workshops vom 17. bis 18. Oktober 2003 in der Internationalen Jugendbegegnungsstätte Ravensbrück. Oranienburg, 39–41.

Greiner, Bettina 2013
  Die Speziallager des NKVD in Deutschland, 1945-1950. In: Greiner, Bettina – Kramer, Alan (eds.), Die Welt der Lager. Zur 'Erfolgsgeschichte' einer Institution. Hamburg, 276-301.

Greiner, Bettina – Kramer, Alan (eds.) 2013
  Die Welt der Lager. Zur 'Erfolgsgeschichte' einer Institution. Hamburg.

Gutman, Israel 1990
  Encyclopedia of the Holocaust. New York.

Herbert, Ulrich 1999
  Das Jahrhundert der Lager. Ursachen, Erscheinungsformen, Auswirkungen. In: Reif-Spereck, Peter – Ritscher, Bodo (eds.), Speziallager in der SBZ. Gedenkstätten mit 'doppelter Vergangenheit'. Berlin, 11-20.

Hirte, Ronald 2000
  Offene Befunde. Ausgrabungen in Buchenwald. Zeitgeschichtliche Archäologie und Erinnerungskultur. Braunschweig.

Hoffmann, Detlef (ed.) 1998
  Das Gedächtnis der Dinge. KZ-Relikte und Kz-Denkmäler 1945-1995. Frankfurt / New York.

Hummel, Juliane 2011
  Der Bau und die baulichen Reste des Kriegsgefangenen- und Konzentrationslagers Bergen-Belsen. In: Wiedemann, Wilfried – Wolschke-Bulmahn, Joachim (eds.), Landschaft und Gedächtnis. Bergen-Belsen, Esterwegen, Falstad, Majdanek. München, 103–124.

Ibel, Johannes 2002
  Konzentrationslager Flossenbürg: Ausgrabungen und Funde. In: Das Archäologische Jahr in Bayern, 147– 149.

Ibel, Johannes 2016
  KZ-Gedenkstätte Flossenbürg – Einbeziehung archäologischer Relikte in die Gedenkstättenpräsentation. In: Kersting, Thomas – Theune, Claudia – Drieschner, Axel – Ley, Astrid – Luth, Thomas (eds.), NS-Lagerstandorte: Erforschen – bewahren – vermitteln. Petersberg, 111-118.

Irlinger, Walter 2012
  Archäologische Bodendenkmalpflege des 20. Jahrhunderts in Bayern. In: Fundberichte aus Österreich 51, 150–155.

Isenberg, Gabriele 1995
  Zu den Ausgrabungen im Konzentrationslager Witten-Annen. In: Ausgrabungen und Funde 40, 33–37.

Jones, Heather 2013
  Eine technologische Revolution? Der Erste Weltkrieg und die Radikalisierung des Kriegsgefangenenlagers. In: Greiner, Bettina – Kramer, Alan, (eds.). Welt Der Lager: Zur 'Erfolgsgeschichte' Einer Institution. Hamburg, 110-133.

Kaltofen, Andrea 2011
  Die Gedenkstätte Esterwegen, Lagertopographie und Landschaftsgestaltung auf dem Gelände des Konzentrations- und Strafgefangenenlagers Esterwegen (1933–1945). In: Wiedemann, Wilfried – Wolschke-Bulmahn, Joachim (eds.), Landschaft und Gedächtnis. Bergen-Belsen, Esterwegen, Falstad, Majdanek. München, 153–177.

Kaienburg, Hermann 2006
  Der Militär- und Wirtschaftskomplex der SS im KZ-Standort Sachsenhausen-Oranienburg. Berlin.

Klein, Ralph 2015
  Das KZ-Außenlager in Witten-Annen. Geschichte, städtebauliche Nutzung und geschichtspolitischer Umgang seit 1945. Berlin.

Klimesch, Wolfgang – Rachbauer, Markus 2007
Veritatem dies aperit – Vernichtet – Vergraben – Vergessen. Archäologische Spurensuche in Schloss Hartheim. In: Archäologie und Landeskunde, 177–189.

Kobialka, Dawidd – Kostyrko, Mikolaj – Kajda, Kornelia 2017
The Great War and its landscapes between memory and oblivion: the case of Prisoner-of war camps in Tuchola and Czersk, Polan. In: International Journal of Historical Archaeology 21, 134-151.

Kogon, Eugen 1946
Der SS-Staat. Das System der Deutschen Konzentrationslager. Frankfurt a. M.

Koła, Andrzej 2000
Bełzec, The Nazi Camp for Jewish in the light of archaeological sources, Excavations 1997–1999. Warsaw, Washington.

Koła, Andrzej 2001
Badania archeologiczne terenu byłego obozu zagłady Żydów w Sobiborze, Przeszłość i Pamięć. In: Biuletyn Rady Ochroni Pamięci Walk i Męczeństwa, 4, 115–122.

Knigge, Volkhard – Scherbakowa, Irina 2012
GULAG. Spuren und Zeugnisse 1929-1956. Weimar.

Kraus, Michael 2015
Tagebuch 1942-1945. Aufzeichnungen eines Fünfzehnjährigen aus dem Holocaust. Berlin.

Leeb, Alexandra 1992
Ravelsbach / Ried Urtlfeld. Ein bedeutender prähistorischer Fundplatz. In: Archäologie Österreichs 3/2, 19–20.

Leeb, Alexandra 1992
Notgrabung auf dem bedeutenden prähistorischen Fundplatz in der Ried Urtlfeld von Ravelsbach. In: Fundberichte aus Österreich 31, 138–149.

Ley, Astrid – Hinz-Wessles, Annette (eds.) 2012
Die Euthanasie-Anstalt Brandenburg an der Havel. Berlin.

Linck, Roland – Faßbinder, Jörg W. E – Ibel, Johannes 2010
Geophysikalische Untersuchungen in der KZ-Gedenkstätte Flossenbürg. In: Das Archäologische Jahr in Bayern, 174–176.

Martin, Angela – Sjöberg, Hanna 2011
Der erzählte Ort. Die Rekonstruktion einer Rüstungsfabrik und ihrer Lager für Zwangsarbeiter/innen und KZ-Häftlinge in zwei Ausstellungen. In: Klei, Alexandra – Stoll, Katrin – Wienert, Annika (eds.), Die Transformation der Lager. Annäherungen an die Orte nationalsozialistischer Verbrechen. Bielefeld, 187-204.

Megargee, Geoffrey P. – The United States Holocaust Memorial Museum (ed.) 2009
Encyclopedia of camps and Ghettos 1933–1945. Vol. 1: Early camps, youth camps, and concentration camps and subcamps and the SS-Business Administration Main Office (WVHA). Bloomington.

Megargee, Geoffrey P. – The United States Holocaust Memorial Museum (ed.) 2012
Encyclopedia of camps and Ghettos 1933–1945. Vol 2: Ghettos in German-Occupied Eastern Europe. Bloomington.

Mitchell, Paul 2017
The concentration camp as built artefact. Buildings archaeology in the Mauthausen-Gusen Complex. In: International Journal of Historical Archaeology, special issue: Carr, Gilly – Theune, Claudia – Jasinski, Marek (eds.), The material culture of Nazi camps.

Morine, Christopher Michael 2016
German POWs Make Colorado Home. Coping by Craft and Exchange. Thesis, University of Denver. [www.academia.edu/25854312/German_POWs_Make_Colorado_Home_Coping_by_Craft_and_Exchange], accessed January 2018.

Münk, Dieter, 1993
Die Organisation des Raumes im Nationalsozialismus. Eine soziologische Untersuchung ideologisch fundierte Leitbilder in Architektur, Städtebau und Raumplanung des Dritten Reichs. Bonn.

Myers, Adrian 2008
Between memory and materiality: an archaeological approach to studying the Nazi Concentration Camps. In: Journal of Conflict Archaeology 4, 231-245.

Myers, Adrian 2013
The archaeology of reform at a German prisoner-of-war camp in a Canadian National Park during the Second World War (1943–1945). PhD-Thesis: Standford University. [(http:// purl.stanford.edu/yc37orj6066], accessed: January 2014.

Myers, Adrian – Moshenska, Gabriel (eds.) 2011
Archaeologies of internment. New York.

Mytum, Harold 2011
A tale of two treatments: the materiality of internment on the Isle of Man in world wars I and II. In: Myers, Adrian –

Moshenska, Gabriel (eds.), Archaeologies of internment. New York, 33-52.

Mytum, Harold 2012
Prisoner-of-war archaeology in an interdisciplinary context. In: Mytum, Harold – Carr, Gilly (eds.), Archaeology, memory, and heritage of 19th and 20th century mass internment. New York, 321-352.

Mytum, Harold – Carr, Gilly (eds.) 2012
Prisoners-of-war: archaeology, memory and heritage of 19th-and 20th century mass internment. New York.

Neerland Soleim, Marinanne (ed.) 2010
Prisoners-of-war and forced labour. Histories of war and occupation. Newcastle upon Tyne.

Neurath, Paul 2005
The society of terror. London.

Nickel, Claudia 2011
Kulturbaracken. Kreative Räume in südfranzösischen Lagern. In: Klei, Alexandra – Stoll, Katrin – Wienert, Annika (eds.), Die Transformation der Lager. Annäherungen an die Orte nationalsozialistischer Verbrechen. Bielefeld.

O'Neil, Robin 1998
Bełżec – The forgotten Death Camp. In: East European Jewish Affairs, 28(2), 49–62.

O'Neil, Robin – Tregenza, Michael 2006
Archaeological investigations. A review by Historians. Acknowledgment to the Torun team of archaeologists and the cartographer. [www.holocaustresearchproject.org/ar/modern/archreview.html], accessed May 2017.

Orth, Karin 2000
Gab es eine Lagergesellschaft? 'Kriminelle' und politische Häftlinge im Konzentrationslager. In: Frei, Norbert – Steinbacher, Sybille – Wagner, Bernd, Ausbeutung, Vernichtung, Öffentlichkeit. München, 109-133.

Pagenstecher, Cord 2017
Through the city of camps: remembering forced labour in Berlin. In: Accessing Campscapes. Inclusive strategies for using European conflicted heritage 2, 4-11 [www.campscapes.org/wp-content/uploads/2017/12/e-journal-ACCESSING-CAMPSCAPES_no2-1.pdf], accessed December 2017.

Pawlicka-Nowak, Łucja 2004
Archaeological research in the grounds of the Chełmno-on-Ner extermination center. In: Pawlicka-Nowak, Łucja (ed.), The Extermination center for Jews in Chełmno-on-Ner in the light of latest research, Symposium Proceedings September 6–7. Konin.

Pawlicka-Nowak, Łucja 2004
Archaeological research in the grounds of the Chełmno-on-Ner former extermination center. In: Pawlicka-Nowak, Łucja (ed.), Chełmno Witnesses Speak. Konin/Łódź.

Pawłoś, Dariusz 2016
Sobibór – Geschichte des deutschen Vernichtungslagers im Kontext der archäologischen Ergebnisse von 2001 bis 2015. In: Kersting, Thomas – Theune, Claudia – Drieschner, Axel – Ley, Astrid – Luth, Thomas (eds.), NS-Lagerstandorte: Erforschen – bewahren – vermitteln. Petersberg, 71-74.

Perz, Bertrand 2013
Verwaltete Gewalt. Der Tätigkeitsbericht des Verwaltungsführers im Konzentrationslager Mauthausen 1941–1944. Mauthausen-Studien Bd. 8. Wien.

Perz, Bertrand 2014
Das Projekt 'Quarz'. Der Bau einer unterirdischen Fabrik durch Häftlinge des KZ-Melk für die Steyr-Daimler-Puch AG 1944-1945. Innsbruck.

Pieler, Franz – Kusternig, Andreas 2016
Archäologie im ehemaligen OFLAG XVIIA Edelbach. In: Archäologie Österreichs 27 (1), 2-13.

Pitzer, Andrea 2017
One long night. A global history of concentration camps. New York.

Pollak, Michael 2016
Die Grenzen des Sagbaren. Lebensgeschichte von KZ-Überlebenden als Augenzeugenberichte und als Identitätsarbeit. Wien.

Pollock, Susan – Bernbeck, Reinhard 2016
The limits of experience: suffering, Nazi Forced Labor camps, and archaeology. In: Archaeological Papers of the American Anthropological Association 27, 22–39.

Prieto, Manuel – Ayán Vila, Xurxo 2014
'Although the loneliness is great, greater yet is the love of my country". Archaeology of a military outpost on the Topain Hillock (Antofagasta Region, Chile). In: Journal of contemporary archaeology 1 (2), 323-350.

Rodrigo, Javier 2013
Der Faschismus und die Lager in Spanien und Italien. In: Greiner, Bettina – Kramer, Alan (eds.) Die Welt der Lager. Zur ,Erfolgsgeschichte' einer Institution. Hamburg, 224-244.

Schnell, Felix 2013
Der Gulag als Systemstelle sowjetischer Herrschaft.
In: Greiner, Bettina – Kramer, Alan (eds.), Die Welt
der Lager. Zur ‚Erfolgsgeschichte' einer Institution.
Hamburg, 134-165.

Schopper, Franz 2016
Zwischen Krieg und Frieden. Waldlager der Roten
Armee in Brandenburg 1945. Archäologisches
Landesmuseum Brandenburg. Begleitheft zur
Sonderausstellung. Berlin.

Schwarz, Gudrun 1996
Die nationalsozialistischen Lager. Frankfurt a. M.

Seitsonen, Oula – Herva, Vesa-Pekka 2013
Forgotten in the wilderness: WWII German PoW camps in
Finnish Lapland. In: Myers, Adrian – Moshenska, Gabriel
(eds.), Archaeologies of internment. New York, 171–190.

Siebrecht, Claudia 2013
Formen von Unfreiheit und Extreme der Gewalt.
Die Konzentrationslager in Deutsch-Südwestafrika,
1904-1908. In: Greiner, Bettina – Kramer, Alan (eds.),
Die Welt der Lager. Zur 'Erfolgsgeschichte' einer
Institution. Hamburg, 87-109.

Sofsky, Wolfgang 1999
The order of terror. The concentration camp.
Princeton.

Sommer, Robert 2009
Das KZ-Bordell. Sexuelle Zwangsarbeit in
nationalsozialistischen Konzentrationslagern.
Paderborn.

Starzmann, Maria Theresia 2015
The Materiality of Forced Labor: An archaeological
exploration of punishment in Nazi Germany. In:
International Journal Historical Archaeology 19, 647–663.

Starzmann, Maria Theresia 2015
Zeitschichten/Bedeutungsschichten: Archäologische
Untersuchungen zur NS-Zwangsarbeit in Berlin-
Tempelhof/ Archaeological Palimpsests: Memory
work at a National Socialist Forced Labor Camp in
Berlin-Tempelhof. In: Historische Archäologie –
Online-Zeitschrift. [www.histarch.uni-kiel.de/2015_
Starzmann.pdf], accessed December 2017.

Starzmann, Maria Theresia 2013
Excavating Tempelhof airfield: objects of memory and the
politcs of absence. In: The Journal of Theory and Practice,
November 2013, 1–19.

Stelzl-Marx, Barbara 2000
Zwischen Fiktion und Zeitzeugenschaft.
Amerikanische und sowjetische Kriegsgefangene im
Stalag XVII B Krems-Gneixendorf. Tübingen.

Stelzl-Marx, Barbara 2012
Das Lager Graz-Liebenau in der NS-Zeit. Graz.

Stensager, Anders Otte 2007
Holocaustarkeologi. En arkæologisk funktionsanalyse
af udryddelseslejrene i Polen 1941-1945. Københavns
Universitet.

Stiftung Topographie des Terrors (ed.) 2010
Topographie des Terrors. Gestapo, SS und
Reichssicherheitshauptamt in der Wilhelm- und Prinz-
Albrecht-Straße. Eine Dokumentation. Berlin.

Stucki, Andreas 2013
Aufbruch ins Zeitalter der Lager?. Zwangsumsiedlung
und Deportation in der spanischen Antiguerilla auf
Kuba, 1868–98. In: Mittelweg 36 20/4, 2011, 20-35.

Sturdy-Collls, Caroline 2012
Holocaust Archaeology: Archaeological approaches
to landscapes of Nazi Genocide and Persecution. In:
Journal of Conflict Archaeology 7/2, 70–104.

Sturdy-Colls, Caroline 2015
Holocaust archaeologies. Approaches and future
directions. New York.

Sturdy-Colls, Caroline 2015
Finding Treblinka. An exhibition of forensic
archaeological research. Staffordshire.

Suderland 2004
Territorien des Selbst. Kulturelle Identität als Ressource
für das tägliche Überleben im Konzentrationslager.
Frankfurt/Main, New York.

Suderland, Maja 2011
'Es bestand nicht die geringste Aussicht, jemals wirklich
für alle ein Niemand zu werden.' – ‚Geschlecht' als
soziale Disposition und Handlungsoption für die
Inhaftierten in Konzentrationslagern. In: Hermann-
Otto, Elisabeth (ed.), Sklaverei – Knechtschaft –
Zwangsarbeit: Untersuchungen zur Sozial-, Rechts- und
Kulturgeschichte, Bd. 8 Sklaverei und Zwangsarbeit
zwischen Akzeptanz und Widerstand. Hildesheim,
Zürich, New York, 491–515.

Suderland, Maja 2013
Inside Concentration Camp. Social Life at the
Extremes. Cambridge.

Theune, Claudia 2010

   Historical Archaeology in National Socialist Concentration Camps in Central Europe. In: Historische Archäologie – Online-Zeitschrift. [www.histarch.uni-kiel.de/2010_Theune_high.pdf], accessed December 2017.

Theune, Claudia 2013

   Archaeological research in former concentration camps. In: Mehler, Natascha (ed.), Historical Archaeology in Central Europe. Society for Historical Archaeology. Special Publication Number 10. Rockville, 241–260.

Theune, Claudia 2017

   Archaeology at the sites of National Socialist terror. Research questions – sources – methodology insights. In: Dziuban, Zuzanna, The forensic turn in Holocaust studies? (Re)thinking the past through materiality. Wien, 121-131.

Thomas, Judith 2013

   Archaeological investigations of Second World War prisoner-of-war camp at Fort Hood, Texas. In: Myers, Adrian – Moshenska, Gabriel (eds.), Archaeologies of Internment. New York, 147–169.

Van Pelt, Robert Jan 2017

   From the last hut of Monowitz to the last hut of Belsen. In: Accessing Campscapes. Inclusive strategies for using European conflicted heritage 2, 4-11 [www.campscapes.org/wp-content/uploads/2017/12/e-journal-ACCESSING-CAMPSCAPES_no2-1.pdf], accessed December 2017.

Vařeka, Pave –Vařeková, Zdeňka 2017

   Archaeology of Zigeunerlager: initial results of the 2016-2017 investigation at the Roma camp in Lety. In: Accessing Campscapes. Inclusive strategies for using European conflicted heritage 2, 4-11 [www.campscapes.org/wp-content/uploads/2017/12/e-journal-ACCESSING-CAMPSCAPES_no2-1.pdf], accessed December 2017.

Wachsmann, Nikolaus 2016

   Die Geschichte der nationalsozialistischen Konzentrationslager. München.

Waters, Michael R. – Long, Mark – Dickens, William 2004

   Lone star Stalag: German prisoners-of-war camp at Hearne. Texas.

Weinmann, Martin (ed.) 1990

   Das nationalsozialistische Lagersystem (Catalogue of Camps and Prisons in Germany and German-Occupied Territories 1939–1945 [CCP]). Frankfurt a. M.

Weishaupt, Johannes 2011

   Lagerarchäologie. Ausgrabungen in den Gedenkstätten Sachsenhausen und Ravensbrück, Lkr. Oberhavel. In: Archäologie in Berlin und Brandenburg 2011, 160–163.

Weishaupt, Johannes 2016

   Archäologie in Gedenkstätten – Anlässe und Ergebnisse. In: Kersting, Thomas – Theune, Claudia – Drieschner, Axel – Ley, Astrid – Luth, Thomas (eds.), NS-Lagerstandorte: Erforschen – bewahren – vermitteln. Petersberg, 63-70.

Weiss, Lindsay 2011

   Exceptional Space: Concentration camps and labor compounds in late nineteenth-century South Africa. In: Myers, Adrian – Moshenska, Gabriel (eds.), Archaeologies of internment. New York, 21-32.

Wienert, Annika 2015

   Das Lager vorstellen. Die Architektur der nationalsozialistischen Vernichtungslager. Berlin.

Wijnen, Jobbe A. T. – Schute, Ivar 2010

   Archeologisch onderzoek in een 'schulig landschap': Concentratiekamp Amersfoort. RAAP-Rapport 2197.

Young, Allison Marie 2013

   An historical archaeological investigation of the Indianola prisoner-of-war camp in Southwestern Nebraska. Master Thesis University of Nebraska. Lincoln.

Zarankin, Andrés – Salerno, Melisa 2011

   The engineering of genocide: An archaeology of dictatorship in Argentina. In: Myers, Adrian – Moshenska, Gabriel (eds.), Archaeologies of internment. New York, 207-228.

Internetlinks: List of detention and internment camps:

Deutsches Bundesarchiv - Haftstättenverzeichnis

   www.bundesarchiv.de/zwangsarbeit/haftstaetten/index.php?tab=1

Verzeichnis der nationalsozialistischen Lager und Haftstätten 1933 bis 1945

   www.deutschland-ein-denkmal.de/ded/start

USHMM (United States Holocaust National Museum)

   www.ushmm.org/

Chapter 7. The archaeology of civilian protest

Badcock, Anna – Johnston, Robert 2013
Protest. In: Graves-Brown, Paul – Harrison, Rodney – Piccini, Angela (eds.), The archaeology of the contemporary world. Oxford, 321-335.

Badcock, Anna – Johnson, Robert 2009
Placemaking through protest: An archaeology of the Lees Cross and Endcliffe Protest Camp, Derbyshire, England. In: Archaeologies 5 (2), 306-322.

Beck, Colleen – Drollinger, Harold – Schofield, John 2007
Archaeology of dissent: landscape and symbolism at the Nevada Peace Camp. In: Schofield, John – Cocroft, Wayne (eds.), A fearsome heritage: diverse legacies of the Cold War. Walnut Creek, 297-320.

Brück, Johanna 2015
Nationalism, gender and memory: internment camp craftwork 1916-1923. In: Godsen, Lisa – Brück, Johanna, Making 1916. Material and visual culture of the Easter Rising. Liverpool, 99-107.

Buchli, Victor – Lucas, Gavin 2001
The absent present. In: Buchli, Victor – Lucas, Gavin, Archaeologies of the contemporary past. London, 3-18.

Burström, Mats et. al. 2009
Memories of a world crisis. The archaeology of a former Soviet nuclear missile site in Cuba. In: Journal of Social Archaeology 9, 295-318.

Cocroft, Wayne – Wilson, Louise 2006.
Archaeology and art at Spadeadam Rocket Establishment (Cumbria). In: Schofield, John. – Klausmeier, Axel – Purbrick, Louise (eds.), Re-mapping the field: new approaches in conflict archaeology. Westkreuz: Berlin, 15–21.

Ehmke, Wolfgang
Wie alles anfing und wohin es führte, 2015 [www.bi-luechow-dannenberg.de/?page_id=9744], accessed October 2015.

Funari, Pedro – Zarankin, Andrés – Salerno, Melisa (eds.) 2009
Memories from darkness: archaeologies of repression and resistance in Latin America. New York.

Godsen, Lisa – Brück, Johanna 2015
Making 1916. Material and visual culture of the Easter Rising. Liverpool.

Gonzáles-Ruibal, Alfredo 2008
Time to destroy. An archaeology of supermodernity. In: Current Anthropology 49,/2, 247-279.

Gonzáles-Ruibal, Alfredo 2014
An archaeology of resistance. Materiality and time in an African borderland. Plymouth.

Graves-Brown, Paul (ed.) 2000
Matter, materiality and modern culture. London.

Hanson, Todd 2010
Uncovering the arsenals of Armageddon: The historical archaeology of North American Cold War Ballistic Missile Launch Sites. In: Archaeological Review from Cambridge 25/1, 157–172.

Hansen, Todd A 2016
The archaeology of the Cold War. Gainesville.

Harrison, Rodney – Schofield, John 2009
After modernity. Archaeological approaches to the contemporary past. Oxford.

Kamien, Susanne – Rheinländer, Max 2008
ÜberMacht & Phantasie. Geschichte(n) des Gorleben Wiederstands. Köln 2008.

Kiddey, Rachael – Schofield, John 2011
Embrace the margins: adventures in archaeology and homelessness. In: Public Archaeology 10 (1), 4-22.

Larkin, Karin – McGuire, Randall H. (eds.) 2009
The archaeology of class war. Boulder.

Laware, Margaret L. 2004
Circling the missiles and staining them red: feminist rhetorical invention and strategies of resistance at the women's peace camp at Greenham Common. In: National Women's Studies Association Journal 16 (3), 18-41.

Leone, Mark P. – Potter, Parker B. – Shakel, Paul A. 1987
Toward a critical archaeology. In: Current Anthropology 28/3, 283-302.

Leone, Mark P. 2010
Critical historical archaeology. Walnut Creek.

Ludlow Collective 2001
Archaeology of the Colorado Coal Field War 1913-1914. In: Buchli, Victor – Lucas, Gavin, Archaeologies of the contemporary past. London, 94-107.

Marshall, Yvonne – Roseneil, Sasha – Armstrong, Kayt 2009
Situating the Greenham archaeology: an autoethnography of a feminist project. In: Public Archaeology: Archaeological Ethnographies 8/2-3, 225-245.

McAtackney, Laura 2014

    An archaeology of the troubles. The dark heritage of Long Kesh/Maze prison. Oxford.

McAtackney, Laura 2015

    Memorials and marching: Archaeological insights into segregation in contemporary Northern Ireland. In: Historical Archaeology 49/3, 110-125.

McGuire, Randall H. 2008

    Archaeology as political action. California series in public anthropology 17. Berkeley.

Müller, Ulrich 2017

    Contested identities. Die Nevada Test Site, Nevada und das Welterbe Le Morne, Mauritius. In: Scholz, Anke K. – Bartelheim, Martin – Hardenberg, Roland – Staecker Jörn (eds.), Resource cultures sociocultural dynamics and the use of resources – theories, methods, perspectives. Tübingen, 271-298.

Müller, Ulrich 2017

    Get up – stand up: The historical archaeology of resistance. In: Hansen, Svend – Müller, Johannes (eds.), Rebellion and inequality in archaeology. Bonn, 304-331.

Myles, Franc 2015

    Beating the retreat: the final hours of the Easter Rising. In: Godsen, Lisa – Brück, Johanna, Making 1916. Material and visual culture of the Easter Rising. Liverpool, 34-48.

O'Farrel, Mick 1999

    A walk through rebel Dublin 1916. Cork.

Purbrick, Louise 2011

    The last murals of Long Kesh: Fragments of political imprisonment at the Maze Prison, Northern Ireland. In: Myers, Adrian – Moshenska, Gabriel (eds.), Archaeologies of internment. New York, 263-284.

Saitta, Dean J. 2007

    The archaeology of collective action. Gainesville.

Saitta, Dean J. – Walker, Mark – Reckner, Paul 2005

    Battlefields of class conflict: Ludlow then and now. In: Journal of Conflict Archaeology 1, 197-213.

Schmidt, Peter R. – Walz, Jonathan R. 2007

    Re-representing African pasts through historical archaeology. In: American Antiquity 72 (1), 53-70.

Schofield, John 2005

    Combat archaeology. Material culture and modern conflict. London.

Schofield, John 2009

    Aftermath. Readings in the archaeology of recent conflict. New York.

Schofield, John 2009

    Peace site: an archaeology of protest at Greenham Common airbase. In: British Archaeology 104, 44-49.

Schofield, John – Anderton, Mike 2000

    The queer archaeology of Green Gate: Interpreting contested space at Greenham Common Airbase. In: World Archaeology 32, 236-251.

Symonds, James – Vařeka, Pavel 2014

    Cowboys and Bohemias. Recreation, resistance, and the tramping movement in West Bohemia. In: Journal of Contemporary Archaeology 1/1, 165-193.

Worman, Frederick 1969

    Archeological investigations at the U.S. Atomic Energy Commission's Nevada Test Site and Nuclear Rocket Development Station. Los Alamos Scientific Laboratory of the University of California: Los Alamos.

Zarankin, Andrés – Funari, Pedro 2008

    'Eternal sunshine of the spotless mind": archaeology and construction of memory of military repression in South America (1960-1980). In: Archaeologies 4/2, 310-327.

Chapter 8. Borders

Baker, Frederick 1993

    The Berlin Wall: production, preservation and consumption of a 20th century monument. In: Antiquity 67, 709-733.

Calame, Jon – Woods, Esther 2009

    Divided cities. Belfast, Beirut, Jerusalem, Mostar, and Nikosia. Philadelphia.

Cramer, Johannes – Rütenik, Tobias – Speiser, Philipp – Tussenbroek, Gabri van 2011

    Die Baugeschichte der Berliner Mauer. Petersberg.

De León, Jason 2013

    Undocumented migration, use wear, and the materiality of habitual suffering in the Sonoran Desert. In: Journal of Material Culture 18 (4), 321-345.

De León, Jason 2015

    The land of open graves. Living and dying on the migrant trail. Oakland.

De León, Victor J. 2012

    Archaeology of the contemporary, and the politics

of researching unauthorized border crossing: a brief and personal history of the undocumented migration project (Gegenwartsarchäologie und die Forschungspolitik der illegalen Grenzübertritte: Eine kurze und persönliche Geschichte des 'Undocumented Migration Project'). In: Kritische Archäologie 1, 141–148 [www.kritischearchaeologie. de/repositorium/fka/2012_1_19_DeLeon.pdf], accessed December 2017.

Dressler, Torsten 2007
Die Mauer ist weg – aber nicht ganz. Spurensuche an der Bernauer Straße, Berlin-Mitte. In: Archäologie in Berlin und Brandenburg, 180–182.

Dressler, Torsten 2010
Grenzerfahrungen. Mauer und Todesstreifen an der Bernauer Straße, Berlin-Mitte. In: Archäologie in Berlin und Brandenburg, 178–181.

Dressler, Torsten – Kersting, Thomas 2011
Ausgang gefunden. Berliner Mauer und Aagaard-Fluchttunnel in Glienicke/Nordbahn, Lkr. Oberhavel. In: Archäologie in Berlin und Brandenburg, 163–167.

Fowler, Martin J. F. 2008
The application of declassified KH-7 GAMBIT satellite photographs to studies of Cold War material culture: a case study from the former Soviet Union. In: Antiquity 317, 714–731.

Klausmeier, Axel – Schlusche, Günter (eds.) 2011
Denkmalpflege für die Berliner Mauer: Die Konservierung eines unbequemen Bauwerks. Berlin.

Löw, Martina 2001
Raumsoziologie. Frankfurt a.M.

McAtackney, Laura 2011
Peace maintenance and political messages: The significance of walls during and after the Northern Irish 'Troubles'. In: Journal of Social Archaeology 11/1, 77-98.

McWilliams, Anna 2013
An archaeology of the Iron Curtain. Material and metaphor. Stockholm.

Pisoni, Luca 2015
What should I bring to Europe. Belongings from the luggage of migrants crossing the Mediterranean Sea from Africa. In: Society of Historical Archaeology – The SHA Newsletter 48/3, 2.

Schofield, John – Cocroft, Wayne (eds.) 2007
A fearsome heritage – diverse legacies of the Cold War. Walnut Creek.

Schroer, Markus 2006
Räume, Orte, Grenzen. Auf dem Weg zu einer Soziologie des Raumes. Frankfurt a. M.

Steiner, Christopher B. 2001
Rights of Passage. On the liminal identiy of art in the border zone. In: Myers, Fred R., The empire of things. Sante Fe, 207-232

Wagner, Karin 2009
Die Berliner Mauer. Ein Geschichtsmonument von hoher Brisanz. In: Archäologie in Deutschland 2009 (1), 70.

Wilson, Thomas M. – Donnan, Hastings (eds.) 2012
A companion to border studies. Chichester.

Chapter 9. Paying tribute to the dead

Anderson, Gail S. – Cervenka, Valerie J. 2002
Insects associated with the body: their uses and analyses. In: Haglund, William D. – Sorg, Marcella H. (eds.), Advances in forensic taphonomy: method, theory and archaeological perspectives. Boca, Raton, London, New York, Washington D.C., 173-200

Cienciala, Anna – Lebedeva, Natalia – Materski, Wojciech (eds.) 2007
Katyn: a crime without punishment. New Haven, London.

Crossland, Zoe 2002
Violent spaces: conflict over the reappearance of Argentina's disappeared. In: Schofield, John – Beck, Colleen M. – Johnson, William Gray (eds.), Matérial culture. The archaeology of 20th century conflict. London, 115-131.

Davidson, James, M. 2008
Identiy and violent death. Contextualizing lethal gun violence within the African American community of Dallas, TX (1900-1907). In: Journal of Social Archaeology 8 (3), 320-354.

Eschebach, Insa – zu Eulenburg, Amélie 2016
'Die Gemeinschaft der Toten'. Bestattungspraktiken an Orten von Gewaltverbrechen in der Moderne. In: Kersting, Thomas – Theune, Claudia – Drieschner, Axel – Ley, Astrid – Luth, Thomas (eds.), NS-Lagerstandorte: Erforschen – bewahren – vermitteln. Petersberg, 87-94.

Fengqi, Qian 2009
Let the dead be remembered: interpretation of the Nanjing Massacre Memorial. In: Logan, William – Reeves, Keir, Places of pain and shame. Dealing with a difficult heritage. London.

Fraser, Alastair H. – Brown, Martin 2013
Mud, blood and missing men: excavations at Serre, Somme, France. In: Journal of Conflict Archaeology 3 (1), 147-171.

Gassend, Jean-Loup – Alberti, Lionel 2015
Soldiers mistakenly reported: killed in action: three German World War II examples related to Operation Dragoon in August 1944. In: Journal of Conflict Archaeology 10 (2), 96-122.

Groen, Mike – Márquez-Grant, Nicholas –Janaway, Robert C. 2015
Forensic archaeology. A global perspective. Chichester.

Haglund, William D. – Connor, Melissa – Scott, Douglas D. 2001
The archaeology of contemporary mass graves. In: Historical Archaeology 35 (1), 57-69.

Haglund, William D. 2001
Archaeology and forensic death investigations, Historical Archaeology 35 (1), 26-34.

Holland, Thomas – Byrd, John – Sava, Vincent 2008
Joint POW /MIA accounting command's central identification laboratory. In: Warren, Michael W. – Walsh-Haney, Heather A. – Freas, Laurel (eds.), The forensic anthropology laboratory. Boca Raton, 47-63.

Hunter, John et al 2001
Forensic archaeology, forensic anthropology and Human Rights in Europe. In: Science & Justice 41/3, 173-178.

Jarvis, Helen (2002
Mapping Cambodia's 'Killing fields'. In. Beck, Colleen M. - Johanson, William Gray – Schofield, John, Matériel culture. The archaeology of twentieth-century conflict. Abdington, 91-102.

Juhl, Kirsten –Olsen, Odd Einar 2006
Societal safety, archaeology and the investigation of contemporary mass graves. In: Journal of Genocide Research 8 (4), 411-435.

Koła, Andrzej 2005
Archeologia zbrodni. Oficerowie Polscy na cmentarzu Ofiar NKWD w Charłwie, [Archäologie des Verbrechens. Polnische Offiziere auf dem Friedhof für die Opfer des NKWD in Charkiw]. Toruń.

Koła, Andrzej 2009
Archäologie des Verbrechens. Das archäologische Know-how im Dienste der Aufklärung von Geheimnissen der jüngsten Vergangenheit (am Beispiel exhumierter Opfer des Stalinismus aus Massengräbern von Charkow und Kiew. In: Jahrbuch des wissenschaftlichen Zentrums der Polnischen Akademie der Wissenschaften in Wien 1, 107-116.

Koła, Andrzej – Sziling, Jan (eds.) 2011
Charków – Katyń – Twer – Bykownia. Torún.

Long, Colin – Reeves, Keir 2009
Dig a hole and bury the past in it: reconciliation and the heritage of genocide in Cambodia. In: Logan, William – Reeves, Keir, Places of pain and shame. Dealing with a difficult heritage. London.

Lyman, R. Lee 2002
Foreword from Paleontology. In: Haglund, William D. – Sorg, Marcella H. (eds.), Advances in forensic taphonomy: Method, theory and archaeological perspectives. Boca, Raton, London, New York, Washington D.C., xxiii-xxiv.

O'Brian, Eadaoin 2011
The exhumation of mass graves by international criminal tribunals: Nuremberg, the former Yogoslavia and Rwanda. PhD Thesis. National University of Ireland. Galway. (https://aran.library.nuigalway.ie/handle/10379/2718, accessd: April 2017).

Powers, Natasha – Sibun, Lucy 2013
Forensic archaeology. In: Graves-Brown, Paul – Harrison, Rodney – Piccini, Angela (eds.), The archaeology of the contemporary world. Oxford, 40-53.

Renshaw, Layla 2010
Missing bodies near-at-hand: the dissonant bodies and dormant graves of the Spanish Civil War. In: Bille, Mikkel – Hastrup, Frida – Sørensen, Tim Flohr (eds.) The anthropology of absence. Materializations of transcendence and loss. New York, 45-61.

Renshaw, Layla 2013
The dead and their public. Memory campaigns, issue networks and the role of the archaeologist in the excavation of mass graves. In: Archaeological Dialogues 20/1, 35–47.

Schmitt, Stefan 2002
Mass graves and the collection of forensic evidence: Genocide, war crimes, and crimes against humanity.

In: Haglund, William D. – Sorg, Marcella H. (eds.), Advances in forensic taphonomy: method, theory and archaeological perspectives. Boca, Raton, London, New York, Washington D.C., 277-292.

Skinner, Mark – Alempijevic, Djordje – Djuric-Srejic, Marija 2003
    Guidelines for international forensic bio-archaeology monitors of mass grave exhumations. In: Forensic Science International 134, 81-92.

Steele, Caroline 2008
    Archaeology and the forensic investigation of recent mass graves. Ethical issues for a new practice of archaeology. In: Archaeologies 4 (3), 414-428.

Theune, Claudia 2011
    Gewalt und Tod in Konzentrations- und Vernichtungslagern. Möglichkeiten und Grenzen der Archäologie. In: Morsch, Günther – Perz, Bertrand, Neue Studien zu nationalsozialistischen Massentötungen durch Giftgas. Berlin, 64-73.

Vanagaite, Ruta 2016
    Mūsiškiai. Vilnius.

Von der Laarse, Rob 2017
    Bones never lie? Unearthing Europ's Age of terror in the age of memory. In: Zuzanna Dziuban (ed.), Mapping the 'Forensic Turn'. Engagements with materialities of mass death in Holocaust. Studies and beyond. Beiträge des VWI zur Holocaustforschung Band 5. Vienna, 143-168.

Chapter 10. The world of small finds

Attfield, Judy (ed.) 2000
    Wild things. The material culture of everyday life. London.

Bergqvist Rydén, Johanna 2017
    When bereaved of everything. Objects from the concentration camp of Ravensbrück as expressions of resistance, memory and identity. In: International Journal of Historical Archaeology, special issue: Carr, Gilly – Theune, Claudia – Jasinski, Marek (eds.), The material culture of Nazi camps.

Bernbeck, Reinhard and Pollock, Susan 2017
    Quotidian and transgressive practices in Nazi Forced Labor Camps: the role of objects. In: International Journal of Historical Archaeology, special issue: Carr, Gilly – Theune, Claudia – Jasinski, Marek (eds.), The material culture of Nazi camps.

Biederer, Benedict 2017
    Medical finds from the concentration camp Sachsenhausen. An attempt to identify treatment methods and the companies involved. In: Historische Archäologie, Online-Zeitschrift. [www.histarch.uni-kiel.de].

Bourdieu, Pierre 1977
    Outline of a Theory of Practice. Cambridge.

Buncíková, Lenka 2017
    Recyclable waste as a maker of everyday life routines. In: Sosna, Daniel – Brunclíková, Lenka, 2017 Archaeologies of waste. Encounters with the unwanted. Oxford, 100-122.

Burström, Mats 2012
    Treasured memories. Tales of buried belongings in wartime Estonia. Lund.

Brück, Joanna 2015
    Nationalism, gender and memory: internment camp craftwork 1916-1923. In: Godson, Lisa – Brück, Joanna (eds.), Making 1916. Material and visual culture of the Easter Rising. Liverpool, 99-108.

Brück, Joanna 2015
    'A good Irishman should blush every time he sees a penny': gender, nationalism and memory in Irish internment camp craftwork, 1916-1923. In: Journal on Material Culture 20 (2), 149-172.

Carr, Gillian 2011
    Engraving and embroidering emotions upon the material culture of internment. In: Myers, Adrian – Moshenska, Gabriel, Archaeologies of internment. New York, 129-146.

Carr, Gilly 2012
    Coins, crest and kings: symbol of identity and resistance in occupied Channel Islands. In: Journal of Material Culture 17 (4), 327-344.

Carr, Gilly 2017
    The small things of life and death: an exploration of value and meaning in the material culture of Nazi camps. In: International Journal of Historical Archaeology, special issue: Carr, Gilly – Theune, Claudia – Jasinski, Marek (eds.), The material culture of Nazi camps.

Carr, Gilly – Jasinski, Marek E. 2013
    Sites of memory, Sites of oblivion: The archaeology of 20th century conflict In Europe. In: Bassanelli, Michela – Postglione, Gennaro (eds.), Re-enacting the Past: Museography for conflict archaeology. Siracusa, 36-55.

Cole, Tim 2013
  The place of things in contemporary history. In: Graves-Brown, Paul – Harrison, Rodney – Piccini, Angela (eds.), The archaeology of the contemporary world. Oxford, 66-81.

Ehresmannm, Andeas 2016
  'Henkelmänner' und Aschehaufen: Archäologie in der musealen und pädagogischen Vermittlung am Beispiel Sandbostel. In: Kersting, Thomas – Theune, Claudia – Drieschner, Axel – Ley, Astrid – Luth, Thomas (eds.), NS-Lagerstandorte: Erforschen – bewahren – vermitteln. Petersberg, 125-130.

Etkind, Alexander et al. (eds.) 2012
  Remembering Katyń. Cambridge.

Forssman, Tim – Louw, Christian 2016
  Leaving a mark: South African war-period (1899–1902) refuge graffiti at telperion shelter in Western Mpumalanga, South Africa. In: South African Archaeological Bulletin 71 (203), 4-13.

Frankl, Viktor 1977
  ...trotzdem Ja zum Leben sagen. München.

Garbe, Detlef 2005
  Selbstbehauptung und Widerstand. In: Benz, Wolfgang – Distel, Barbara, Der Ort des Terrors – Geschichte der nationalsozialistischen Konzentrationslager 1. München, 242-255.

Gassen, Jean-Loup 2014
  What can be learned from shell fragments? Examples from World War II battlefields in the Maritime Alps. In: Journal of Conflict Archaeology 9:1,16-32.

Griessel, Fabien 2015
  Soldatenkunst – auch ein deutsches Phänomen. Von Krieg, Granatenhülsen und Fingerringen. In: Mitteilungen der Deutschen Gesellschaft für Archäologie des Mittelalters und der Neuzeit 28, 147–154.

Haibl, Michaela (ed.) 2007
  Zeit Raum Beziehung. Menschen und Dinge im Konzentrationslager Dachau. Wien.

Härtl, Ursula (ed.) 2005
  Überlebensmittel, Zeugnis, Kunstwerk, Bildgedächtnis. Weimar.

Hausmair, Barbara 2016
  Jenseits des 'Sichtbarmachens' – Überlegungen zur Rclcvanz matcricllcr Kultur für dic Erforschung nationalsozialistischer Lager am Beispiel Mauthausen. In: Kersting, Thomas – Theune, Claudia – Drieschner, Axel – Ley, Astrid – Lutz, Thomas (eds.), Archäologie und Gedächtnis: NS-Lagerstandorte erforschen – bewahren – vermitteln. Petersberg, 31-46.

Hausmair, Barbara 2017
  Identity destruction or survival in small things? Reconsidering prisoner tags from the Mauthausen concentration camp. In: International Journal of Historical Archaeology, special issue: Carr, Gilly – Theune, Claudia – Jasinski, Marek (eds.), The material culture of Nazi camps.

Hinterndorfer, Peter 2017
  Material remains of telecommunication at the forced labour camp in Kirchbichl (Tyrol, Austria). In: Historische Archäologie, Online-Zeitschrift. [http://www.histarch.uni-kiel.de].

Hirte, Ronald 2000
  Offene Befunde. Ausgrabungen in Buchenwald. Zeitgeschichtliche Archäologie und Erinnerungskultur. Braunschweig.

Hoffmann, Detlef (ed.) 1998
  Das Gedächtnis der Dinge. KZ-Relikte und Kz-Denkmäler 1945-1995. Frankfurt / New York.

Kobiałka Dawid – Fraçkowiak, Maksymilian – Kajda, Kornelia 2015
  Tree memories of the Second World War: a case study of common beeches from Chycina, Poland. In: Antiquity 89, 683-696.

Kopytoff, Igor 1986
  The cultural biography of things: commoditization as process. In: Appadurai, Arjun, The social life of things: commodities in cultural perspective. Cambridge, 64-91.

Kriechbaum, Anna-Maria 2017
  Nutrition in Nazi concentrations camps. A comparison between the SS and prisoners at the Concentration Camp Mauthausen. In: Historische Archäologie, Online-Zeitschrift.

Landau, Julia Franziska – Langeheine, Romy 2014
  'An Gefäßen für das essen gab es nichts'. Keramikfunde zur Geschichte der sowjetischen Speziallager Mühlberg und Buchenwald. Weimar.

Ley, Astrid – Morsch, Günther 2007
  Mcdizin und Vcrbrcchcn. Das Krankcnrcvicr dcs KZ Sachsenhausen 1936-1945. Berlin.

Loistl, Simone – Schwanninger, Florian 2017
Vestiges and Witnesses: archaeological finds from the Nazi euthanasia institution of Hartheim as objects of research and education. In: International Journal of Historical Archaeology, special issue: Carr, Gilly – Theune, Claudia – Jasinski, Marek (eds.), The material culture of Nazi camps.

McAtackney, Laura 2015
Female prison autograph books: (re)remembering the Easter Rising through the experience of Irish Civil War Imprisonment. In: Godson, Lisa – Brück, Joanna (eds.), Making 1916. Material and visual culture of the Easter Rising. Liverpool, 108-116.

Miller, Daniel (ed.) 1998
Material cultures. Chicago.

Miller, Daniel 2008
The comfort of things. Cambridge.

Müller, Anne-Kathrin 2010
Entsorgte Geschichte – Entsorgte Geschichten. Die Funde aus einer Abfallgrube auf dem Gelände der Gedenkstätte Sachsenhausen und die Bedeutung zeitgeschichtlicher Archäologie. Unpublished master thesis. Berlin.

Müller, Anne-Kathrin 2015
Die Qual der Wahl? Zum Umgang mit Funden aus Grabungen zeitgeschichtlichen Komplexen. In: Kersting, Thomas – Theune, Claudia – Drieschner, Axel – Ley, Astrid – Lutz, Thomas (eds.), Archäologie und Gedächtnis: NS-Lagerstandorte erforschen – bewahren – vermitteln. Petersberg, 75-86.

Müller, Anne-Kathrin 2017
A tough choice? Suggestions for dealing with finds from the contemporary past. In: Historische Archäologie, Online-Zeitschrift. [www.histarch.uni-kiel.de].

Myers, Adrian 2008
Between memory and materiality: an archaeological approach to studying the Nazi concentration camps. In: Journal of Conflict Archaeology 4 (1-2), 231-245.

Myers, Adrian 2011
The things of Auschwitz. In: Myers, Adrian – Moshenska, Gabriel (eds.), Archaeologies of internment. New York, 75-88.

Myers, Adrian
Contemporary archaeology in transit: The artifacts of a 1991 van. International Journal of Historical Archaeology 15/1, 138-161.

Myers, Adrian – Dodson, Timothy 2014
Prisoners-of-war and dreams of freedom: dugout canoes at Second World War Work Camp in Manitoba, Canada. In: Manitoba Archaeological Journal 24 (1-2), 93-112.

Myers, Fred R. (ed.) 2001
The empire of things. Regimes of value and material culture. Santa Fe.

Mytum, Harold 2011
A tale of wo treatments: the materiality of internment on the Isle of Man in World Wars I and II. In: Myers, Adrian – Moshenska Gabrieal, Archaeologies of internment. New York, 33-53.

Orth, Karin 2000
Gab es eine Lagergesellschaft? 'Kriminelle' und politische Häftlinge im Konzentrationslager. In: Frei, Norbert – Steinbacher, Sybille – Wagner, Bernd, Ausbeutung, Vernichtung, Öffentlichkeit. München, 109-133.

Pisoni, Luca 2015
What should I bring to Europe. Belongings from the luggage of migrants crossing the Mediterranean Sea from Africa. In: Society of Historical Archaeology – The SHA Newsletter 48/3, 2.

Pototschnig, Thomas 2014
Autor unbekannt. Schriftzeugnisse aus der Zeit des Zweiten Weltkriegs aus einem Schwechater Luftschutzkeller (Author unknown. Written sources dating to the Second World War from an air-raid shelter in Schwechat, Austria. Historische Archäologie. Online-Zeitschrift.

Reich, Ines 2006
'Bittersüß'. Geschichte(n) des Hungers: Zuckerdosen aus dem sowjetischen Speziallager Sachsenhausen 1945–1950': Eine Sonderausstellung in der Gedenkstätte und Museum Sachsenhausen. In: Gedenkstättenrundbrief 132, 34–40.

Samida, Stefanie – Eggert, Manfred K.H. – Hahn, Hans Peter 2015
Handbuch Materielle Kultur. Stuttgart/Weimar.

Saunders, Nicholas 2011
Trench art. Barnsley.

Schofield, John 2005
Matériel Culture: the archaeology of twentieth-century conflict. London.

Schofield, John 2005
Combat archaeology. Material culture and modern conflict. London.

Schute Ivar 2017

Collecting artefacts on Holocaust sites: a critical review of archaeological research in Ybenheer, Westerbork and Sobibor camps. In: International Journal of Historical Archaeology, special issue: Carr, Gilly – Theune, Claudia – Jasinski, Marek (eds.), The material culture of Nazi camps.

Schütze, Marlene 2013

Löffel, Zigarettenetui, Erkennungsmarke. Theses University of Vienna. http://othes.univie.ac.at/26541/, access October 2017.

Sosna, Daniel – Brunclíková, Lenka, 2017

Archaeologies of waste. Encounters with the unwanted. Oxford.

Starzmann, Maria Theresia 2015

The materiality of forced labor: an archaeological exploration of punishment in Nazi Germany. In: International Journal of Historical Archaeology 19, 647-663.

Starzmann, Maria Theresia 2017

The fragment and the testimony: reflections on absence and time in the archaeology of prisons and camps. In: International Journal of Historical Archaeology, special issue: Carr, Gilly – Theune, Claudia – Jasinski, Marek (eds.), The material culture of Nazi camps.

Stockhammer, Philipp – Hahn, Hans Peter 2015

Lost in things. Fragen an die Welt des Materiellen. Münster.

Suderland, Maja 2013

Inside Concentration Camp. Social Life at the Extremes. Cambridge.

Theune, Claudia 2011

Das Gedächtnis der Dinge. In: Berger, Heinrich – Dejnega, Melanie – Fritz, Regina – Prenninger, Alexander (eds.), Politische Gewalt und Machtausübung im 20. Jahrhundert. Zeitgeschichte, Zeitgeschehen und Kontroversen. Wien, Köln, Weimar, 543-560.

Theune, Claudia 2015

Archäologische Fundmassen und Massenfunden aus ehemaligen Konzentrationslagern. In: Hofer, Nikolaus (ed.), Massenfunde – Fundmassen. Strategien und Perspektiven im Umgang mit Massenfundkomplexen. Fundberichte aus Österreich, Tagungsband 2. Wien, 37–42.

Theune, Claudia 2017

Clothes as expression of action in former concentration camps. In: International Journal of Historical Archaeology, special issue: Carr, Gilly – Theune, Claudia – Jasinski, Marek (eds.), The material culture of Nazi camps.

Tilley, Christopher, 1990

Reading material culture. Oxford.

Wemhoff, Matthias (ed.) 2012

Der Berliner Skulpturenfund. 'Entartete Kunst' im Bombenschutt. Entdeckung, Deutung, Perspektive. Regensburg.

Woodward, Ian 2007

Understanding material culture. London.

Chapter 11. A global perspective

Appadurai, Arjun 2001

The globalisation of archaeology and heritage: a discussion with Arjun Appadurai. In: Journal of Social Archaeology 1 (1), 35-49.

Brooks, Alasdair – Conlin Casella, Eleanor 2013

Globalization, immigration, transformation. In: Historical Archaeology 47/1.

Burström, Mats – Gustafsson, Anders – Karlsson, Håkan 2011.

World crisis in ruin. The archaeology of the former Soviet nuclear missile sites in Cuba. Lindome.

Funari, Pedro Paulo 1999

Historical archaeology from a world perspective. In: Funari, Pedro, Paulo – Hall, Martin – Jones, Siân (eds.), Historical Archaeology. Back from the edge. London, 37-66.

Hahn, Hans Peter 2017

Güterexpansion und Kulturwandel. Anmerkungen zu einer transparenten Globalgeschichte des Sachbesitzes. In: Cremer, Annette Caroline – Mulsow, Martin (eds.), Objekte als Quellen der historischen Kulturwissenschaften. Göttingen, 47-62.

Hodos, Tamar (ed.) 2016

The Routledge handbook of archaeology and globalization. London.

Horning, Audrey 2016

Transatlantic currents: exploring the past, present, and future of global historical archaeology. In: Historical Archaeology 50 (3) 111-126.

Horning, Audrey – Schweikart, Eric 2016
Globalization and the spread of capitalism: material resonances. In: Postmedieval Archaeology 50, 34-52.

Mehler, Natascha 2013
Globalization, Immigration and transformation: thought from a European perspective. In: Brooks, Alasdair – Conlin Casella, Eleanor, Globalization, immigration, transformation. In: Historical Archaeology 47 (1), 38-49.

Müller, Ulrich 2017
Globalisierung in der Archäologie: Weltsysteme, Scapes und Netzwerke. In: Globalisierung. Mitteilungen der Deutschen Gesellschaft für Archäologie des Mittelalters und der Neuzeit 30, 9-24.

Olsen, Bjørnar Julius 2001
The end of history? Archaeology and the politics of identity in a globalised world. In: Layton, Robert – Stone, Peter G. – Thomas, Julian, The destruction and conservaton of cultural property. London, 42-54.

Orser, Charles E. 2002
Globalization. In: Orser, Charles E. (ed.), Encyclopedia of Historical Archaeology. New York, 282-283.

Scholte, Jan Aart 2000
Globalization. A critical introduction. New York.

Chapter 12. Contemporary archaeology beyond war

Andreassen, Elin – Bjerck, Hein Bjartmann – Olsen, Bjørnar 2010
Persistent memories: Pyramiden – A Soviet mining town in the High Arctic. Trondheim.

Augé, Marc 1992
Non-Places: An Introduction to Anthropology of Supermodernity. Le Seuil.

Buchli, Victor 2001
The archaeology of alienation: A late 20th century British council house. In: Buchli, Viktor – Lucas, Gavin (eds.), Archaeologies of the contemporary past. London, 158-167.

Burström, Mats – Gelderblom, Bernhard 2011
Dealing with difficult heritage. The case of Brückeberg, site of the Third Reich Harvest Festival. In: Journal of Social Archaeology 2011 (3), 266-282.

Dezhamkhooy, Maryam 2011
The Interaction of body, things and the others in constituting feminine identity in lower socio-economic ranks of Bam, Iran. In: Archaeologies 7 (2), 372-86.

Finneran, Niall 2017
Beside the seaside. The archaeology of the twentieth-century English seaside holiday experience: a phenomenological context. In: International Journal of Historical Archaeology 21, 533-557.

Fogle, Kevin R. – Nyman, James A. – Beaudry, Mary C. 2015
Beyond the walls: New perspectives on the archaeology of historical households. Gainesville.

González Alonso, Pablo – González Álvarez, David 2016
A contemporary archaeology of cultural change in rural North-Western Spain: from traditional domesticity to postmodern individualisation. In: International Journal of Historical Archaeology 20, 23-44.

González-Ruibal, Alfredo 2014
Archaeology of the contemporary past. In: Claire Smith (ed.), Encyclopedia of global archaeology. New York, 1683 1694.

Gorleben-Archiv
Archiv einer Geschichte, die noch Geschichte ist [www.gorleben-archiv.de], access October 2015.

Gould, Richard – Schiffer, Michael (eds.) 1981
Modern material culture: the archaeology of us. New York.

Harrison, Rodney 2002
The archaeology of 'Lost places': ruin, memoriy and the heritage of the Aboriginal diaspora in Australia. In: Historical Environment 17 (1), 18-23.

Hopp, Detlef (ed.) 2011
Industrie. Archäologie. Essen. Industriearchäologie in Essen. Essen.

Jürgens, Fritz – Schade, Tobias – Wolpert, Nils 2017
Ist das Müll oder kann das weg? Die Relikte eines Truppenmanövers der Nachkriegszeit bei Borgenteich (Kr. Höxter). In: Globalisierung. Mitteilungen der Deutschen Gesellschaft für Archäologie des Mittelalters und der Neuzeit 30, 251-261.

Kerscher, Hermann 2012
Kulturlandschaftsforschung oder Topografie des Terrors? Über nationalsozialistische Thingstätten in Bayern. In: Denkmalpflege Informationen Bayerisches Landesamt für Denkmalpflege 151, 25–27.

Kiddey, Rachael – Schofield, John 2011
Embrace the margins: adventures in archaeology and homelessness. In: Public Archaeology 10 (1), 4-22.

Klápště, Jan (ed.) 2002
The rural house from the migration period to the oldest still standing buildings. Ruralia IV= Památky Archaologické Supplementum 15. Prag.

Klein, Ulrich 2015
Archäologische Untersuchungen an der Marburger Synagoge. In: Mitteilungen der Deutschen Gesellschaft für Archäologie des Mittelalters und der Neuzeit 28, 155–164.

Krabath, Stefan – Schöneburg, Peter 2015
Ein bedeutender Depotfund des 20. Jahrhunderts – Repräsentative Ausstattungsstücke aus dem Schloss im Fürst-Pückler Park von Bad Muskau (Sachsen). In: Blickpunkt Archäologie 2015 (3), 200-209.

Lehmann, La Vergne 2015
The garbage project revisited: From a 20th century archaeology of food waste to a contemporary study of food packaging waste. In: Sustainability 7/6, 6994-7010.

Lucas, Gavin 2013
Ruins. In: Graves-Brown, Paul – Harrison, Rodney – Piccini, Angela (eds.), The archaeology of the contemporary world. Oxford, 192-203.

Lucas, Gavin – Hreiðarsdóttir, Elín Ósk 2012
The archaeology of capitalism in Iceland: The view from Viðey. In: International Journal of Historical Archaeology 16 (3), 604-621.

MacDonald, Sharon 2006
Words in Stone? Agency and identity in a Nazi Landscape. In: Journal of Material Culture 11 (1/2), 105-126.

McAtackney, Laura and Krysta Ryzewski (eds.) 2017
Contemporary archaeology and the city. Creativity, ruination, and political action. Oxford.

Mehler, Natascha 2015
Die Archäologie des 19. und 20. Jahrhunderts zwischen Akzeptanz und Relevanz. In: Mitteilungen der Deutschen Gesellschaft für Archäologie des Mittelalters und der Neuzeit 28, 23-28.

Myers , Adrian 2011
Contemporary archaeology in transit. The artifacts of a 1991 van. In: International Journal of Historical Archaeology 15 (1), 138-161.

Nevell, Michael 2014
What's the point of recording 20th-century industrial archaeology? In: Industrial Archaeological review 36, 1-2.

Pétursdóttir, Þóra 2012
Concrete matters: ruins of modernity and the things called heritage. In: Journal of Social Archaeology 13 (1), 31.53.

Reno, Joshua 2013
Waste. In: Graves-Brown, Paul – Harrison, Rodney – Piccini, Angela (eds.), The archaeology of the contemporary world. Oxford, 261-272.

Ricci, Glenn Arthur 2011
The archaeology of a contemporary 'Leichenhalle' in Berlin, Germany. In: Historische Archäologie – Online-Zeitschrift [www.histarch.uni-kiel.de/2011_Ricci_low.pdf], accessed December 2017.

Przybilla, Heinz-Jürgen – Grünkemeier, Antje (eds.) 2009
Denkmäler3.de – Industriearchäologie. Tagungsband des interdisziplinären Kolloquiums vom 5.–7. November 2008 in Essen, Zollverein School. Aachen.

Rathje, William 1979
Modern Material-Culture Studies. In: Advances in archaeological method and theory 2, 1-37.

Rathje, William – Murphy, Cullen 2001
Rubbish! The archaeology of garbage. Tucson.

Rahtje, William 2001
Integrated archaeology: a garbage paradigm. In: Buchli, Viktor – Lucas, Gavin (eds.), Archaeologies of the contemporary past. London, New York, 63-76.

Ruiz, Rita 2016
Modern road archaeology: identification and classification proposal. In: International Journal of Historical Archaeology 20, 437-462.

Scholz , Ansgar 1998
Siedlungsentwicklung und Baugeschichte bäuerlicher Gehöfte in Breunsdorf. Breunsdorf 1. Dresden.

Shackel, Paul A. – Palus, Matthew 2006
Remembering an industrial landscape. In: International Journal of Historical Archaeology 10 (1), 49-71.

Smolnik, Regina (ed.) 2011
Breunsdorf – Ein verschwundenes Dorf im westsächsischen Braunkohlenrevier. Archäologischer Befund und schriftliche Überlieferung. Breunsdorf 3. Dresden.

Symonds, James 2004
Historical archaeology and the recent urban past. In: International Journal of Heritage Studies 10 (1), 33-48.

Tesch, Sebastian 2016
Hitlers Architekten. Albert Speer (1905-1981). Köln, Wien, Weimar.

Theune, Claudia 2013
Goldbergbau im Gasteiner Tal. In: Theune, Claudia et al. (eds.), Stadt – Land – Burg. Festschrift für Sabine Felgenhauer-Schmiedt zum 70. Geburtstag. Rahden/Westf., 395–404.

Trier, Markus – Naumann-Deckner, Friederike 2014
Archäologie der Moderne in Köln. Köln.

Trier, Markus – Naumann-Steckner, Friederike 2014
Archäologie der Moderne in Köln. Sonderausstellung des Römisch-Germanischen Museums der Stadt Köln. Köln,

Vařeka, Pawel (ed.) 2013
Archeologie 19. a 20. století. Přístupy – Metody – Témata [Archäologie des 19. und 20. Jahrhunderts. Zugriff – Methoden – Themen]. Plzeň.

Vařeka, Pawel – Vařeková, Zdeňka 2016
Contemporary cemeteries in the district of Tachov/Taschau (Western Bohemia) as an evidence of population and settlement discontinuity in the 2nd half of the 20th century. In: Siedlungsforschung. Archäologie – Geschichte – Geographie: Tod und Gedenken in der Landschaft 33, 225-244.

Voss, Barbara 2015
The historical experience of labor: archaeological contributions to interdisciplinary research on Chinese railroad workers. In: Historical Archaeology 49 (1), 4-23.

Williams, Bryn – Voss, Barbara 2008
The archaeology of Chinese immigrant and Chinese American communities. In: Historical Archaeology 42/3, 1–4.

Yazdi, Leila Papoli 2010
Public and private lives in Iran: an introduction to the archaeology of the 2003 Bam earthquake. In: Journal of the World Archaeological Congress 29-47.

Ylimaunu, Timo et al. 2013
Memory of barracks: World War II German 'Little Berlins' and post-war urbanization in Northern Finnish towns. In: Scandinavian Journal of History 38 (4), 525-548.

Zimmermann, Larry J. 2013
Homelessness. In: Graves-Brown, Paul – Harrison, Rodney – Piccini, Angela (eds.), The archaeology of the contemporary world. Oxford, 33-350.

Chapter 13. Archaeology and commemoration

Allmeier, Daniela – Manka, Inge – Mörtenböck, Peter – Scheuvens, Rudolf (eds.) 2016
Erinnerungsorte in Bewegung. Zur Neugestaltung des Gedenkens an Orten nationalsozialistischer Verbrechen. Bielefeld.

Asmuss, Burkhard (ed.) 2002
Holocaust. Der nationalsozialistische Völkermord und die Motive seiner Erinnerung. Berlin.

Assmann, Aleida 1999
Erinnerungsräume. Formen und Wandlungen des kulturellen Gedächtnisses. München.

Assmann, Aleida 2007
Geschichte im Gedächtnis. Von der individuellen Erfahrung zur öffentlichen Inszenierung. München.

Assmann, Aleida 2013
Das neue Unbehagen an der Erinnerungskultur. München.

Assmann, Jan – Czaplicka, John 1995
Collective memory and cultural identity. In: New German Critique 65, 125–133.

Auwera von der, Sigrid – Schramme, Annick 2014
Commemoration of the Great War: a global phenomenon or a national agenda? In: Journal of Conflict Archaeology 9, 3-15.

Bassanelli, Michaela – Gravano, Viviana – Grechi, Giulia – Postiglione, Gennaro (eds.) 2014
Recall. European conflict archaeological landscape re-appropriation. Milano.

Benton, Tim (ed.) 2010
Understanding heritage and memory. Manchester.

Bevan, Robert 2016
The destruction of memory. Architecture at war. London

Bolin, Annalisa 2012
On the side of light: performing morality at Rwanda's genocide memorials. In: Journal of Conflict Archaeology 7/3, 199 207.

Brooks, Alasdair – Mehler, Natascha 2017
  The country where my hearts is. Historical archaeologies of nationalism and national identity. Gainesville.

Connerton, Paul 1989
  How societies remember. Cambridge

Crooke, Elizabeth 2016
  Artefacts as agents for change: commemoration and exchange via material culture. In: Irish Political Studies 31/1, 86–100.

Defreese, Michelle 2009
  Kosovo: cultural heritage in conflict. In: Journal of Conflict Archaeology 5:1, 257-269.

Dziuban, Zuzanna 2017
  Landscape: Unpacking the Cultural Concept. In: Accessing Campscapes. Inclusive strategies for using European conflicted heritage 2, 4-11 [www.campscapes.org/wp-content/uploads/2017/12/e-journal-ACCESSING-CAMPSCAPES_no2-1.pdf], accessed December 2017.

Erll, Astrid 2011
  Kollektives Gedächtnis und Erinnerungskulturen. Stuttgart, Weimar.

Fehn, Klaus 2016
  Erinnerungsorte und Erinnerungslandschaften im nationalsozialistischen Deutschen Reich 1933-1945. In: Siedlungsforschung. Archäologie – Geschichte – Geographie: Tod und Gedenken in der Landschaft 33, 295-318.

François, Étienne – Schulze, Hagen (eds.) 2009
  Deutsche Erinnerungsorte. 3 Bände. München.

Giblin, John Daniel 2015
  Towards an archaeology of recent conflict in Western Great Lakes Africa. In: Journal of Conflict Archaeology 10 (2), 123 146.

González Ruibal, Alfredo – Hall, Martin 2015
  Hertitage and violence. In: Meskell, Lynn (ed.), Global heritage: a reader. Chichester, 150-170.

Graves-Brown, Paul 2013
  Authenticity. In: Graves-Brown, Paul – Harrison, Rodney – Piccini, Angela (eds.), The archaeology of the contemporary world. Oxford, 219-231.

Gryglewski, Elke – Haug, Verena – Kößler, Gottfried – Luth, Thomas – Schikorra, Christa 2015
  Gedenkstättenpädagogik. Kontext, Theoric und Praxis der Bildungsarbeit zu NS-Verbrechen. Berlin.

Halbwachs, Maurice 1941
  On collective memory. Chicago, London.

Harrison, Rodney (eds.) 2010
  Understanding the politics of heritage. Manchester.

Harrison, Rodney 2013
  Heritage. In: Graves-Brown, Paul – Harrison, Rodney – Piccini, Angela (eds.), The archaeology of the contemporary world. Oxford, 273-288.

Hettlage, Robert (ed.) 2003
  Verleugnen, Vertuschen, Verdrehen. Leben in der Lügengesellschaft. Konstanz.

Hummel, Juliane 2016
  Aspekte und Perspektiven im Umgang mit den archäologischen Relikten der Gedenkstätte Bergen-Belsen. In: Kersting, Thomas – Theune, Claudia – Drieschner, Axel – Ley, Astrid – Luth, Thomas (eds.), NS-Lagerstandorte: Erforschen – bewahren – vermitteln. Petersberg, 137-144.

Jones, Siân – Russell, Lynette 2012
  Archaeology, memory and oral tradition. In: International Journal of Historical Archaeology, special issue: archaeology, memory and oral tradition 16 (2), 267-283.

Jong de, Ferdinand – Rowlands, Michael 2008
  Postconflict heritage. In: Journal of Material Culture 13-29.

Kaltofen, Andrea 2016
  Lagerreste zeigen, Die Gedenkstätte Esterwegen. In: Kersting, Thomas – Theune, Claudia – Drieschner, Axel – Ley, Astrid – Luth, Thomas (eds.), NS-Lagerstandorte: Erforschen – bewahren – vermitteln. Petersberg, 95-110.

Kidron, Carol A. 2012
  Breaching the wall of traumatic silence: Holocaust survivor and descendant person-object relations and the material transmission of the genocidal past. In: Journal of Material Culture 17 (1), 3-21.

Kersting, Thomas – Theune, Claudia – Drieschner, Axel – Ley, Astrid – Luth, Thomas (eds.) 2016
  NS-Lagerstandorte: Erforschen – bewahren – vermitteln. Petersberg.

Klei, Alexandra – Stoll, Katrin – Wienert, Annika (eds.) 2011
  Die Transformation der Lager. Annäherungen an die Orte nationalsozialistischer Verbrechen. Bielefeld.

Le Goff, Jacques 1992
  History and memory. New York.

Logan, William – Reeves, Keir (eds.) 2009
Places of pain and shame. Dealing with 'difficult heritage'. London.

Loistl, Simone 2016
Museale Präsentation und museumspädagogische Vermittlung. Die Rolle archäologischer Fundstücke an Gedenkstätten am Beispiel von Schloss Hartheim. In: Kersting, Thomas – Theune, Claudia – Drieschner, Axel – Ley, Astrid – Luth, Thomas (eds.), NS-Lagerstandorte: Erforschen – bewahren – vermitteln. Petersberg, 119-125.

Lucas, Gavin 1997
Forgetting the past. In: Anthropology today 13, 8–14.

May, Sarah – Orange, Hilary – Penrose, Sefryn (eds.) 2012
The good, the bad and the unbuilt: Handling heritage of the recent past. Studies in Contemporary and Historical Archaeology. BAR int. Ser. 2362. Oxford.

McGuire, Randall H. 2008
Archaeology as political action. Berkley, Los Angeles, London.

Meier, Hans-Rudolf – Wohlleben, Marion (eds.) 1998
Bauten und Orte als Träger von Erinnerung. Die Erinnerungsdebatte und die Denkmalpflege. Zürich.

Morsch, Günter 2016
Die Bedeutung der Archäologie für die historische Forschung, für Ausstellungen – Pädagogische Vermittlung und Neugestaltung in den NS-Gedenkstätten. In: Kersting, Thomas – Theune, Claudia – Drieschner, Axel – Ley, Astrid – Luth, Thomas (eds.), NS-Lagerstandorte: Erforschen – bewahren – vermitteln. Petersberg, 17-30.

Nora, Pierre 1989
Between memory and history. Les lieux de mémoire, Représentations 26, 7-24.

Nora, Pierre (eds.) 2001
Zwischen Geschichte und Gedächtnis. Frankfurt a. M.

Olsen, Bjørnar 2013
Memory. In: Graves-Brown, Paul – Harrison, Rodney – Piccini, Angela (eds.), The archaeology of the contemporary world. Oxford, 204-2018.

O'Ríagáin, Russell – Popa, Cătălin Nicolae (eds.) 2012
Archaeology and the (de)construction of national and supra-national polities. In: Archaeological Review from Cambridge 27 (2). Cambridge.

Perz, Bertrand 2006
Die KZ-Gedenkstätte Mauthausen 1945 bis zur Gegenwart. Innsbruck.

Pollack, Martin 2014
Kontaminierte Landschaften. St. Pölten.

Porombka, Stephan – Schmundt, Hilmar (eds.) 2005
Böse Orte. Stätten nationalsozialistischer Selbstdarstellung – heute. Berlin.

Rass, Christoph – Lohmeier, Jens 2011
Transformations: Post-battle processes of the Hürtgenwald battlefield. In: Journal of Conflict Archaeology 6/3, 179-199.

Scham, Sandra – Yahya, Adel 2003
Heritage and reconciliation. In: Journal of Social Archaeology 3 (3), 399-416.

Schofield, Arthur – Cocroft, Wayne (eds.) 2009
A fearsome heritage. Diverse legacies of the Cold War. Walnut Creek.

Seidenspinner, Wolfgang 2007
Authentizität. In: Kunsttexte.de 4/2007, 1–20.

Skeates, Robin 2000
Debating the archaeological heritage. London.

Snead, James E. 2012
Teaching the archaeology of war. In: Rockman, Marcy – Flatman, Joe (eds.), Archaeology in society. Its relevance in the modern world. New York, 217–229.

Sturdy Colls, Caroline 2017
The archaeology of cultural genocide. In: Dziuban, Zuzanna, The forensic turn in Holocaust studies? (Re)thinking the past through materiality. Wien, 119-142.

Sturdy Colls, Caroline – Branthwaite, Michael 2017
'This is proof'? Forensic evidence and ambiguous material culture at Treblinka extermination camp. In: International Journal of Historical Archaeology, special issue: Carr, Gilly – Theune, Claudia – Jasinski, Marek (eds.), The material culture of Nazi camps.

Tauschek, Markus
Kulturerbe. Eine Einführung. Berlin 2013.

Theune, Claudia 2012
Identity establishing heritage sites? Memory, remembrance and commemoration at monuments and memorials. In: O'Ríagáin, Russell – Popa, Cătălin Nicolae (eds.) Archaeology and the (de)construction of national and supra-national polities, Archaeological Review from Cambridge 27/2, 161–177.

Theune, Claudia 2013
Archaeology and remembrance: the contemporary archaeology of concentration camps, prisoner-of-war

camps, and battlefields. In: Mehler, Natascha (ed.),
Historical archaeology in Central Europe. Society
of Historical Archaeology, Special publication 10.
Rockville, 241-259.

Theune, Claudia 2016
Unsichtbarkeiten. Aufgedeckte Spuren und Relikte.
Archäologie in ehemaligen Konzentrationslager
Mauthausen. In: Allmeier, Daniela – Manka, Inge –
Mörtenböck, Peter – Scheuvens, Rudolf (eds.),
Erinnerungsorte in Bewegung. Zur Neugestaltung

des Gedenkens an Orten nationalsozialistischer
Verbrechen. Bielefeld, 199-218.
Wegener, Wolfgang 2016
Kulturlandschaft – Erinnerungskultur –
Erinnerungslandschaft. Projekt Hürtgenwald:
Eine kritische Betrachtung von Erinnerungskultur
und Kulturlandschaft des Zweiten Weltkriegs. In:
Siedlungsforschung. Archäologie – Geschichte –
Geographie: Tod und Gedenken in der Landschaft 33,
163-176.

SELECTION OF MEMORIALS AND MUSEUMS

see also:
www.ushmm.org
www.gedenkstaetten-uebersicht.de
www.memorialmuseums.org

FIRST WORLD WAR

Belgium
In Flanders Fields Museum,
Sint-Maartensplein 3, 8900 Ypern
www.inflandersfields.be

France
Historial de la Grande Guerre
(Museum des Ersten Weltkriegs/1914–1918),
Château de Péronne, B. P. 20063,
80201 Péronne Cedex
www.historial.org

Mémorial de Verdun,
1, avenue du Corps Européen,
55100 Fleury-Devant-Douaumont
www.memorialde-verdun.fr

Musée de la Grande Guerre du Pays de Meaux,
Route de Varreddes,
77100 Meaux
www.museedelagrandeguerre.eu

Great Britain
Imperial War Museum London,
Lambeth Road, London SE16HZ
ww.iwm.org.uk

Italy
Museo Storico Italiano della Guerra
(Kriegsmuseum Rovereto),
via Castelbarco 7,
38068 Rovereto
www.museodellaguerra.it

Austria
MUSEUM 1915–1918,
Kötschach 390,
9640 Kötschach
www.dolomitenfreunde.at

NATIONAL SOCIALIST ERA AND SECOND WORLD WAR

Argentinia
Museo del Holocausto,
Montevideo 919,
1019 Buenos Aires
www.museodelholocausto.org.ar

Austria
Lern- und Gedenkort Schloss Hartheim,
Schlossstraße 1,
4072 Alkoven
www.schloss-hartheim.at

Mauthausen Memorial KZ-Gedenkstätte Mauthausen,
Erinnerungsstraße 1,
4310 Mauthausen
www.mauthausen-memorial.at

Zeitgeschichte Museum und KZ-Gedenkstätte Ebensee,
Kirchengasse 5,
4802 Ebensee
www.memorial-ebensee.at

KZ-Gedenkstätte Gusen,
Georgestraße 6,
4222 Langen- stein/Oberösterreich
www.gusen-memorial.at

Belarus
Дзяржаўны мемарыяльны комплекс « атын »
(The memorial complex »Khatyn«),
Logojskij Kreis, Minskaja Gebiet;
223110 Chatyn
www.khatyn.by

Belgium
Kazerne Dossin, Gedenkstätte Museum und
Dokumentationszentrum Holocaust und
Menschenrechte,
Goswin de Stassartstraat 153,
2800 Mecheln
www.kazernedossin.eu

Musée de la Résistance et des Camps de concentration,
Chaussée Napoléon, 4500 Huy
www.fortdehuy.be

Nationaal Gedenkteken Fort Breendonk, Brandstraat 57,
2830 Willebroek
www.breendonk.be/

Canada
Musée Holocauste Montréal
(Montreal Holocaust Museum),
5151 Ch de la Côte-Sainte-Catherine,
Montreal, QC H3W 1M6
http://museeholocauste.ca

The Nikkei Internment Memorial Centre,
306 Josephine St. New Denver, BC
http://newdenver.ca/nikkei/

Croatia
Spomen Područje Jasenovac Memorial Site,
Braće Radić 147,
44324 Jasenovac
www.jusp-jasenovac.hr

Czech Republic
Památník Terezín,
Princi- pova alej 304,
41 155 Terezín
www.pamatnik-terezin.cz

Denmark
Frøslevlejrens Museum,
Lejrvej 83,
6330 Frøslev
www.froeslevlejrensmuseum.dk

France
Centre de la Mémoire Oradour-sur Glane village martyr,
87520 Oradour-sur-Glane
www.oradour.org

Le Centre Européen du Résistant Déporté et le Musée du Struthof
www.struthof.fr

Mémorial de l'internement et de la déportation Camp de Royallieu,
2 bis, avenue des Martyrs de la Liberté,
60200 Compiègne
www.memorial-compiegne.fr

Mémorial de la Shoah – Musée,
Centre de documentation, 17, rue Geoffroy l'Asnier, 75004 Paris
www.memorialdelashoah.org

Site-Mémorial du Camp des Milles,
40, chemin de la Badesse,
13547 Aix-en-Provence
www.campdesmilles.org

Germany

Baden-Wuerttemberg
Dokumentations- und Kulturzentrum deutscher Sinti und Roma,
Bremeneckgasse 2,
69117 Heidelberg
www.sintiundroma.de/zentrum/ausstellungen/heidelberg.html

Gedenkstätte Grafeneck,
Grafeneck 3,
72532 Gomadingen
www.gedenkstaette-grafeneck.de

Bavaria
Dokumentation Obersalzberg,
Salzbergstraße 41,
83471 Berchtesgaden
www.obersalzberg.de/obersalzberg-home.html

Dokumentationszentrum Reichparteitagsgelände,
Bayernstraße 110,
90478 Nürnberg
https://museen.nuernberg.de/dokuzentrum/

KZ-Gedenkstätte Dachau,
Alte Römerstraße 75,
85221 Dachau
www.kz-gedenkstaette-dachau.de

KZ-Gedenkstätte Flossenbürg,
Gedächtnisallee 5,
92696 Flossenbürg
www.gedenkstaette-flossen buerg.de

NS-Dokumentationszentrum München;
Max-Mannheimer-Platz 1,
80333 München
www.ns-dokuzentrum-muenchen.de

Berlin
Denkmal für die ermordeten Juden Europas und Ort der Information
(Holocaustdenkmal),
Cora-Berliner Straße 1,
10117 Berlin
www.stiftung-denkmal.de

Dokumentationszentrum NS-Zwangsarbeit Berlin, Britzer Straße 5,
12439 Berlin
www.dz-ns-zwangs arbeit.de

Dokumentationszentrum Topographie des Terrors,
Niederkirchnerstraße 8,
10963 Berlin
www.topographie.de

Brandenburg
Gedenkstätte und Museum Sachsenhausen, Straße der Nationen 22,
16515 Oranienburg
www.stiftung-bg.de

Mahn- und Gedenkstätte Ravensbrück,
Straße der Nationen,
16798 Fürstenberg/Havel
www.ravensbrueck.de

Hamburg
KZ-Gedenkstätte Neuengamme,
Jean-Dolidier-Weg 75,
21039 Hamburg
www.kz-gedenkstaette- neuengamme.de

Lower Saxony
Gedenkstätte Bergen-Belsen,
Anne-Frank-Platz,
29303 Lohheide
http://bergen-belsen.stiftung-ng.de

Stiftung Gedenkstätte Esterwegen,
Hinterm Busch 1,
26897 Esterwegen
www.gedenkstaette- esterwegen.de

North Rhine-Westphalia
NS-Dokumentationszentrum der Stadt Köln,
Appellhofplatz 23–25,
50667 Köln
www.museenkoeln.de/ ns-dokumentationszentrum

Rhineland-Palatinate
NS-Dokumentationszentrum Rheinland-Pfalz,
Gedenkstätte KZ Osthofen,
Ziegelhüttenweg 38,
67574 Osthofen
www.gedenkstaette-osthofen-rlp.de

Saxony
Gedenkstätte Pirna-Sonnenstein,
Schlosspark 11,
01796 Pirna
www.stsg.de/cms/pirna/startseite

Thuringia
Gedenkstätte Buchenwald,
99427 Weimar
www.buchenwald.de

KZ-Gedenkstätte Mittelbau-Dora,
Kohnsteinweg 20,
99734 Nordhausen
www.buchcnwald.dc

Great Britain
Imperial War Museum,
Lambeth Road,
London SE16HZ
www.iwm.org.uk

Greece
Εβραϊκό Μουσείο Θεσσαλονίκης
(Jewish Museum of Thessaloniki),
11 Agiou Mina Street,
546 46 Thessaloniki
http://www.jmth.gr/

Hungary
Holokauszt Emlékközpont,
Páva utca 39,
1094 Budapest
http://www.hdke.hu/

Israel
Yad Vashem - The Holocaust Martyrs' and Heroes'
Remembrance Authority,
Har Hazikaron,
P.O.B. 3477,
Jerusalem 9103401
http://www.yadvashem.org/

Italy
Museo della deportazione e centro di documentazione
della deportazione e della resistenza,
Via di Cantagallo 250,
59100 Prato
www.museodelladeportazione.it

Museo della Risiera di San Sabba,
Via Giovanni Palatucci 5,
34148 Trieste
http://www.risierasansabba.it/

Japan
広島平和記念資料館
(Hiroshima Peace Memorial Museum)
1-2 Nakajima-cho, Naka-ku,
Hiroshima 730-081
http://hpmmuseum.jp/

Latvia

Rīgas geto un Latvijas Holokausta muzejs (Riga Ghetto and Lativan Holocaust museum), Maskavas 14a, Rīga
www.rgm.lv

Lithuania

Valstybinis Vilniaus Gaono žydų muziejus
(The Vilna Gaon Jewish State Museum),
Naugarduko gatvė 10/2,
01114 Vilnius
www.jmuseum.lt

Luxembourg

Mémorial de la Déportation Gare Hollerich
(Deportationsdenkmal und Museum Bahnhof Hollerich),
3 A, rue de la Déportation,
1415 Luxembourg
www.musees.lu/de/2/bid,196394

Musée national de la Résistance,
Place de la Résistance,
4041 Esch-sur-Alzette
http://www.esch.lu/culture/musee/fr/Pages/default.aspx

Netherlands

Herinneringscentrum Kamp Westerbork, Oosthalen 8,
9414 TG Hooghalen
www.kampwesterbork.nl

Nationaal Monument Kamp Amersfoort,
Loes van Overeemlaan 19,
3832 RZ Amersfoort
www.kampamersfoort.nl

Nationaal Monument Kamp Vught
(Nationale Gedenkstätte Lager Vught), Lunettenlaan 600,
5263 NT Vught
www.nmkampvught.nl

Norway

The Falstadsenteret – Minnested og senter for menneskerettigheter,
7624 Ekne
falstadsenteret.no

Poland

Muzeum Byłego niemieckiego Obozu Zagłady Kulmhof w Chełmnie nad Nerem,
62–663 Chełmno
www.muzeum.com.pl/en/chelmno.htm

Muzeum Byłego Obozu Zagłady w Sobiborze, Stacja Kolejowa 1,
22–200 Sobibór
www.sobibor-memorial.eu

Muzeum Gross-Rosen w Rogoźnicy,
Rogoźnica,
58–150 Rogoźnica
www.grossrosen.eu

Muzeum Katyńskie,
Aleje Jerozolims- kie 3,
00–495 Warszawa
www.muzeumkatynskie.pl

Muzeum Miejsce Pamięci w Bełżcu,
Ul. Ofiar obozu 4,
22–670 Bełżec
www.belzec.eu

Muzeum Stutthof w Sztutowie, ul. Muzealna 6, 82–110 Sztutowo
www.stutthof.org

Muzeum Walki i Męczeństwa w Treblince,
Kosów Lacki,
08–330 Treblinka
www.treblinka.bho.pl

Muzeum II Wojny Światowej
(Museum of the Second World War),
W. Bartoszewskiego Square 1 ,
80-862 Gdańsk
http://muzeum1939.pl/

Państwowe Muzeum na Majdanku,
ul. Droga Męczenników Majdanka 67,
20–325 Lublin
www.majdanek.pl

Państwowe Muzeum Auschwitz-Birkenau,
ul. Więźniów Oświęci- mia 20,
32–603 Oświęcim
www.auschwitz.org.pl

Republic of South Africa
Cape Town Holocaust Centre,
88 Hatfield Street Gardens,
Cape Town 800
http://www.ctholocaust.co.za/

Russia
Memorial »Katyn«,
Katyn;
214522 Katyn
www.katyn-memorial.ru
Slovakia

Múzeum Slovenského národného povstania (Museum of Slovak National Uprising),
Kapitulská 23,
975 59 Banská Bystrica
http://www.muzeumsnp.sk/

Slovenia
Spominski park taborišča Mauthausen-Ljubelj,
Loiblpassstraße,
Podljubelj

United States of America
United States Holocaust Memorial Museum,
100 Raoul Wallenberg Place,
SW, Washington,
DC 20024-2126
https://www.ushmm.org/

USS Arizona Memorial,
1 Arizona Memorial Place,
Honolulu, HI 96818
https://www.nps.gov/valr/index.htm

Honouliuli National Monument,
1845 Wasp Blvd, Bld 176,
Honolulu HI, 96818
https://www.nps.gov/hono/index.htm

Bainbridge Island Japanese American Memorial, 4192 Eagle Harbor Drive,
Bainbridge Island,
WA 98110
http://www.bijac.org/index.
php?p=MEMORIALIntroduction

COLD WAR

Germany
BlackBox Kalter Krieg,
Friedrichstraße 47/Ecke Zimmerstraße,
10117 Berlin
www.bfgg.de/zentrum-kalter- krieg/blackbox-kalter-krieg.html

Gedenkstätte Berliner Mauer,
Bernauer Straße 119,
13355 Berlin
www.berliner-mauer-gedenkstaette.de

Gedenkstätte Bautzen,
Weigangstraße 8a,
02625 Bautzen
www.stsg.de/cms/bautzen/startseite

Museum Sowjetisches Speziallager Nr. 7/Nr. 1 (1945–1950) in Sachsenhausen,
Gedenkstätte und Museum Sachsenhausen, Straße der Nationen 22,
16515 Oranienburg
www.stiftung-bg.de

Russia
Музей истории гулАГа (Muzey istorii GULAGa, GULAG History Museum),
1-й Самотечный пер., д.9, стр.1,
127473 Москва
(1-y Samotechnyy per. 9, 127473 Moskva)
http://www.gmig.ru/

FURTHER MEMORIALS

Armenia
Armenian Genocide Museum-Institute, Tsitsernakaberd
memorial complex RA,
Armenia Yerevan 0028
http://www.genocide-museum.am/eng/

Bosnia and Herzegovina
Memorijalni Centar Srebrenica – Potočari (Srebrenica
Genocide Memorial),
Potocari bb,
75430 Srebrenica
http://www.potocarimc.org/

Cambodia
The Documentation Center of Cambodia,
66 Preah sihanouk Boulevard,
P.O. Box 1110, Phnom Penh
http://www.dccam.org/

Romania
Memorialul Victimelor Comunismului şi al Rezistenţei
(Memorial of the Victims of Communism and of the
Resistance),
Str. Corneliu Coposu,
Nr. 4 Sighet Jud. Maramureş
http://www.memorialsighet.ro/

Rwanda
Kigali Genocide Memorial,
KG 1 Ave, Kigali
http://www.kgm.rw/

Spain
Museo de la paz de Gernika
(Gernika Peace Museum),
Foru Plaza, 1,
48300 Gernika-Lumo
http://www.museodelapaz.org/